ASPEN
PUBLISHERS

Bittker on the Regulation of Interstate and Foreign Commerce

by Boris I. Bittker

With its *Lopez* ruling in 1995, the U.S. Supreme Court signaled a new era in interpretation of the Commerce Clause of the Constitution. Boris Bittker, long one of the nation's pre-eminent tax authorities, turned his attention to analyzing this area of constitutional law, responding to the many unanswered questions in the wake of the *Lopez* decision, as well as the dramatic changes in other commerce areas, such as electronic commerce.

Bittker on the Regulation of Interstate and Foreign Commerce is the only up-to-date treatise to examine the scope of the Commerce Clause, which is regarded as "the king of the constitutional castle." The book analyzes the entire unruly tangle of judicial opinions enunciating, refining, applying, and occasionally rejecting the dormant Commerce Clause, along with the Commerce Clause's other features and the four commerce-related provisions of the Constitution—the Import-Export Clause, the Tonnage Clause, the Federal Export Clause, and the Port Preference Clause. Together, the five constitutional provisions have the same target—state restrictions on national commerce. The book also explores and explains the effect of the interpretation of the commerce power on various industries, such as aviation, banking and financial services, insurance, and shipping.

Highlights of the 2006 Cumulative Supplement

Brannon P. Denning, who teaches at Samford University's Cumberland School of Law, and who originally collaborated with Boris Bittker on the book, has authored the 2006 Cumulative Supplement. The 2006 Cumulative Supplement reflects the developments in the law since publication of the original work. It features:

- Extensive discussion and analysis of *Gonzales v. Raich*, the medical marijuana case that upheld the federal government's power, under the Commerce Clause, to regulate local, noncommercial production, possession, and use of marijuana.
- Description and analysis of *Granholm v. Heald*, in which the Court held that states could not discriminate between in-state and out-of-state alcohol producers in laws banning direct shipment to consumers by the latter.
- The latest lower court decisions applying *Lopez* and *Morrison* to nine frequently litigated federal statutes.
- A discussion of *Cuno v. DaimlerChrysler*, a Sixth Circuit opinion striking down a state economic development incentive under the dormant Commerce Clause doctrine, which may have national implications for similar economic incentive plans in other states.

All tables and the Index have been updated to reflect these changes.

11/05

For questions concerning this shipment, billing, or other customer service matters, call our Customer Service Department at 1-800-234-1660.

For toll-free ordering, please call 1-800-638-8437.

a Wolters Kluwer business

BITTKER ON THE REGULATION OF INTERSTATE AND FOREIGN COMMERCE

2006 Cumulative Supplement

BITTKER ON THE REGULATION OF INTERSTATE AND FOREIGN COMMERCE

2006 Cumulative Supplement

Prepared by

BRANNON P. DENNING

Cumberland School of Law,
Samford University, Birmingham, Alabama

ASPEN

PUBLISHERS

111 Eighth Avenue, New York, NY 10011
www.aspenpublishers.com

Printed in the United States of America

ISBN 0-7355-5528-1

1 2 3 4 5 6 7 8 9 0

Library of Congress Cataloging-in-Publication Data

Bittker, Boris I.
Bittker on the regulation of interstate and foreign commerce /
by Boris I. Bittker and contributing editor, Brannon P. Denning.
p. cm.
Includes bibliographical references and index.
ISBN 0-7355-0364-8 (alk. paper)
1. Interstate commerce—Law and legislation—United States.
2. Foreign trade regulation—United States. I. Denning, Brannon P.
II. Title.
KF4606 .B58 1999
343.73′088—dc21 99-19483
CIP

About Aspen Publishers

Aspen Publishers, headquartered in New York City, is a leading information provider for attorneys, business professionals, and law students. Written by preeminent authorities, our products consist of analytical and practical information covering both U.S. and international topics. We publish in the full range of formats, including updated manuals, books, periodicals, CDs, and online products.

Our proprietary content is complemented by 2,500 legal databases, containing over 11 million documents, available through our Loislaw division. Aspen Publishers also offers a wide range of topical legal and business databases linked to Loislaw's primary material. Our mission is to provide accurate, timely, and authoritative content in easily accessible formats, supported by unmatched customer care.

To order any Aspen Publishers title, go to *www.aspenpublishers.com* or call 1-800-638-8437.

To reinstate your manual update service, call 1-800-638-8437.

For more information on Loislaw products, go to *www.loislaw.com* or call 1-800-364-2512.

For Customer Care issues, e-mail *CustomerCare@aspenpublishers.com*; call 1-800-234-1660; or fax 1-800-901-9075.

Aspen Publishers
a Wolters Kluwer business

SUBSCRIPTION NOTICE

This Aspen Publishers product is updated on a periodic basis with supplements to reflect important changes in the subject matter. If you purchased this product directly from Aspen Publishers, we have already recorded your subscription for the update service.

If, however, you have purchased this product from a bookstore and wish to receive future updates and revised or related volumes billed separately with a 30-day examination review, please contact our Customer Service Department at 1-800-234-1660, or send your name, company name (if applicable), address, and title of the product to:

Aspen Publishers
7201 McKinney Circle
Frederick, MD 21704

TABLE OF CONTENTS

CONTENTS
[New Only]

IN MEMORIAM

Boris Irving Bittker
Late Sterling Professor of Law, Yale University
1916-2005

CHAPTER 1

BACKGROUND AND EARLY HISTORY

§1.01 INTRODUCTION

Page 1-6, add to the end of note 14:

For an account of the role that a young legal historian, James Willard Hurst, played in researching and writing Professor Frankfurter's widely cited book on the Commerce Clause, *see* Ernst, Willard Hurst and the Administrative State: From Williams to Wisconsin, 18 Law & Hist. Rev. 1, 17 (2000).

Page 1-6, add to the end of note 15:

For a slightly different conclusion, *see* Nelson & Pushaw, Rethinking the Commerce Clause: Apply First Principles to Uphold Federal Commercial Regulations but Preserve State Control Over Social Issues, 85 Iowa L. Rev. 1, 57–63 (1999) (arguing that the Framers intended for Congress to have both negative and affirmative power over various commercial activities that affected more than one state); *but see* Barnett, The Original Meaning of the Commerce Clause, 68 U. Chi. L. Rev. 101 (2001) (arguing that, according to the original meaning of the word "commerce," Congress may prescribe rules by which people (1) exchange or trade goods from one state to another; (2) remove obstructions on commerce erected by states; and (3) regulate and restrict the flow of goods from and into the U.S. to and from other countries; arguing that broader constructions of the word "commerce" have no foundation in the original meaning of the word as adopted by the Framers in Philadelphia); Johnson, The Panda's Thumb: The Modest and Mercantilist Original Meaning of the Commerce Clause, 13 Wm. & Mary Bill Rts. J. 1 (2004) (arguing in favor of a narrow meaning of "commerce"). For Professors Nelson and Pushaw's reply to Professor Barnett, *see* Pushaw & Nelson, A Critique of the Narrow Interpretation of the Commerce Clause, 96 Nw. U. L. Rev. 695 (2002). For Professor Barnett's response, see Barnett, New Evidence of the Original Meaning of the Commerce Clause, 55 Ark. L. Rev. 847 (2003); *see also* Pushaw, Methods of Interpreting the Commerce Clause: A Comparative Analysis, 55 Ark. L. Rev. 1185, 1199-1202 (2003) (responding, in part, to Barnett's new evidence). For an international perspective on the scope of the commerce power, *see* Smith, Interstate Commerce and the Principles of the Law of Nations, 2004 Utah L. Rev. 111 (2004).

§ 1.02 THE COMMERCE CLAUSE IN CHIEF JUSTICE MARSHALL'S DAY

Page 1-7, add to note 19, before "White":

Newmyer, John Marshall and the Heroic Age of the Supreme Court (L.S.U. Press, 2001), pp. 302-315;

[A] *Gibbons v. Ogden*

Page 1-7, add to note 19 after "(Knopf, 1972)" *and before* "The New York":

; Williams, *Gibbons*, 79 N.Y.U. L. Rev. 1398 (2004).

Page 1-7, add to the end of note 19:

For a discussion of *Gibbons*, as well as a thorough canvassing of the evidence of original intent of the Commerce Clause, *see* Nelson & Pushaw, Rethinking the Commerce Clause: Apply First Principles to Uphold Federal Commercial Regulations but Preserve State Control Over Social Issues, 85 Iowa L. Rev. 1, 57-63 (1999); *see also* Pushaw & Nelson, A Critique of the Narrow Interpretation of the Commerce Clause, 96 Nw. U. L. Rev. 695 (2002).

Page 1-11, add to the end of note 30:

Professor Barnett suggests a third, unarticulated support for Marshall's conclusion that navigation was included within the term "commerce": the Necessary and Proper Clause. *See* Barnett, *supra* note 15, at 127 ("the admitted power to pass navigation laws is most accurately conceived as an implied power that was embraced by the Necessary and Proper Clause").

Page 1-11, add to the end of note 33:

For a recent reexamination of the phrase "among the several states," which concludes that Marshall's "concerns more states than one" formulation is too broad a construction, *see* Barnett, *supra* note 15, at 132-139.

Professor Barnett writes, "Marshall's vague formulation has improperly permitted the expansion of the power to regulate commerce beyond that which actually crosses state lines." *Id.* at 137.

Page 1-13, add to the end of note 43:

For a recent case whose facts and result resemble *Gibbons*, *see* Young v. Coloma-Agaran, 2001 WL 1677259 (D. Hawaii) (Dec. 27, 2001) (concluding that tour boat operator's federal license preempted state efforts to block operation of tour boats, but not other boats, in Hanalei Bay, Hawaii).

Page 1-15, add to the end of note 49:

Marshall's most recent biographer emphasizes the unsettled, indeterminate nature of *Gibbons*, noting that, "unlike *McCulloch*, [it] put the Court on the side of nationalism without calling forth retaliation from states' rights extremists." Newmyer, *supra* note 19, at 315; *see also id.* at 313–314 (pointing out the questions left hanging fire in *Gibbons*).

Page 1-15, add to the end of note 52:

For a revisionist analysis of *Gibbons* which suggests, among other things, that Marshall's *Gibbons* opinion was rather unremarkable and owed its popularity to the widespread hatred for the steamboat monopoly, *see* Klarman, How Great Were the "Great" Marshall Court Opinions?, 87 Va. L. Rev. 1111, 1126-1137 (2001); *see also* Newmyer, *supra* note 19, at 315 (crediting *Gibbons'* popularity "in the midst of the greatest Court-bashing rampage in American history" to Jacksonian Democrats' hatred of monopolies).

CHAPTER 2

SCOPE OF THE POWER TO "REGULATE"

§ 2.01 THE POWER TO "REGULATE"

Page 2-3, add to the end of note 2:

; *see also* Barnett, The Original Meaning of the Commerce Clause, 68 U. Chi. L. Rev. 101, 139-147 (2001); Pushaw & Nelson, A Critique of the Narrow Interpretation of the Commerce Clause, 96 Nw. U. L. Rev. 695, 714 (2002); *see also* Barnett, New Evidence of the Original Meaning of the Commerce Clause, 55 Ark. L. Rev. 847, 863-865 (2003) (discussing further evidence on meaning of "regulate"); Johnson, The Panda's Thumb: The Modest and Mercantilist Original Meaning of the Commerce Clause, 13 Wm. & Mary Bill Rts. J. 1 (2004) (arguing in favor of a narrow meaning of "commerce").

§ 2.03 PROHIBITIONS AS "REGULATIONS" OF INTERSTATE COMMERCE

Page 2-8, add to the beginning of note 20:

Gonzales v. Raich, ___ U.S. ___, 125 S. Ct. 2195 (2005) (divided court) (power of Congress to eliminate interstate market in controlled substance included power to reach noncommercial, intrastate production of medical marijuana for private consumption);

Page 2-9, add to the end of note 25:

Professor Barnett's study of the Commerce Clause's original meaning concludes that while the power to prohibit is inherent in Congress's ability to "regulate" commerce so as to eliminate barriers to interstate trade *and* to prohibit certain foreign trade, it does not necessarily follow that Congress was intended to possess a similar power to prohibit certain interstate trade. *See* Barnett, *supra* note 2, at 144; *but see* Pushaw & Nelson, A Critique of the Narrow Interpretation of the Commerce Clause, 96 Nw. U. L. Rev. 695, 714 (2002) (disputing Barnett's interpretation). For Barnett's reply, *see* Barnett, New Evidence of the Original Meaning of the Commerce Clause, 55 Ark. L. Rev. 847, 863-865 (2003) (discussing further evidence on meaning of "regulate").

Page 2-14, add to the end of note 42:

In fact, the Court recently reaffirmed *Darby*'s prohibition-as-regulation foundation. *See* Gonzales v. Raich, __ U.S. __, 125 S. Ct. 2195 (2005) (divided court) (power of Congress to eliminate interstate market in controlled substance included power to reach noncommercial, intrastate production of medical marijuana for private consumption); Reno v. Condon, 528 U.S. 141, 120 S. Ct. 666 (2000) (upholding the federal Driver's Privacy Protection Act prohibiting states from selling driver's license data in interstate commerce). Scholars, however, have not been so reticent. *See* Barnett, *supra* note 2, at 139-146 (concluding that it is unlikely that the Framers intended the power to "regulate" interstate commerce to include the power to prohibit certain types of commerce); *see also* Barnett, New Evidence of the Original Meaning of the Commerce Clause, 55 Ark. L. Rev. 847, 863-865 (2003) (discussing further evidence on meaning of "regulate").

§ 2.04 REGULATING INTERSTATE COMMERCE FOR "NON-COMMERCIAL" OR "ULTERIOR" PURPOSES: THE NATIONAL POLICE POWER

Page 2-20, add to the end of note 60:

For a thorough account of the 1964 Civil Rights Act's public accommodation provisions, and their eventual approval by the Supreme Court in *Heart of Atlanta Motel, Inc. v. U.S.*, 379 U.S. 241, 85 S. Ct. 348 (1964), and *Katzenbach v. McClung*, 379 U.S. 294, 85 S. Ct. 377 (1964), *see* Cortner, Civil Rights and Public Accommodations: The *Heart of Atlanta Motel* and *McClung* Cases (Univ. Press of Kansas, 2001).

§ 2.05 COMMERCIAL LAW AS A "REGULATION" OF COMMERCE: INTRODUCTION

Page 2-23, add to note 69, after "see also":

Nelson, A Commerce Clause Standard for the New Millennium: "Yes" to Broad Congressional Control over Commercial Transactions; "No" to Federal Legislation on Social and Cultural Issues, 55 Ark. L. Rev. 1213, 1243 (2003) (proposing federal commercial code to preempt Uniform

Commercial Code); Overby, Our New Commercial Law Federalism, 76 Temple L. Rev. 297 (2003);

[B] The Unification of State Commercial Law

Page 2-30, add to the end of note 94:

The myriad issues regarding "electronic commerce," which can occur without regard for geographical or jurisdictional boundaries, offers an occasion to revisit some of the issues raised in this section. *See, e.g.*, Symposium, Annual Regulation of Business Focus: Regulation of Electronic Commerce, 51 Admin. L. Rev. 769 (1999); Overby, Our New Commercial Law Federalism, 76 Temple L. Rev. 297 (2003); Tomaszewski, The Pandora's Box of Cyberspace: State Regulation of Digital Signatures and the Dormant Commerce Clause, 33 Gonzaga L. Rev. 417 (1997-1998); *see also infra* § 3.06[C] (discussing Internet commerce as "interstate commerce"). For articles discussing the phenomenon of Internet gambling, *see, e.g.*, Keller, The Game's the Same: Why Gambling in Cyberspace Violates Federal Law, 108 Yale L.J. 1569 (1999); Kailus, Note, Do Not Bet on Unilateral Prohibition of Internet Gambling to Eliminate Cyber-Casinos, 1999 Ill. L. Rev. 1045 (1999).

CHAPTER 3

THE MEANING OF "COMMERCE"

§ 3.01 INTRODUCTION: THE MEANING OF "COMMERCE"

Page 3-3, add to the end of note 3:

; *but see* Barnett, The Original Meaning of the Commerce Clause, 68 U. Chi. L. Rev. 101 (2001) (arguing that the original meaning of the Clause was narrower); Barnett, New Evidence of the Original Meaning of the Commerce Clause, 55 Ark. L. Rev. 847 (2003); *see also* Johnson, The Panda's Thumb: The Modest and Mercantilist Original Meaning of the Commerce Clause, 13 Wm. & Mary Bill Rts. J. 1 (2004) (arguing in favor of a narrower meaning of "commerce"). Responses to Barnett can be found in Pushaw & Nelson, A Critique of the Narrow Interpretation of the Commerce Clause, 96 Nw. L. Rev. 695 (2002) and in Pushaw, Methods of Interpreting the Commerce Clause: A Comparative Analysis, 55 Ark. L. Rev. 1185, 1199-1202 (2003) (responding, in part, to Barnett's new evidence).

§ 3.02 MODES OF TRANSPORTATION

[A] By Sea

Page 3-6, add to the end of note 15:

More recently, the Supreme Court stated that "the federal interest [in navigation] has been manifest since the beginning of our Republic and is now well established." Moreover, it continued, "[t]he authority of Congress to regulate interstate navigation, without embarrassment from intervention of the separate States and resulting difficulties with foreign nations was cited in the Federalist Papers as one of the reasons for adopting the Constitution." United States v. Locke, 529 U.S. 89, 99, 120 S. Ct. 1135, 1143 (2000). For the difference between navigation as commerce, and the use of a waterway for commercial activity sufficient to maintain federal admiralty jurisdiction, *see* Le Blanc v. Cleveland, 198 F.3d 353 (2d Cir. 1999) (no jurisdiction over personal injury case occurring at a place in the Hudson river which was not "navigable"); Fahnestock v. Reeder, 223 F. Supp. 2d 618, 624 (E.D. Pa. 2002) (holding that the "appropriate standard for determining the navigability of a body of water for the purpose of conferring admiralty jurisdiction . . . is whether the body of water is actually navigable or susceptible to being navigated without modification from its current state").

[C] Distinctions between Navigation and Land Transportation

Page 3-7, add to the end of note 19:

; Bederman, Admiralty Jurisdiction, 31 J. Mar. L. & Com. 189 (2000).

[D] The Coming of the Iron Horse

Page 3-8, add to the end of note 23:

For a panoramic account of the changes to American law wrought by the advent of the railroads, see Ely, Railroads and American Law (Kansas Univ. Press, 2001); Ely, "The Railroad Has Burst Through State Limits": Railroads and Interstate Commerce, 1830-1920, 55 Ark. L. Rev. 933 (2003).

[E] Motor Vehicles

Page 3-13, add to the end of note 36:

For the Court's approval of an expression of the "will of Congress" that states not be permitted to sell the information they collect from driver's licenses, *see* Reno v. Condon, 528 U.S. 141, 120 S. Ct. 666 (2000) (upholding the federal Driver's Privacy Protection Act prohibiting states from selling driver's license data in interstate commerce); *see generally* Preiser, Note, Staking Out the Border Between Commandeering and Conditional Preemption: Is the Driver's Privacy Protection Act Constitutional Under the Tenth Amendment?, 98 Mich. L. Rev. 514 (1999).

§ 3.04 MANUFACTURING VS. "COMMERCE"

Page 3-25, add to the end of note 74:

For a recent argument that the *Kidd* majority and Justice Thomas got it right, and that Professor Crosskey was mistaken, *see* Barnett, *supra* note 3, at 125-132; *see also* Barnett, New Evidence of the Original Meaning of the Commerce Clause, 55 Ark. L. Rev. 847 (2003). *But see* Pushaw & Nelson,

A Critique of the Narrow Interpretation of the Commerce Clause, 96 Nw. U. L. Rev. 695 (2002) (disputing Barnett's conclusions) and Pushaw, Methods of Interpreting the Commerce Clause: A Comparative Analysis, 55 Ark. L. Rev. 1185, 1199-1202 (2003) (responding, in part, to Barnett's new evidence).

§ 3.06 TELECOMMUNICATIONS

[B] Later Technological Devices: Telephones and Radios

Page 3-33, add to the end of note 106:

For a recent reaffirmation of the government's power to regulate even intrastate radio broadcasts, *see* United States v. Butterfield, 91 F. Supp. 2d 704, 705 (D. Vt. 2000) ("The Defendant argues that Congress has no authority to regulate intrastate radio broadcasts under the Commerce Clause. However, radio broadcasts have impact upon interstate commerce, regardless of whether those broadcasts are interstate or intrastate in scope."); *see also* Miller & Biggerstaff, Application of the Consumer Protection Act to Intrastate Telemarketing Calls and Faxes, 52 Fed. Comm. L.J. 667 (2000). Telephones and telephonic components are also "instrumentalities" of interstate commerce, whose regulation by Congress is widely acknowledged, and, indeed, was not questioned by the Supreme Court's 1995 *Lopez* decision. *See, e.g.,* United States v. Edmondson, 175 F. Supp. 2d 889, 894 (S.D. Miss. 2001) (holding that cellular telephone identification numbers and account numbers are instrumentalities of commerce and thus affect interstate commerce under federal fraud statute). For more on *Lopez*'s tri-partite classification of Congress's regulatory power, *see infra* § 5.04.

Page 3-35, add to the end of note 110:

; *but see* Cable Plus Co., L.P. v. Arizona Dept. Rev., 4 P.3d 1050, 1052-1053 (Ct. App. Ariz. 2000) (rejecting state argument that "electronically process[ed] raw satellite programming from out of state" can be taxed under a statute providing for the taxation of intrastate telecommunications services; state view would mean that the transmission of "television programming by way of a satellite in an orbit 23,000 miles above the equator is always an exclusive intrastate business").

[C] Internet Commerce as "Interstate Commerce"

Page 3-36, add to the end of note 115:

But *see* Goldsmith & Sykes, The Internet and the Dormant Commerce Clause, 110 Yale L.J. 785, 787 (2001) (seeking to "deflate the emerging conventional wisdom" that the dormant Commerce Clause doctrine renders invalid most state attempts to regulate the Internet "and to show that the dormant Commerce Clause, properly understood, leaves states with much more flexibility to regulate Internet transactions than is commonly thought"). *See also* Ribstein & Kobayashi, State Regulation of Electronic Commerce, 51 Emory L.J. 1 (2002) (arguing that state regulation is preferable to federal regulation).

Page 3-36, add to the end of note 116:

Deciding where, in fact, the Internet activity *does* originate presents its own set of interesting issues. *See* Boland & Gwin, The Internet and Personal Jurisdiction Under the Constitution: In What State, Exactly, Is the Internet Located?, Boston Bar J., Jan./Feb. 2000, at 6; Stein, Personal Jurisdiction and the Internet: Seeing Due Process Through the Lens of Regulatory Precision, 98 Nw. U. L. Rev. 411 (2004).

Page 3-36, add to third line of note 117 before "American Civil Liberties Union v. Johnson":

PSINET, Inc. v. Chapman, 362 F.3d 227, ___-___ (4th Cir. 2004) (divided court) (striking down Virginia statute prohibiting use of Internet to display or provide access to offensive materials by juveniles; burdens on interstate commerce clearly excessive compared to local benefits); American Bookseller's Foundation v. Dean, 342 F.3d 96, 102-104 (2d Cir. 2003) (striking down Vermont's statute governing sexually explicit content on the Internet; concluding that statute is impermissible extraterritorial regulation; predicting that "it [is] likely that the internet will soon be seen as falling within that class of subjects that are protected from State regulation because they 'imperatively demand[] a single uniform rule'" (quoting Cooley v. Board of Wardens, 53 U.S. (12 How.) 299, 319 (1851))); Southeast Booksellers Ass'n v. McMaster, 2005 WL 1322849 (D.S.C. 2005), at *10-11 (South Carolina statute prohibiting dissemination of material "harmful to minors" over the Internet invalid "because the burdens that it imposes on interstate commerce are excessive in relation to the local benefit conferred" and because act "regulat[es] commerce occurring wholly outside of South Carolina"); Center for Democracy & Technology v. Pappert, 2004 WL 2005938 (E.D. Pa. 2004), at __ (striking down state law requiring Internet service providers to remove or disable access to child pornography either stored on or available through its service; little evidence law is effective while "there is evidence that this Act places a substantial burden on interstate commerce" and has the "practical effect of exporting Pennsylvania's domestic policies"); Cyberspace Communications, Inc. v. Engler, 55 F. Supp. 2d 737 (E.D. Mich. 1999), *aff'd* 238 F.3d 420 (6th Cir. 2000) (enjoining Michigan statute prohibiting the use of computers or the Internet to disseminate sexually explicit materials to minors; relying in part on the dormant Commerce Clause doctrine);

Page 3-36, add to sixth line of note 117 after "grounds)":

, *aff'd* American Civil Liberties Union v. Johnson, 194 F.3d 1149, 1163 (10th Cir. 1999) (upholding district court's grant of preliminary injunction). On remand from the Sixth Circuit, the Michigan statute struck down in *Cyberspace Communications v. Engler, supra,* was permanently enjoined. *See* Cyberspace Communications, Inc. v. Engler, 142 F. Supp. 2d 827, 830-831 (E.D. Mich. 2001) (concluding that the statute impermissibly regulated extraterritorial activity). *But see* State v. Backlund, 672 N.W.2d 431, 436-438 (N.D. 2003) (rejecting Commerce Clause challenge to state law prohibiting use of the Internet to "lure" minors; "it is difficult to ascertain any legitimate commerce that is derived from the willful transmission of explicit or implicit sexual communications to a person believed to be a minor in order to willfully lure that person into sexual activity"); Hatch v. Superior Court, 94 Cal. Rptr. 2d 453, 473 (Ct. App. Cal. 2000) (divided court) (upholding California statute making it illegal to send by any means certain material "with the intent or for the purpose of seducing a minor," as applied to Internet communications). For a critique of the majority opinion, *see id.* at 278-295 (McDonald, J., concurring and dissenting). *See also* State v. Cunningham, 2004 WL 829881 (Ct. App. Ohio) (April 16, 2004) (unpublished), at *5-*6 (rejecting Commerce Clause challenge to state law prohibiting use of the Internet to "lure" minors); State v. Snyder, 2003 WL 22838714 (Ct. App. Ohio) (Dec. 1, 2003), at *8 (same); People v. Hsu, 82 Cal. App. 4th 976, 983-985 (Cal. Ct. App. 2000) (rejecting dormant Commerce Clause challenge to state statute prohibiting persons from sending "harmful material" to a person known to be a minor with the intent to arouse or appeal to the sexual desires of that person, and with the intent of seducing the minor; costs to interstate commerce do not clearly exceed putative benefits, and because statute does not presume to operate outside the borders of the state, no extraterritoriality problem exists); People v. Barrows, 709 N.Y.S.2d 573, 574 (N.Y. Sup. Ct. 2000) (relying on *Foley, infra,* to uphold conviction of defendant convicted of using material sent over Internet to lure minor into sexual activity); People v. Foley, 94 N.Y.2d 668 (Ct. App. N.Y. 2000) (upholding state law prohibiting dissemination of certain images to minors to "lure" them into engaging in sexual activity not prohibited by the dormant Commerce Clause doctrine). *See generally* Pann, The Dormant Commerce Clause and State Regulation of the Internet: Are Laws Protecting Minors from Sexual Predators Constitutionally Different than Those Protecting Minors from Sexually Explicit Materials? 2005 Duke L. & Tech. Rev. 8 (2005); Stanger, Comment, Salvaging States' Rights to Protect Children from Internet Predation: State Power to Regulate Internet Activity under the Dormant Commerce Clause, 2005 B.Y.U. L. Rev. 191 (2005).

Page 3-36, add to the end of the first paragraph of note 117:

; *see also* Symposium, Jurisdiction to Tax Income and Consumption in the New Economy: International, National, and Subnational Perspectives, 38 Ga. L. Rev. 1 (2003) (articles by Hellerstein, Cockfield, Freidman, Libin & Gillis, and Swain); Symposium, Debating the Prospect of E-Commerce Taxation, 13 Harv. J.L. & Tech. 549-657 (2000) (articles by Hellerstein, McClure, Bick, Groves, and Varian); Symposium on Taxation of Electronic Commerce, 2000 B.Y.U. L. Rev. 1-183 (articles by Fleming, Houghton and Hellerstein, McLure, and McKeown); Camilli, Run for the Border!: Evasion of Sales and Use Taxes by Mail-Order and Internet Sellers, 19 J.L. & Comm. 137 (1999) (recommending that Congress pass legislation permitting states and localities to collect sales and use taxes); Clevenger, Internet Pharmacies: Cyberspace Versus the Regulatory State, 15 J.L. & Health 165 (2000-2001) (discussing difficulties posed by regulation of Internet pharmacies); Cockfield, Transforming the Internet into a Taxable Forum: A Case Study in E-Commerce Taxation, 85 Minn. L. Rev. 1171 (2001); Davidson & Banthin, Untangling the Web: Legal and Policy Tools to Restrict Online Cigar Advertisement, 35 U. S. F. L. Rev. 1, 37-45 (2000) (discussing dormant Commerce Clause doctrine obstacles to state regulation); Farber, Expressive Commerce in Cyberspace: Public

Goods, Network Effects, and Free Speech, 16 Ga. St. U. L. Rev. 789, 818 (2000) (urging restraint in the application of the dormant Commerce Clause doctrine to Internet cases, but arguing that approach is to be preferred to decisions based on the First Amendment because Congress can overturn a judicial decision based on the dormant Commerce Clause doctrine); Fogo, The Postman Always Rings 4,000 Times: New Approaches to Curb Spam, 18 J. Marshall J. Computer & Info. L. 915 (2000); Goldsmith & Sykes, *supra* note 115; Fagan, Note, Taxation of Electronic Commerce: Avoiding an Inroad Upon Federalism, 49 Drake L. Rev. 441 (2001); Morris & Booher, A Case for National E-Mail Regulation: State UCE Statutes Have Infirmities, 70 Def. Counsel J. 1 (2003); Lanin, Note, Who Controls the Internet?: States' Rights and the Reawakening of the Dormant Commerce Clause, 73 S. Cal. L. Rev. 1423 (2000); Liazos, Comment, Can States Impose Registration Requirements on Online Charitable Solicitors, 67 U. Chi. L. Rev. 1379 (2000); Masterson, Note, Collecting Sales and Use Tax Electronic Commerce: E-Confusion or E-Collection, 79 N.C. L. Rev. 203 (2000); Moorefield, Note, Spam— It's Just Not for Breakfast Anymore: Federal Legislation and the Fight to Free the Internet from Unsolicited Commercial E-mail, 5 B.U. J. Sci. & Tech. L. 10 (1999); Morris, Commentary, Interstate Commerce and the Future of State Sales and Use Taxes, 54 Ala. L. Rev. 1393 (2003); Smith, Comment Internet Taxes: Congressional Efforts to Control States' Ability to Tax the World Wide Web, 7 Rich. J.L. & Tech. 3 (2000); Swartout, Comment, The Tooth Fairy, the Easter Bunny, and Tax-Free Holiday Gifts On-Line: Who Picks Up the Sales Tax Tab?, 47 Wayne L. Rev. 1027 (2001); Symposium, Annual Regulation of Business Focus: Regulation of Electronic Commerce, 51 Admin. L. Rev. 769 (1999); Amaditz, Canning "Spam" in Virginia: Model Legislation to Control Junk E-mail, 4 Va. J.L. & Tech. 4 (1999); Burk, How State Regulation of the Internet Violates the Commerce Clause, 17 Cato J. 147 (1997); Kass, Regulation and the Internet, 26 So. U. L. Rev. 93 (1998); Simmons, No Seconds on Spam: A Legislative Prescription to Harness Unsolicited Commercial E-Mail, 3 J. Small & Emerging Bus. L. 389, 411-412 (1999) (suggesting that many state laws aimed at regulating unsolicited commercial e-mail— "spam" to the cognoscenti—are at risk of invalidation under the dormant Commerce Clause doctrine); Tomaszewski, The Pandora's Box of Cyberspace: State Regulation of Digital Signatures and the Dormant Commerce Clause, 33 Gonzaga L. Rev. 417 (1997-1998); Ann, Comment, A More Convenient Crime: Why States Must Regulate Internet-Related Criminal Activity Under the Dormant Commerce Clause, 20

Pace L. Rev. 189 (1999); Gaylord, Note, State Regulatory Jurisprudence and the Internet: Letting the Dormant Commerce Clause Lie, 52 Vand. L. Rev. 1095 (1999); Bassinger, Note, Dormant Commerce Clause Limits on State Regulation of the Internet: The Transportation Analogy, 32 Ga. L. Rev. 889 (1998). For articles on the regulation of Internet gambling *see* Keller, The Game's the Same: Why Gambling in Cyberspace Violates Federal Law, 108 Yale L.J. 1569 (1999); Kailus, Note, Do Not Bet on Unilateral Prohibition of Internet Gambling to Eliminate Cyber-Casinos, 1999 Ill. L. Rev. 1045; *see also* Hellwege, Law Enforcement, Legislators Grapple with Child Sexual Exploitation on the Net, Trial, March, at 13, 16 (2000) (noting dormant Commerce Clause doctrine problems with state laws designed to safeguard children from Internet predators); Stanger, Comment, Salvaging States' Rights to Protect Children from Internet Predation: State Power to Regulate Internet Activity under the Dormant Commerce Clause, 2005 B.Y.U. L. Rev. 191 (2005); Kaplan, State Internet Laws Face a Different Constitutional Challenge, N.Y. Times, July 2, 1999, available at http://nytimes.com/library/tech/99/07/cyber/cyberlaw/02law.html. For an interesting debate on whether Congress could use its commerce power to create property rights in new information, *see* Benkler, Constitutional Bounds of Database Protection: The Role of Judicial Review in the Creation and Definition of Private Rights in Information, 15 Berkeley Tech. L.J. 535, 548-552 (2000), and Hamilton, A Response to Professor Benkler, 15 Berkeley Tech. L.J. 605, 621-625 (2000) (suggesting that *Lopez* and *Morrison* limit congressional power to create such new rights).

Page 3-37, add to the end of note 120:

For a cogent critique of the *Pataki* court's assumptions about the architecture of the Internet, and an argument that technological advances since that decision make its conclusions about state regulation of the Internet obsolete, *see* Goldsmith & Sykes, *supra* note 115, at 813-818.

Page 3-38, add to note 125 before "see generally":

See also American Bookseller's Foundation v. Dean, 342 F.3d 96, 102-104 (2d Cir. 2003) (predicting that "it [is] likely that the internet will soon be seen as falling within that class of subjects that are protected from State regulation because they 'imperatively demand[] a single uniform rule'" (quoting Cooley v. Board of Wardens, 53 U.S. (12 How.) 299, 319 (1851)));

Page 3-38, add to the end of note 127:

; Schulte, *Abracadabra International, Ltd. v. Abracadabra Creations, Inc.*—Internet Advertising Just Federalized the Nation's Service Mark Law, 22 Hamline L. Rev. 563 (1999) (describing the effects the Internet has on the scope of federal trademark legislation). On the other hand, recent state attempts to regulate unsolicited e-mail advertisements—"spam"—have been upheld by courts in Washington and California. *See* State v. Heckel, 24 P.3d 404, 836-840 (Wash. 2001) (concluding that Washington anti-spam law did not violate the dormant Commerce Clause doctrine); Ferguson v. Friendfinders, Inc., 115 Cal. Rptr.2d 258, 262-269 (Ct. App. Cal. 2002) (relying in part on *Heckel* to uphold similar California law). *See generally* Recent Cases, 115 Harv. L. Rev. 931 (2002) (discussing *Heckel*).

Page 3-38, add to note 128 following "see generally":

Symposium, Jurisdiction to Tax Income and Consumption in the New Economy: International, National, and Subnational Perspectives, 38 Ga. L. Rev. 1 (2003) (articles by Hellerstein, Cockfield, Freidman, Libin & Gillis, and Swain); Symposium, Debating the Prospect of E-Commerce Taxation, 13 Harv. J.L. & Tech. 549-657 (2000) (articles by Hellerstein, McClure, Bick, Groves, and Varian); Symposium on Taxation of Electronic Commerce, 2000 B.Y.U. L. Rev. 1-183 (articles by Fleming, Houghton and Hellerstein, McLure, and McKeown); Cockfield, Transforming the Internet into a Taxable Forum: A Case Study in E-Commerce Taxation, 85 Minn. L. Rev. 1171 (2001); Camilli, Run for the Border!: Evasion of Sales and Use Taxes by Mail-Order and Internet Sellers, 19 J.L. & Comm. 137 (1999) (recommending that Congress pass legislation permitting states and localities to collect sales and use taxes); Forgione, Weaving the Continental Web: Exploring Free Trade, Taxation, and the Internet, 9 L. & Bus. Rev. Am. 513 (2003); McClure, Sales and Use Taxes on Electronic Commerce: Legal, Economic, Administrative, and Political Issues, 24 Urb. Law. 449 (2002);

Page 3-39, add to note 128 before "For the ironic use of uniform state laws":

; Fagan, Note, Taxation of Electronic Commerce: Avoiding an Inroad Upon Federalism, 49 Drake L. Rev. 441 (2001); Masterson, Note,

Collecting Sales and Use Tax Electronic Commerce: E-Confusion or E-Collection, 79 N.C. L. Rev. 203 (2000); Morris, Commentary, Interstate Commerce and the Future of State Sales and Use Taxes, 54 Ala. L. Rev. 1393 (2003); Way, Note, State and Local Sales Tax on Internet Commerce: Developing a Neutral and Efficient Framework, 19 Va. Tax Rev. 115 (1999); Wilde, Comment, *Western Wireless Corp. v. Department of Revenue*: State Taxation on Interstate Transactions and How to Comply with the Dormant Commerce Clause, 49 S.D. L. Rev. 341 (2003-2004); *see also* Gray, Comment, The Constitutionality of Federal Preemption of State Taxation of Internet Transactions, 17 St. Louis U. Pub. L. Rev. 451 (1998) (arguing that the federal moratorium on state taxation of Internet commerce was unconstitutional); Smith, Comment Internet Taxes: Congressional Efforts to Control States' Ability to Tax the World Wide Web, 7 Rich. J.L. & Tech. 3 (2000).

Page 3-39, add to the end of note 128:

The Clinton Administration had proposed that the World Trade Organization impose a permanent, global ban on taxes and tariffs that target Internet commerce. Associated Press, U.S. Seeking Ban on Internet Taxes, N.Y. Times, Oct. 1, 1999, available at http://nytimes.com/aponline/w/AP-Internet-Taxes.html.

Internet crime is also receiving attention at the state and federal level. *See* Braun, Drobny & Gessner, www.commercial_terrorism.com: A Proposed Federal Criminal Statute Addressing the Solicitation of Commercial Terrorism Through the Internet, 37 Harv. J. on Legis. 159 (2000); Ann, Comment, A More Convenient Crime: Why States Must Regulate Internet-Related Criminal Activity Under the Dormant Commerce Clause, 20 Pace L. Rev. 189 (1999).

Page 3-39, replace third sentence of note 129 with the following:

In 1998, Congress passed, and the President signed into law, a three-year moratorium on state and local Internet taxes, which was extended in November of 2001 for another two years. It expired in October, 2003 and Congress is considering whether to make it permanent.

Page 3-39, add to the end of note 129:

As part of the moratorium, an Advisory Commission on Electronic Commerce was established to draft tax policies for the Internet. For more on its work and the political problems inherent in proposing taxes on Internet commerce, *see* Clausing, Debate on Internet Taxes Takes Political Turn, N.Y. Times, Sept. 13, 1999, at C1. With the end of the moratorium in sight, Congress is having to face the issue once again and is under considerable pressure from traditional "brick and mortar" retailers and from state and local governments to end the moratorium and the *de facto* subsidy of Internet commerce. *See generally* Congress Wrestles Again with Internet Sales Taxes, CNN, April, 30, 2001, available at http://www.cnn.com/2001/ALLPOLITICS/04/30/internet.taxes.ap/index.html; McCaleb, States Argue for Taxing Internet Transactions, CNN, March 14, 2001, available at http://www.cnn.com/2001/ALLPOLITICS/03/14/internet.taxes/index.html. The current administration, however, favors a broad ban on Internet taxes, as do many members of Congress. *See generally* Cheney Calls for Permanent Internet Tax Ban, CNN, April 19, 2001, available at www.cnn.com/2001/ALLPOLITICS/tech.cheney.reut/index.html.

Page 3-39, add new paragraph after carryover paragraph:

Recent lower court cases have exhibited a more tolerant attitude toward state regulation of electronic commerce than might be expected from cases involving cyberporn. In a case involving a statute combining governmental desires to take in revenue and control vice, the Second Circuit Court of Appeals reversed a district court enjoining a New York statute that had the effect of prohibiting the sale of cigarettes by phone, through the mail, or over the Internet.[129.1] The district court had concluded that "the statute in effect bars out-of-state retailers of tobacco products in favor of in-state tobacco products. . . ."[129.2] Since the statute discriminated against interstate commerce, it was subject to strictest scrutiny; the court concluded that none of the state's asserted justifications — including preventing adults from evading state taxes and preventing minors from obtaining cigarettes — saved the statute.[129.3]

The Second Circuit, however, held that only discrimination that prevented other out-of-state suppliers from stepping in to fill the void left by suppliers who, because of the legislation, must stop selling in the state, violated the dormant Commerce Clause.[129.4] "The fact that these particular Plaintiffs may be priced out of the retail cigarette market does not establish a discriminatory effect," wrote the court.[129.5] Though the statute "eliminate[s] *all* sales of cigarettes to New York consumers that do not involve face-to-face sales or the transportation of fewer than four cartons of cigarettes to any one consumer," the court continued, the dormant Commerce Clause doctrine does not "'protect[] the particular structure or methods of operation in a retail market.'"[129.6]

The Fifth Circuit recently upheld efforts by the Texas legislature to insulate in-state automobile dealers from electronic competition by automobile makers. In *Ford Motor Co. v. Texas Department of Transportation* (2001), the challenged law prohibited automotive manufacturers from selling cars to consumers via the Internet.[129.7] Texas law prohibited sales of used vehicles to Texas consumers without a license.[129.8] Ford Motor Company, which operated a website that offered used cars to consumers, could not obtain the license since the law prohibited automotive manufacturers and distributors from owning and interest in, operating, or acting as an automotive dealer.[129.9] Ford sued, alleging, *inter alia,* that the Texas law impermissibly discriminated in its effects.[129.10]

The purpose of the statute, the court found, was "to prevent manufacturers from utilizing their superior market position to compete against dealers in the retail car market. The legislature's concern was fueled by the recent opening of several dealerships owned by manufacturers and the perceived detriment to the public from vertical integration of the automobile market."[129.11] Despite this fairly blatant announcement by the legislature of its protectionist aims, the court of appeals rejected Ford's discriminatory effects argument.

While conceding that a facially neutral statute (which Texas's was) may have discriminatory effects, the court maintained that "[t]he [Supreme] Court's jurisprudence finds discrimination only when a State discriminates among similarly situated in-state and out-of-state interests."[129.12] The court explained that a "State statute or regulation is discriminatory [in its effects] when it provides for differential treatment of similarly situated entities based on their contacts with the State or has the effect of providing a competitive advantage to in-state interests vis-à-vis similarly situated out-of-state interests."[129.13] In the case of the Texas statute, though the state sought to advantage in-state dealers over out-of-state manufacturers, it did not prevent out-of-state auto dealers seeking to establish themselves in Texas. "Consequently," the court held, the statute "does not protect dealers from out-of-state competition, it protects dealers from competition from manufacturers,"[129.14] despite the fact that Texas had no automobile manufacturers.[129.15]

[129.1] Brown & Williamson Tobacco Co. v. Pataki, 320 F.3d 200 (2d Cir. 2003) (divided court). For the district court's opinion, *see* Santa Fe Tobacco Co., Inc. v. Spitzer, 2000 WL 1694307 (S.D.N.Y. 2000).

[129.2] *Santa Fe Tobacco Co., Inc.,* 2000 WL 1694307, at *1.

[129.3] *Id.* at *2-*5.

[129.4] *Brown & Williamson,* 320 F.3d at 208.

[129.5] *Id.* at 213.

[129.6] *Id.* (quoting *Exxon v. Maryland,* 437 U.S. 117, 127 (1978) (divided court)); Oltra, Inc. v. Pataki, 273 F. Supp. 2d 265 (W.D.N.Y. 2003) (applying *Brown and Williamson* to reject claims by direct retailers of cigarettes that New York direct shipment ban violates the dormant Commerce Clause).

[129.7] For an overview of the Texas legislation and similar laws, *see* generally Empie, Comment, The Dormant Internet: Are State Regulations of Motor Vehicle Sales by Manufacturers on the Information Superhighway Obstructing Interstate and Internet Commerce?, 18 Ga. St. U. L. Rev. 827 (2002); *see also* Forehand & Forehand, Motor Vehicle Dealers and Motor Vehicle Manufacturers: Florida Reacts to Pressures in the Marketplace, 29 Fla. St. U. L. Rev. 1057 (2002).

[129.8] *Ford Motor Co.,* 264 F.3d at 498.

[129.9] *Id.* at 498.

[129.10] *Id.* at 499.

[129.11] *Id.* at 500.

[129.12] *Id. But see* Oregon Waste Systems, Inc. v. Dept. Eviron. Quality, 511 U.S. 93, 99 (1994) (defining discrimination as "differential treatment of in-state and out-of-state economic interests that benefits the former and burdens the latter").

[129.13] *Id.* at 501.

[129.14] *Id.* at 502.

[129.15] *Cf.* International Truck and Engine Corp. v. Bray, 372 F.3d 717, 726 (5th Cir. 2004) (upholding Texas law prohibiting truck manufacturers from acting as new or used vehicles dealers or as used truck dealers; in-state dealers and out-of-state manufacturers not similarly situated); Alliance of Automobile Mfrs. v. Hull, 137 F. Supp.2d 1165, 1174 (D. Ariz. 2001) (rejecting motion for injunction against Arizona law that, *inter alia,* prohibits automobile manufacturers from selling services in competition with in-state dealers).

§ 3.07 TRANSMISSION OF POWER

Page 3-42, add to the end of note 140:

See generally Robertson, Bringing the Camel into the Tent: State and Federal Power over Electricity Transmission, 49 Clev. St. L. Rev. 71 (2001).

Page 3-45, add to second line of note 155, after "See also":

Engel, The Dormant Commerce Clause Threat to Market-Based Environmental Regulation: The Case of Electricity Deregulation, 26 Ecology L.Q. 243 (1999);

Page 3-45, add to end of note 155:

; Dennis, Federalism, Electric Industry Restructuring, and the Dormant Commerce Clause: *Tampa Electric Co. v. Garcia* and State Restrictions on the Development of Merchant Power Plants, 43 Nat. Res. J. 615 (2003) (student work).

Page 3-45, add to end of note 157:

However, states may not discriminate against interstate commerce in the regulation of utilities; *see, e.g.,* Kentucky Power Co. v. Huelsmann, 352 F. Supp. 2d 777, 784-787 (E.D. Ky. 2005) (striking down Kentucky law requiring utilities to curtail service to out-of-state customers instead of in-state customers in the event of a disruption of energy supply; *held,* statute has a discriminatory effect on interstate commerce).

§ 3.08 REGULATION OF INSURANCE

[C] Congressional Withdrawal from the Arena: The McCarran-Ferguson Act

Page 3-51, add to note 176 after "see generally":

Guenter, Rediscovering the McCarran-Ferguson Act's Commerce Clause Limitation, 6 Conn. Ins. L.J. 253 (1999-2000);

Page 3-52, add to the end of note 178:

For a call to revisit the McCarran-Ferguson Act regime of exclusive state regulation in light of other recent changes to the federal regulation of financial institutions, *see* Sinder, The Gramm-Leach-Bliley Act and State Regulation of the Business of Insurance—Past, Present and . . . Future?, 5 N.C. Banking Inst. 49 (2001).

[E] Other Constitutional Restrictions on State Legislation

Page 3-55, insert new paragraph after carryover paragraph and before § 3.09:

To the limitations of the Due Process and Equal Protection Clauses, the Supreme Court, in *American Insurance Association v. Garamendi* (2003), held that the President's responsibility for the conduct of foreign affairs, too, limited state regulation of insurance, despite the McCarran-Ferguson Act.[186.1]

At issue was the constitutionality of California's Holocaust Victim Insurance Relief Act ("HVIRA"), which required all insurers doing business in California to disclose information about policies sold in Europe between the years 1920 and 1945. The Ninth Circuit had upheld the statute against a variety of challenges; in particular, the court rejected a challenge under the Commerce Clause, holding that "Congress has expressly delegated to the states the power to regulate insurance, free from the constraints of the dormant Commerce Clause. [The challenged statute] is a California regulation of California insurance companies that affects foreign commerce only indirectly. Consequently, the McCarran Act applies and the dormant Commerce Clause does not."[186.2]

The Supreme Court reversed, concluding that "HVIRA interferes with foreign policy of the Executive Branch" as expressed in a number of executive agreements with countries whose companies were affected by the California law.[186.3] The Court rejected the argument that Congress had authorized laws like HVIRA through the McCarran-Ferguson Act. "[T]he point of McCarran-Ferguson's legislative choice of leaving insurance regulation generally to the States," the Court explained, "was to limit congressional preemption under the commerce power, whether dormant or exercised."[186.4] Leaving aside the question whether HVIRA *was* a "regulation of the business of insurance," which the Court seemed to question, "a federal statute directed to implied preemption by domestic commerce legislation cannot sensibly be construed to address preemption by executive conduct in foreign affairs."[186.5]

[186.1] American Ins. Ass'n v. Garamendi, 539 U.S. 396, 123 S. Ct. 2374 (2003) (divided court); *see generally* Denning, International Decisions—*American Insurance Association v. Garamendi* and *Deutsch v. Turner Corp.*, 97 Am. J. Int'l L. 950.

[186.2] Gerling Global Reinsurance Corporatino of America v. Low, 240 F.3d 739, 746 (9th Cir. 2001), *rev'd sub nom.* American Ins. Ass'n v. Garamendi, 539 U.S. 396, 123 S. Ct. 2374 (2003) (divided court).

186.3 *Garamendi,* 539 U.S. at 396, 123 S. Ct. at 2386.

186.4 539 U.S. at 396, 123 S. Ct. at 2394.

186.5 539 U.S. at 396, 123 S. Ct. at 2394. The dissenting Justices did not take issue with the majority's disposal of the McCarran-Ferguson argument. *See* 539 U.S. at ___, 123 S. Ct. at 2394 (Ginsburg, J., dissenting). For criticism of this portion of the Court's decision, *see* Denning & Ramsey, *American Insurance Association v. Garamendi* and Executive Preemption in Foreign Affairs, ___ Wm. & Mary L. Rev. ___ (forthcoming 2004).

§ 3.10 LABOR AND PERSONAL SERVICES AS "COMMERCE"

Page 3-59, add to the end of note 198:

; Sullivan, Note, "A Derelict in the Stream of Law": Overruling Baseball's Antitrust Exemption, 48 Duke L.J. 1265 (1999).

Page 3-60, add to the end of note 202:

See generally Piraino, A Proposal for the Antitrust Regulation of Professional Sports, 79 B.U. L. Rev. 889 (1999).

§ 3.11 MOVEMENT OF PERSONS AS "COMMERCE"

Page 3-63, add to the end of note 213:

; Palmore, The Not-So-Strange Career of Interstate Jim Crow: Race Transportation, and the Dormant Commerce Clause, 1878-1946, 83 Va. L. Rev. 1173 (1997). The Supreme Court, without "identify[ing] the source of that particular right in the text of the Constitution . . . ," recently reaffirmed the right to travel, striking down a state durational residency requirement that limited the welfare benefits of new state residents. Saenz v. Roe, 526 U.S. 489, 501, 119 S. Ct. 1518, 1525 (1999); *see generally* Hills, Poverty, Residency, and Federalism: States' Duty Impartiality Toward Newcomers, 1999 S. Ct. Rev. 277; Nzelibe, Free Movement: A Federalist Reinterpretation, 49 Am. U. L. Rev. 433 (1999); Montejano, Note, When Welfare Reform Crosses the Line: A Look Behind the Scenes of *Saenz v. Roe* and California's Battle over Durational Residency Requirements, 4 Tex. F. on C.L. & C.R. 275 (1999). For an argument that the failure of states to recognize same-sex marriages that might be permitted in other states violates the right to travel, *see* Strasser,

The Privileges of National Citizenship: On *Saenz,* Same-Sex Couples, and the Right to Travel, 52 Rutgers L. Rev. 553 (2000).

[B] Transporting Oneself

Page 3-66, add to the end of note 223:

For a recent rejection of a state's argument that the taxation of out-of-state commuters had no demonstrable effect on any interstate market, *see* New York v. State, 94 N.Y.2d 577, 584 (Ct. App. N.Y. 2000) ("It has long been recognized . . . that the movement of persons across State lines is a form of commerce.").

Page 3-67, add to the end of note 227:

But see John Doe No. 1 v. Georgia Dept. Pub. Safety, 147 F. Supp. 2d 1369, 1374 (N.D. Ga. 2001) (concluding that state law prohibiting illegal aliens from obtaining state driver's license was not subject to strict scrutiny under the Fourteenth Amendment).

Page 3-67, add to the end of note 228:

For an interesting twist on a "right to travel" case, *see John Doe No. 1 v. Georgia Department of Public Safety,* 147 F. Supp. 2d 1369 (N.D. Ga. 2001). Georgia's law prohibiting illegal aliens from receiving a driver's license was challenged under the Equal Protection Clause. Refusing to apply strict scrutiny, the judge first noted that illegal aliens were not a suspect class under Supreme Court precedent. *Id.* at 1373. Though recognizing that there existed a fundamental right to travel (citing *Edwards v. California*), the judge nevertheless found that illegal aliens did not enjoy "the same fundamental rights as a citizen or lawful resident alien. . . . It would be curious indeed if the law gave illegal aliens a fundamental right to travel about this country where their mere presence here is a violation of federal law." *Id.* Moreover, the court regarded Justice Jackson's connection of travel with the perquisites of citizenship in *Edwards* as further evidence that illegal aliens did not possess similar rights. *Id.* at 1374. The court further distinguished the "waiting period" cases, such as *Dunn v. Blumstein,* by noting that "[t]he state does not require a new resident to wait a certain period before applying for a new license. The state simply requires that an applicant establish residency before demanding state services." *Id.* at 1375. Finally, the court held that if an illegal alien *does* possess the right to travel, restrictions on a single mode of transportation do not violate that right. *Id.* at 1375 (citing cases from other circuits and noting that "[a] legal resident of Georgia does not have a constitutional right to a driver's license"). The court also rejected a claim that the state was incompetent to legislate on matters touching immigration, since that power resided with the federal government. *Id.* at 1375-1376.

Page 3-68, add new sentence following note 232 and before **"[C] Travel for Pleasure and Other Non-Profit Purpose"***:*

Another recent example is a federal statute, 18 U.S.C. § 2423(b), which prohibits traveling in interstate or foreign commerce for purposes of engaging in sex with minors.[232.1]

[C] Travel for Pleasure and Other Non-Profit Purposes

Page 3-69, add to the end of note 240:

Cf. United States v. Griffith, 284 F.3d 338, 347 (2d Cir. 2002) (upholding conviction under federal statute prohibiting use of minors to perform sex acts where the depiction will be transported in interstate commerce; no requirement that the tape had to have been produced or transported for economic purposes); Ramirez v. United States, 286 F. Supp. 2d 243, 244 (S.D.N.Y. 2003) (holding that federal kidnapping statute requiring transportation in interstate commerce applied despite kidnapping victim's transportation by noncommercial means, *i.e.,* in a private automobile).

Page 3-69, add to the end of note 241:

; Baden, Note, When the Open Road Is Closed to Juveniles: The Constitutionality of Juvenile Curfew Laws and the Inconsistencies Among the Courts, 37 Val. U. L. Rev. 831 (2003). *But see* Florida State Conference of NAACP Branches v. Daytona Beach, 54 F. Supp. 2d 1283, 1286 (M.D. Fla. 1999) (city plan to regulate traffic during Black College reunion by closing bridges to all beaches except for employees of certain businesses and residents held to violate the dormant Commerce Clause doctrine, in part because ordinance aimed at out-of-state visitors).

[232.1] *See* United States v. Bredimus, 352 F.3d 200, 204-208 (5th Cir. 2003) (upholding 18 U.S.C. § 2423(b) against Commerce Clause challenge); Andrews, Comment, U.S. Domestic Prosecution of the American International Sex Tourist: Efforts to Protect Children from Sexual Exploitation, 94 J. Crim. L. & Criminology 415 (2004).

§ 3.12 SHIPMENT OF DELETERIOUS PRODUCTS AS "COMMERCE"

Page 3-73, add to the end of note 250:

But see Predka v. Iowa, 186 F.3d 1082, 1083 (8th Cir. 1999) (holding that "property which it is unlawful to possess" was contraband and thus "not an object of interstate trade protected by the Commerce Clause," *held,* conviction of defendant for transporting marijuana without a state tax stamp did not violate the dormant Commerce Clause doctrine); CSX Transportation, Inc. v. Williams, 2005 WL 902130, at *21 (D.D.C. 2005) (upholding District prohibition of transportation of certain hazardous materials within 2.2 miles of the U.S. Capitol; suggests that "mere movement" risks harm, unlike in *Philadelphia v. New Jersey*).

Page 3-73, add to the end of note 252:

For a state court's recent use of the quarantine "exception" to the dormant Commerce Clause doctrine, *see* Hagener v. Wallace, 47 P.3d 847, 855-857 (Mont. 2002) (upholding permanent injunction by state agency against transfer of game farm elk to Indian reservation; state efforts to "reduce the risk of spreading [Chronic Wasting Disease], genetic pollution, interbreeding between wild and game-farm bred elk, and the establishment of feral populations" qualify as "quarantine laws" exempt from dormant Commerce Clause scrutiny); *cf.* Bean v. Bredesen, 2005 WL 1025767 (Tenn. Ct. App. 2005), at *7 (upholding state ban on private possession of white-tailed deer).

§ 3.13 CRIME AS "COMMERCE"

Page 3-73, add to the end of note 253:

See also Gonzales v. Raich, ___ U.S. ___, 125 S. Ct. 2195 (2005) (divided court) (congressional power to reach intrastate, noncommercial production of medical marijuana for personal use stemmed from combination of power of Congress to eliminate national market in illicit drugs under the Commerce Clause with the Necessary and Proper Clause); *id.* (Scalia, J., concurring) (emphasizing this argument).

[B] Expansion of Federal Criminal Jurisdiction

Page 3-76, add to the end of note 265:

For recent commentary on the federalization of crime, *see* Beale, The Unintended Consequences of Enhancing Gun Penalties: Shooting Down the Commerce Clause and Arming Federal Prosecutors, 51 Duke L.J. 1641 (2002); Bradley, Federalism and Federal Criminal Law, 55 Hastings L.J. 573 (2004) (arguing that the Supreme Court "is in the process of making a meaningful, but not dramatic or disastrous, trimming of federal jurisdiction under the Commerce Clause" but that the Court's intent has been frustrated by recalcitrant lower courts); Calabresi, Federal and State Courts: Restoring a Workable Balance, 78 N.Y.U. L. Rev. 1293 (2003) (former Yale Law School Dean and current Second Circuit Judge Calabresi expressing doubts whether courts can impose meaningful limits); Ehrlich, The Increasing Federalization of Crime, 32 Ariz. St. L.J. 825 (2000) (critique by a state appeals court judge); Klein, Independent-Norm Federalism in Criminal Law, 90 Cal. L. Rev. 1541 (2002); Maroney, Fifty Years of Federalization of Criminal Law: Sounding the Alarm or "Crying Wolf?," 50 Syracuse L. Rev. 1317 (2000) (criticizing the trend, but suggesting that the problem is not quite as great as is often portrayed); O'Hear, Federalism and Drug Control, 57 Vand. L. Rev. 783 (2004); Simons, Prosecutorial Discretion and Prosecution Guidelines: A Case Study in Controlling Federalization, 75 N.Y.U. L. Rev. 893 (2000) (arguing that guidelines for federal prosecutors could remedy problems of over-federalization of crimes); Chorba, Note, The Danger of Federalizing Hate Crimes: Congressional Misconceptions and the Unintended Consequences of the Hate Crimes Prevention Act, 87 Va. L. Rev. 319 (2001); Green, Note, Guns, Drugs, and Federalism: Rethinking Commerce-Enabled Regulation of Mere Possession, 72 Fordham L. Rev. 2543 (2004).

Page 3-77, add to tenth line of note 268, between "kickbacks);" and "see generally":

United States v. Kovach, 208 F.3d 1215, 1217 (10th Cir. 2000) (sustaining conviction under federal statute prohibiting making or possessing of counterfeited security of any organization whose activities affect interstate or foreign commerce; court considered amount in the case, $6400, to be "significant," but added that "our conclusion would be the same even if the amount were considered de minimis").

Page 3-77, add to the end of note 268:

For an interesting aside from a federal judge who disapproves of the expansion of federal criminal jurisdiction under the auspices of the Commerce Clause, *see* United States v. Claiborne, 92 F. Supp. 2d 503, 509 (E.D. Va. 2000). A criminal defendant was seeking dismissal of an indictment, under federal law, for crimes for which the defendant was tried and acquitted under *state* law. While recognizing that the dual sovereignty exception to the constitutional prohibition against double jeopardy applied, and that the exception was "deeply rooted in tradition," the judge commented that

> in view of the expansion of the Commerce Clause as it relates to federal crimes, perhaps the dual sovereignty doctrine should be reconsidered. Where the Commerce Clause has been broadly expanded and the line between federal and state crimes has been blurred to allow virtually every crime to be prosecuted in federal court under the auspice of "affecting interstate commerce," the rationale of the dual sovereignty doctrine is nullified and thus, the doctrine should be eliminated.

Id. Perhaps the judge can take some comfort from United States v. Morrison, 529 U.S. 598, 120 S. Ct. 1740 (2000) (divided court) (holding that the civil suit remedy for victims of "gender-based animus" contained in the Violence Against Women Act exceeded Congress's power under the Commerce Clause and the Fourteenth Amendment) and Jones v. United States, 529 U.S. 848, 120 S. Ct. 1904 (2000) (refusing to apply federal arson statute containing "in or affecting interstate commerce" jurisdictional nexus to arson of private resident not otherwise used in commerce).

Page 3-79, add to the end of note 273:

; *but see* Calabresi, Federal and State Courts: Restoring a Workable Balance, 78 N.Y.U. L. Rev. 1293 (2003) (former Yale Law School Dean and current Second Circuit Judge Calabresi expressing doubts whether courts can impose meaningful limits); Maroney, Fifty Years of Federalization of Criminal Law: Sounding the Alarm or "Crying Wolf?," 50 Syracuse L. Rev. 1317 (2000) (criticizing the trend, but suggesting that the problem is not quite as great as is often portrayed); Simons, Prosecutorial Discretion and Prosecution Guidelines: A Case Study in Controlling Federalization, 75 N.Y.U. L. Rev. 893 (2000) (arguing that guidelines for federal prosecutors could remedy problems of over-federalization of crimes).

Page 3-79, add new paragraph before § 3.14:

The Court's decision in *Lopez,* however, has given those charged with federal crimes a new opportunity to challenge the validity of their indictments and convictions. For example, the Supreme Court recently used *Lopez* to announce an outer limit to the reach of 18 U.S.C. § 844(i), the federal arson statute. In *Jones v. United States* (2000), the Court unanimously held that, under *Lopez,* arson of "an owner-occupied residence not used for any commercial purpose does not qualify as property 'used in' commerce or commerce-affecting activity" and was not subject to federal prosecution.[275.1] The Court rejected the reasoning of the government, which had been accepted by a number of other jurisdictions,[275.2] that a private residence was "used in" interstate commerce by, *inter alia,* using the house as collateral to secure a mortgage from an out-of-state lender; using the house to obtain insurance from an out-of-state insurer; and using the house to receive natural gas from outside the state.[275.3] "Were we to adopt the Government's expansive interpretation," wrote Justice Ginsburg, "hardly a building in the land would fall outside the federal statute's domain. Practically every building in our cities, towns, and rural areas is constructed with supplies that have moved in interstate commerce, served by utilities that have an interstate connection . . . or bears some other trace of interstate commerce."[275.4] *Lopez,* the "rule of lenity" that counsels narrow construction of penal statutes, and *Bass*'s reluctance to interpret federal statutes so as to upset the federal-state balance in crime control all counseled a more narrow reading of the statute than that which the government urged upon the Court.[275.5]

Following *Jones,* a number of defendants have appealed their various federal convictions. As was true following the *Lopez* decision, federal courts have been loath to give *Jones* an expansive interpretation. While some arson convictions have been set aside when the government has been unable to prove the requisite "use" of property in interstate commerce,[275.6] the courts have divided on whether, for example, churches are "used in" interstate commerce and whether their activities "substantially affect" interstate commerce.[275.7] At least one court has likewise interpreted *Jones* to mean that arson of rental property will sustain a conviction under the statute because rental property is, by definition, "used in" interstate commerce.[275.8] Attempts to increase the burden on the government in securing convictions under other federal criminal statutes, such as those criminalizing possession of firearms by convicted felons,[275.9] federal drug laws,[275.10] as well as federal racketeering[275.11] and gambling statutes,[275.12] have largely been unsuccessful — so much so that some courts have held that it is not ineffective assistance of counsel to raise a "fruitless" constitutional challenge to federal drug laws in light of the circuits' consistency in upholding those statutes.[275.13]

Moreover, despite the suggestions in *United States v. Lopez* (1995) and *United States v. Morrison* (2000) that the Court was poised to revise the holdings of cases like *Perez, Gonzales v. Raich* (2005) reaffirmed *Perez's* holding. The Court in *Raich* held that since Congress could eliminate the interstate market in illicit drugs, like marijuana, it could also prohibit intrastate, noncommercial production and possession of medical marijuana for personal use. As long as Congress could have rationally concluded that such activities, if aggregated, had a substantial effect on interstate commerce, then it can reach them as means "necessary and proper" to the permitted end — the elimination of the interstate market in illegal drugs.[275.14] The Court rejected arguments that since the production and possession of medical marijuana had been authorized by state statute, and since it was not specifically mentioned in the findings accompanying the federal Controlled Substances Act, Congress had not demonstrated that it affected interstate commerce.[275.15]

[275.1] Jones v. United States, 529 U.S. 848, 850-851, 120 S. Ct. 1904, 1912 (2000).

[275.2] *See, e.g.,* United States v. Jones, 178 F.3d 479 (7th Cir. 1999) (conviction for arson of private residence constitutional), *rev'd* Jones v. United States, 529 U.S. 848, 859, 120 S. Ct. 1904, 1912 (2000); United States v. Rea, 169 F.3d 1111 (8th Cir. 1998); United States v. Serang, 156 F.3d 910 (9th Cir. 1998); *but see* United States v. McGuire, 178 F.3d 203 (3d Cir. 1999); United States v. Papadopolous, 64 F.3d 522 (9th Cir. 1995).

[275.3] *See Jones,* 529 U.S. at 855-856, 120 S. Ct. at 1910.

275.4 529 U.S. at 857, 120 S. Ct. at 1911.

275.5 529 U.S. at 857, 120 S. Ct. at 1912. Justice Stevens concurred to emphasize his belief that "we should interpret narrowly federal criminal laws that overlap with state authority unless congressional intention to assert its jurisdiction is plain." 529 U.S. at 860, 120 S. Ct. at 1912-1913 (Stevens, J., concurring). Justice Thomas also concurred to emphasize the fact that he (and Justice Scalia, who joined him) "express no view on the question whether the federal arson statute . . . as there construed, is constitutional in its application to all buildings used for commercial activities." 529 U.S. at 860, 120 S. Ct. at 1913 (Thomas, J., concurring). *Compare* United States v. Armstrong, 2004 WL 1763907 (9th Cir.) (Aug. 5, 2004) (unpublished), at *1 (rejecting constitutional challenge to conviction under federal statute of arson involving a business); United States v. Corum, 362 F.3d 489, 494 (8th Cir. 2004) (rejecting constitutional challenge to 18 U.S.C. § 844(e), which prohibits use of instrumentality of interstate commerce to make threats to damage or destroy a building by use of fire or explosives; because Congress was regulating use of instrumentalities of interstate commerce, no need to demonstrate substantial effects on interstate commerce); United States v. Laton, 352 F.3d 286, 302 (6th Cir. 2003) (divided court) (concluding that a local fire station was a building whose use in an activity affecting interstate commerce — fighting fires — was sufficient to support a conviction of one who burned down the fire station); *but see id.* at 302 (Sutton, C.J. dissenting); United States v. Parsons, 314 F.3d 745,752 (5th Cir. 2002), (arson of hotel sufficient to come under federal arson statute "[d]espite the fact that Parson's hotel may have been closed for the winter season, a temporary cessation of activity does not place the hotel beyond the reach of [the federal statute] if there is an intent to return to the stream of commerce"); United States v. Williams, 299 F.3d 250, 256 (3d Cir. 2002) (upholding conviction, under federal statute, for arson of a building available for rent, but not actually leased); United States v. Cristobol, 293 F.3d 134, 144-146 (4th Cir. 2002) (upholding federal arson conviction of defendant who placed explosive devices under automobiles used in interstate commerce; vehicles owned by commercial businesses engaged in interstate commerce); United States v. Geiger, 263 F.3d 1034 (9th Cir. 2001) (upholding conviction under federal arson statute where defendant attached a bomb to victim's leased truck killing victim and destroying truck; noting that victim's "truck was subject to an out-of-state lease and insured by an out-of-state insurance company" and concluding that "a leased truck is owned by someone other than the user, and it may be used again for a business purpose . . . .And the leasing market, like the rental market, is a national one that substantially effects interstate commerce."); Tawalbeh v. United States, 2001 WL 1274562 (W.D. Va.) (Oct. 19, 2001), at *2 (concluding that arson of a competitor's convenience store that bought and sold goods in interstate commerce was covered by federal arson statute, 18 U.S.C. § 844(i)); United States v. Silverwood Realtors, 2000 WL 631373 (N.D. Ill. 2000), at *3 (upholding Toxic Substance Control Act and Residential Lead-Based Paint Hazard Reduction Act, as applied against owner of residential rental properties, against Commerce Clause challenge; "residential rental properties categorically substantially affect interstate commerce"). *See also* United States v. Ballinger, 395 F.3d 1218, 1228 (11th Cir. 2005) (en banc) (divided court) (holding that federal statute criminalizing church burning could be constitutionally applied to a defendant who used channels and instrumentalities of interstate commerce to accomplish acts prohibited by statute).

275.6 *See, e.g.,* United States v. Davies, 394 F.3d 182, 194-196 (3d Cir. 2005) (fact that church operated a small school whose students attended out-of-state universities, which purchased supplies in interstate commerce, which raised money to support other churches and fund mission projects, did not mean that church was "used in" interstate commerce for purpose of federal arson statute); United States v. Lamont, 330 F.3d 1249 (9th Cir. 2003) (concluding that "a church building used by a church that simply engages in ordinary religious activities is neither used in interstate commerce nor in any activity affecting interstate commerce within the meaning of the federal arson statute"); United States v. Ballinger, 312 F.3d 1264 (11th Cir. 2002) (divided court) (upholding Church Arson Prevention Act on its face, but not as applied to "the arson of five, rural churches in Georgia, because there was an insufficient connection between these arsons and interstate commerce"); United States v. Rea, 300 F.3d 952, 960-963 (8th Cir. 2002) (reversing federal arson conviction for arson of church annex; insufficient facts presented to permit conclusion annex either used in or affected interstate or foreign commerce); United States v. Odom, 252 F.3d 1289, 1297 (11th Cir. 2001) (reversing conviction under federal arson statute; evidence presented by government to establish use in and affect on interstate commerce "too passive, too minimal, and too indirect to substantially affect interstate commerce"); United States v. Ryan, 227 F.3d 1058, 1063-1064 (8th Cir. 2000) (reversing conviction for arson of abandoned fitness center; no proof of "use" in interstate commerce; court rejected government argument that *Jones* was inapplicable because of commercial nature of property); United States v. Ramey, 217 F.3d 842 (4th Cir. 2000) (vacating sentence under federal arson conviction in light of *Jones*); United States v. Rayborn, 138 F. Supp. 2d 1029 (W.D. Tenn. 2001) (denying motion to reconsider dismissal of indictment for arson of church; evidence presented by government to establish effect on interstate commerce insufficient), *aff'd* 312 F.3d 229 (6th Cir. 2002).

[275.7] Compare *Lamont,* 330 F.3d at 1254-1257; *Odom,* 252 F.3d at 1297; and *Rayborn,* 138 F. Supp. 2d at 1032-1036 *with* United States v. Rayborn, 312 F.3d 229.1 (6th Cir. 2002) (evidence that building used as church also recorded worship services for radio broadcast sufficient to bring it within scope of federal arson statute); United States v. Grassie, 237 F.3d 1199, 1209 (10th Cir. 2001) (concluding that churches "are major participants in interstate markets for goods and services, use of interstate communications and transportation, raising and distributing revenues . . . interstate, and so on"; *Jones* did not require court to change position that *de minimis* connection to interstate commerce is all that is necessary to sustain conviction under federal arson statute); United States v. Corum, 2002 WL 1285078 (D. Minn.) (June 5, 2002) (unpublished) (rejecting facial challenges to church arson statute and statute prohibiting threats made using telephone); United States v. Tush, 151 F. Supp. 2d 1246, 1253 (D. Kan. 2001) (presence of occasional out-of-state guests show that church is "actively employed or used in an activity affecting interstate commerce"). *See also* United States v. Ballinger, 395 F.3d 1218, 1228 (11th Cir. 2005) (en banc) (divided court) (holding that federal statute criminalizing church burning could be constitutionally applied to a defendant who used channels and instrumentalities of interstate commerce to accomplish acts prohibited by statute).

[275.8] *See* United States v. Sawyer, 133 F. Supp. 2d 969, 970-971 (E.D. Mich. 2001). *See also* United States v. Parsons, 314 F.3d 745, 752 (5th Cir. 2002) (arson of hotel sufficient to come under federal arson statute "[d]espite the fact that Parson's hotel may have been closed for the winter season, a temporary cessation of activity does not place the hotel beyond the reach of [the federal statute] if there is an intent to return to the stream of commerce"); United States v. Williams, 299 F.3d 250, 256 (3d Cir. 2002) (upholding conviction, under federal statute, for arson of a building available for rent, but not actually leased).

[275.9] *See, e.g.*, United States v. Boles, 2001 WL 22985 (4th Cir. 2001), at *1 ("We agree with our sister circuits that [18 U.S.C.] § 922(g) does not offend the Commerce Clause because it requires a particularized finding of a link to interstate commerce.").

[275.10] *See, e.g.*, Gonzales v. Raich, ___ U.S. ___, 125 S. Ct. 2195 (2005) (divided court) (holding that Congress can prohibit noncommercial, intrastate production and possession of medical marijuana through the Controlled Substances Act); United States v. Brown, 221 F.3d 1336 (6th Cir. 2000) (upholding conviction under federal drug trafficking charges against Commerce Clause challenge).

[275.11] *See, e.g.*, United States v. Riddle, 249 F.3d 529, 537-538 (6th Cir. 2001) (upholding convictions under both federal racketeering conspiracy statute, 18 U.S.C. § 1962, and statute punishing violence committed in furtherance of racketeering, 18 U.S.C. § 1959).

[275.12] *See, e.g.,* United States v. Vlanich, 2003 WL 22213951 (3d Cir.) (Sept. 24, 2003), at *2 (rejecting Commerce Clause arguments challenging constitutionality of 18 U.S.C. § 1955; noting that "[a]ll of the circuit courts of appeal which have considered the issue since *Lopez* have concluded that Section 1955 continues to be valid under the Commerce Clause"); United States v. Brieno, 2001 WL 290618 (N.D. Ill. 2001), at *2 (upholding conviction under 18 U.S.C. § 1955, which prohibits "running an illegal gambling business").

[275.13] *See* Caicedo v. United States, 2003 WL 22681437 (S.D.N.Y.) (Nov. 12, 2003) (failure to raise constitutional challenges to federal drug laws not ineffective assistance of counsel); United States v. Handschu, 2001 WL 641078 (D. Del.) (June 1, 2001), at *7 n.4 (rejecting argument that failure to challenge constitutionality of drug statutes constituted ineffective assistance of counsel "[g]iven the abundance of case law upholding . . . these laws under the Commerce Clause"); United States v. Butler, 2001 WL 311209 (E.D. Pa. 2001), at *4 (failure to raise constitutional challenge to federal drug laws not ineffective assistance of counsel because argument "fruitless" in light of various circuits having upheld acts' constitutionality). *See also* United States v. Fields, 2004 WL 3037960 (D. Kan. 2004), at *5 (failure to raise challenge to Hobbs Act conviction and to urge plea of guilty in light of "well-established law . . . that drug trafficking affects interstate commerce and that robbing a drug dealer satisfies" the Hobbs Act not ineffective assistance of counsel); Meeks v. United States, 2003 WL 1989653 (N.D. Ill.) (April 30, 2002) (failure to raise constitutional challenge to Hobbs Act not ineffective assistance of counsel given circuit precedent); United States v. Hernandez, 190 F. Supp. 2d 773 (E.D. Pa. 2002) (holding that defense counsel not ineffective for failure to raise constitutional challenge to 18 U.S.C. § 922(g), which prohibits felons from possessing firearms); Beamon v. United States, 189 F. Supp. 2d 350, 358 (E.D. Va. 2002) (failure to challenge federal felon-in-possession statute at trial in light of circuit court precedents rejecting such challenges not ineffective assistance). For more on the aftermath of *Morrison* and *Jones, see infra* § 5.04[G]. For further discussion of challenges to specific federal statutes in light of *Lopez, Morrison,* and *Jones, see infra* § 5.04[H].

[275.14] Gonzales v. Raich, __ U.S. __, __, 125 S. Ct. 2195, 2205 (2005) (divided court) ("Our case law firmly establishes Congress' power to regulate purely local activities that are part of an economic [class of activities] that have a substantial effect on interstate commerce."). For more on *Raich, see infra* § 5.04[C].

[275.15] *Raich*, __ U.S. at __, 125 S. Ct. at 2208 ("While congressional findings are certainly helpful in reviewing the substance of a congressional statutory scheme, particularly when the connection to commerce is not self-evident, and while we will consider congressional findings in the analysis when they are available, the absence of particularized findings does not call into question Congress' ability to regulate.") (footnote omitted).

§ 3.14 NON-PROFIT ACTIVITIES AS "COMMERCE"

Page 3-81, add to note 281 after "See also" and before "Lopez v. United States":

Gonzales v. Raich, __ U.S. __, 125 S. Ct. 2195 (2005) (divided court) (concluding that noncommercial nature of marijuana grown for medicinal use did not render it beyond the scope of Congressional power under the federal Controlled Substances Act);

Page 3-81, add to the end of note 281:

In deciding whether churches are engaged in interstate commerce, for purposes of determining whether church burning prosecutions may be brought under the federal arson statute, 18 U.S.C. § 844(i), or a similar statute, 18 U.S.C. § 247, which criminalizes arsons of churches, a few federal courts have specifically relied upon *Camps Newfound/Owatonna*'s conclusion that church activities are "commercial" in nature. *See, e.g.,* United States v. Grassie, 237 F.3d 1199, 1209 (10th Cir. 2001); United States v. Tush, 151 F. Supp. 2d 1246, 1252 (D. Kan. 2001).

CHAPTER 4

INTRASTATE VS. INTERSTATE COMMERCE

§4.04 EXPORTS: WHEN DOES INTERSTATE COMMERCE BEGIN?

[B] When Are Goods "Launched" on Way to Destination?

Page 4-20, add to the end of note 64:

; *compare* Ammex, Inc. v. Dept. Treasury, 603 N.W.2d 308, 314 (Ct. App. Mich. 1999) (noting that "an article does not constitute an 'export' if there exists a practical possibility of diversion to domestic markets. . . . Similarly, an article cannot be considered an 'export' within the meaning of the Import-Export Clause if 'it will be used in this country for its designed purpose, before being shipped abroad'"; therefore, state tax on gasoline sold at station located close to Canadian border not an "export" within the meaning of the Import-Export Clause).

CHAPTER 5

FEDERALIZATION OF LOCAL ACTIVITIES

§5.01 COMMERCE "AMONG THE SEVERAL STATES": INTRODUCTION

Page 5-3, add to the end of note 1:

For a recent argument that Marshall's conception of what constituted "interstate commerce" was too broad, *see* Barnett, The Original Meaning of the Commerce Clause, 68 U. Chi. L. Rev. 101, 137 (2001); Barnett, New Evidence of the Original Meaning of the Commerce Clause, 55 Ark. L. Rev. 847 (2003). Responses to Barnett can be found in Pushaw & Nelson, A Critique of the Narrow Interpretation of the Commerce Clause, 96 Nw. L. Rev. 695 (2002) and in Pushaw, Methods of Interpreting the Commerce Clause: A Comparative Analysis, 55 Ark. L. Rev. 1185, 1199-1202 (2003) (responding, in part, to Barnett's new evidence). *See also* Johnson, The Panda's Thumb: The Modest and Mercantilist Original Meaning of the Commerce Clause, 13 Wm. & Mary Bill Rts. J. 1 (2004) (arguing in favor of a narrow meaning of "commerce").

Page 5-3, add to note 3 after "see also" and before "Harrison":

Currie, The Constitution in Congress: The Jeffersonians 1801-1829 (2001);

Page 5-4, add to note 5, after "see":

Cushman, *Lochner*, Liquor and Longshoremen: A Puzzle in Progressive Era Federalism, 32 J. Maritime L. & Comm. 1 (2000);

Page 5-4, rename section [A] as follows, add new subsection [1]:

[A] Expansion of Federal "Affirmative" Power

[1] Early Interpretations

Page 5-6, add to note 13, after "See also":

Cushman, Formalism and Realism in Commerce Clause Jurisprudence, 67 U. Chi. L. Rev. 1089 (2000) (noting that constitutional doctrine in the Commerce Clause area progressed synchronically, not topically; stressing the connection between the Court's jurisprudence regarding Congress's affirmative power under the Commerce Clause, and its cases regarding the restrictions on state power, *viz.*, the "dormant" Commerce Clause doctrine).

Page 5-6, add new paragraph following note 14:

[2] The Modern View

Summarizing Congress's affirmative power under the Commerce Clause in the watershed case of *United States v. Lopez* (1995), the Supreme Court found that Congress may act in any one of three distinct sets of circumstances.[1]

> First, Congress may regulate the use of the channels of interstate commerce. . . . Second, Congress is empowered to regulate and protect the instrumentalities of interstate commerce, or persons or things in interstate commerce, even though the threat may come only from intrastate activities. . . . Finally, Congress' commerce authority includes the power to regulate those activities . . . that substantially affect interstate commerce. . . . [2]

While *Lopez, United States v. Morrison* (2000), and *Gonzales v. Raich* (2005) concern what was constitutionally necessary for Congress to regulate intrastate activity that allegedly "substantially affected" interstate commerce, the other two categories of regulation still leave Congress considerable latitude to regulate what Marshall referred to as a state's "internal concerns."[3]

The power of Congress to regulate "instrumentalities" of interstate commerce, though the instrumentality operated solely within one state, was affirmed as far back as the Court's 1870 case of *The Daniel Ball.*[4] The early twentieth century, moreover, saw the Court criminalize activity that crossed state lines — even if the ulterior motive (or even the activity itself) was "non-commercial" — on the theory that the channels of interstate commerce could be closed to harmful or injurious uses.[5] Recently, the Court implicitly confirmed what many lower courts had inferred from *Lopez* and *Morrison*; that congressional power over instrumentalities and channels of interstate commerce remained potent.[5.1] In *Pierce Co. v. Guillen* (2003), the Court unanimously upheld a federal statute that prohibited the use of highway safety data collected by states pursuant to federal law in federal and state trials.[5.2] Reversing the Washington

Supreme Court, which had held the statute unconstitutional, the Court wrote of the "well established" authority to regulate channels and instrumentalities of interstate commerce.[5.3] The challenged law did both. "Congress could reasonably believe that adopting a measure eliminating an unforeseen side effect of the information-gathering requirement [contained in another statute] would result in more diligent efforts to collect the relevant information, more candid discussions of hazardous locations, better informed decisionmaking, and . . . greater safety on our Nation's roads," Justice Thomas wrote.[5.4] "Consequently," he continued, the privilege "can be viewed as legislation aimed at improving safety in the channels of commerce and increasing protection for the instrumentalities of interstate commerce" and thus squarely within Congress's power.[5.5]

Perhaps anticipating *Guillen*, several courts of appeals have upheld the federal Child Support Recovery Act, 18 U.S.C. § 228, which makes it a federal crime for a parent in one state to fail to make a court-ordered payment of support to an ex-spouse or child in another state, holding that the statute either regulates the channels of interstate commerce or that the obligation is a "thing" in interstate commerce that should have been honored.[6] Following signals from the Supreme Court that *Lopez*'s attempt to limit congressional power to regulate intrastate conduct "affecting commerce" was not a passing fancy, many lower courts have looked for ways to fit challenged congressional legislation into the other two categories.[7]

[1] United States v. Lopez, 514 U.S. 549, 558-559, 115 S. Ct. 1624, 1629-1630 (1995) (divided court).

[2] *Id.* The Court's tri-partite classification was not completely original with Chief Justice Rehnquist. *Compare* Hodel v. Virginia Surface Min. & Reclamation Ass'n, Inc., 425 U.S. 264, 276-277, 101 S. Ct. 2352, 2360 (1981); Perez v. United States, 402 U.S. 146, 150-152, 91 S. Ct. 1357, 1360-1361 (1971) (divided court). For a helpful description of the evolution of the first two categories, *see* Young, The Significance of Border Crossings: *Lopez, Morrison*, and the Fate of Congressional Power to Regulate Goods, and Transactions Connected with Them, Based on Prior Passage Through Interstate Commerce, 61 Md. L. Rev. 177 (2002).

[3] United States v. Morrison, 529 U.S. 598, 120 S. Ct. 1740 (2000) (divided court); *see, e.g.*, Pierce Co. v. Guillen, 537 U.S. 129, 123 S. Ct. 720, 731-732 (2003) (upholding, as regulation of channels and instrumentalities of interstate commerce, federal law prohibiting the use of certain highway safety data collected by states pursuant to federal law in federal or state trials); Reno v. Condon, 528 U.S. 141, 148-149, 120 S. Ct. 666, 671 (2000) (upholding federal Driver's Privacy Protection Act prohibiting states from selling driver's license data in interstate commerce); Slavin v. United States, 2005 WL 742707 (8th Cir. 2005), at *1 (per curiam) (rejecting challenge to federal statute prohibiting

transport of birds in interstate commerce for purposes of having them participate in a "fighting venture"); United States v. Ballinger, 395 F.3d 1218, 1228 (11th Cir. 2005) (en banc) (divided court) (holding that federal statute criminalizing church burning could be constitutionally applied to a defendant who used channels and instrumentalities of interstate commerce to accomplish acts prohibited by statute); United States v. Hornaday, 392 F.3d 1306, 1310-1311 (11th Cir. 2004) (holding that statute prohibiting use of facility of interstate commerce to induce minor to engage in unlawful sexual activity; "The internet is an instrumentality of interstate commerce. Congress clearly has the power to regulate the internet, as it does other instrumentalities and channels of interstate commerce, and to prohibit its use for harmful or immoral purposes regardless of whether those purposes would have a primarily intrastate impact."); United States v. Bredimus, 352 F.3d 200, 204-208 (5th Cir. 2003) (upholding 18 U.S.C. § 2423(b), prohibiting traveling in interstate or foreign commerce for the purpose of engaging in sexual act with person under 18 years of age; statute regulates channels of interstate commerce, "substantially affects" test inapplicable; *Lopez*'s three categories are analytically distinct); Nebraska v. Environmental Protection Agency, 331 F.3d 995, 998 (D.C. Cir. 2003) (rejecting facial Commerce Clause challenge to EPA order regarding arsenic levels in drinking water; fact that EPA regulation applies to water that is sold in interstate commerce sufficient to defeat facial attack); United States v. Deaton, 2003 WL 21357305 (4th Cir.) (June 12, 2003), at *6 (rejecting challenge to EPA jurisdiction over wetlands ditch that flowed into navigable waterway; regulation of navigable waterways permissible under congressional power to regulate channels of interstate commerce); Dailey v. Veneman, 2002 WL 31780191 (6th Cir.) (Dec. 3, 2002) (unpublished), at *4 (upholding federal meat and poultry inspection acts; congress did not strip itself of authority to regulate state-inspected meat and poultry processing plants where it prohibited state-inspected meat and poultry from crossing state lines; "Congress's power to regulate things in interstate commerce surely includes the power to ensure that a commodity does not become a thing in interstate commerce"); Riley v. Merrill, Lynch, Pierce, Fenner & Smith, Inc., 292 F.3d 1334, 1346-1347 (11th Cir. 2002) (upholding Securities Litigation Uniform Standards Act; regulates both channels of interstate commerce, national securities markets, as well as things in interstate commerce, the securities trade on those markets); Ickes v. Federal Aviation Administration, 299 F.3d 260, 263 (3d Cir. 2002) (rejecting challenge to FAA authority to regulate intrastate flights of Ultralight aircraft; "Congress's power over interstate commerce includes the power to regulate use of the nation's navigable airspace, which is a channel of interstate commerce"; authority also supported by fact that airplanes are instrumentalities of interstate commerce); United States v. Karamanos, 2002 WL 626780 (3d Cir.) (April 18, 2002) (unpublished) (rejecting Commerce Clause challenge to conviction under federal wire fraud statute, 18 U.S.C. § 1343; wire fraud statute regulates "channels" and "instrumentalities" of interstate commerce); United States v. Al-Zubaidy, 283 F.3d 804, 811-812 (6th Cir. 2002) (upholding federal interstate stalking statute, 18 U.S.C. § 2261A, against Commerce Clause challenge; "[a] statute that punishes persons for using the channels of interstate commerce to bring 'the spread of any evil or harm to the people of other states from the state of origin' is directly within Congress's Commerce Clause power"); United States v. Han, 230 F.3d 560, 562-563 (2nd Cir. 2000) (rejecting *Lopez* challenge to federal statute criminalizing the traveling in interstate commerce for the purpose of engaging in a sex act with a minor); Tocher v. Santa Ana, 219 F.3d 1040, 1052 (9th Cir. 2000) (upholding federal preemption of state and local regulation of motorcarriers: "automobiles are instrumentalities of interstate commerce even when used solely for intrastate purposes"); United States v. Kammersell, 196 F.3d 137, 139 (10th Cir. 1999) (upholding conviction of defendant for sending threatening communication in interstate commerce over the Internet, even though defendant and recipient were in the same state when the transmission occurred; *Lopez* permitted regulation of channels of interstate commerce); United States v. Borchert, 2004 WL 2278551 (N.D. Ill.) (Oct. 7, 2004), at *4 (rejecting constitutional challenge to federal statute criminalizing crossing of state lines to engage in criminal sexual conduct; "[s]uch conduct clearly falls within [*Lopez*'s] first category of activity); United States v. Perez, 2004 WL 24722 (D. Conn. 2004), at *4 (holding that, for purposes of conviction under 18 U.S.C. § 1958, prohibiting murder for hire using "facility of interstate commerce," use of interstate phone call was use of "facility of interstate commerce" even though call was made intrastate); Ramirez v. United States, 286 F. Supp. 2d 243, 244 (S.D.N.Y. 2003) (holding that federal kidnapping statute requiring transportation in interstate commerce applied despite kidnapping victim's transportation by noncommercial means); United States v. Shahani-Jahromi, 286 F. Supp. 2d 723, 732-736 (E.D. Va. 2003) (upholding International Parental Kidnapping Crime Act, 18 U.S.C. § 1204, criminalizing intentional obstruction of parental rights by removing a child from the U.S. or retaining them outside the U.S. was valid exercise of congressional power to regulate channels of interstate and foreign commerce); United States v. Corum, 2003 WL 21010962 (D. Minn.) (Apr. 17, 2003), *aff'd*, 362 F.3d 489, 493-494 (8th Cir. 2004); (rejecting defendant's claim that *de minimis* connection to interstate commerce insufficient to sustain conviction under 18 U.S.C. § 247, outlawing attempt to obstruct free exercise of religion through threats of force; Congress has authority to regulate telephone calls, even if intrastate, under authority to regulate instrumentalities of commerce); United States v. Angleton, 221 F. Supp. 2d 696, 731-733 (S.D. Tex. 2002) (rejecting challenge to 18 U.S.C. § 1958, federal murder-for-hire statute; statute, requiring travel in interstate commerce, "is based on Congress's power to regulate either the channels of interstate commerce or the subjects of interstate commerce" and thus within Congress's acknowledged power); United States v. Reynard, 220 F. Supp. 2d 1142, 1171-1174 (S.D. Cal. 2002) (upholding federal law requiring, as mandatory condition of supervised release, submission of DNA sample for use in federal database; samples are "things in" interstate commerce); United States v. Edmondson, 175 F. Supp. 2d 889, 894 (S.D. Miss. 2001) (holding that cellular telephone identification numbers and account numbers are instrumentalities of commerce and thus affect interstate commerce under federal fraud statute); United States v. Crawford, 2001 WL 185140 (D. Me. 2001), at *1 (upholding provision of Violence Against Women Act, 18 U.S.C. § 2261, which makes it a federal crime to stalk someone across state lines). For more on the "affecting commerce" category after *Lopez* and *Morrison*, see *infra* § 5.04. For the "affecting commerce" category more generally, *see infra* § 5.04[B].

For a debate over whether the federal murder-for-hire statute requires that the defendant use an instrumentality of interstate commerce *capable* of being used in interstate commerce, or whether the defendant must actually *use* that instrumentality in interstate commerce, *compare* United States v. Drury, 344 F.3d 1089, 1104 (11th Cir. 2003) (divided court) (concluding that "a defendant must actually use a facility in a *manner* that implicates interstate commerce, not just that the facility itself possess the *capability* of affecting interstate commerce) *with id.* at 1110-1123 (Marcus, C.J., dissenting) (concluding that the statute only requires that the instrumentality have the capability of being so used). *See also* United States v. Perez, 2004 WL 24722 (D. Conn. 2004), at *4 (holding that, for purposes of conviction under 18 U.S.C. § 1958, prohibiting murder for hire using "facility of interstate commerce," use of interstate phone call was use of "facility of interstate commerce" even though call was made intrastate). *Cf.* United States v. Corum, 362 F.3d 489, 493-494 (8th Cir. 2004) (holding that, for purposes of 18 U.S.C. § 844(e), which prohibits use of instrumentality of interstate commerce to make threats to damage or destroy a building by use of fire or explosives, the instrumentality need not have actually been used in interstate commerce); *accord* United States v. R.J.S., 366 F.3d 960, 961 (8th Cir. 2004).

[4] The Daniel Ball, 77 (10 Wall.) U.S. 557 (1870) (upholding power of Congress to regulate ships carrying interstate commerce even if traveling entirely within a single state).

[5] Caminetti v. United States, 242 U.S. 470, 37 S. Ct. 192 (1917) (divided court) (upholding the power of Congress to punish those transporting women in interstate commerce for "immoral" purposes); Champion v. Ames, 188 U.S. 321, 23 S. Ct. 321 (1903) (divided court) (upholding power of Congress to prohibit shipment of lottery tickets in interstate commerce).

[5.1] For an excellent argument that the breadth of the instrumentalities and channels categories sap much of the force of *Lopez* and *Morrison*'s limitations on the "affecting commerce" category, *see* Klein, Note, Commerce Clause Questions After *Morrison*: Some Observations on the New Formalism and the New Realism, 55 Stan. L. Rev. 571, 584-596 (2002).

[5.2] Pierce Co. v. Guillen, 537 U.S. 129, 123 S. Ct. 720 (2003). The statute privileging the information is found at 23 U.S.C. § 409. For an insightful discussion of *Guillen*, *see* Berman, *Guillen* and Gullibility: Piercing the Surface of Commerce Clause Doctrine, 89 Iowa L. Rev. 1487 (2004).

[5.3] *Guillen*, 537 U.S. at 129, 123 S. Ct. at 731.

[5.4] 537 U.S. at 129, 123 S. Ct. at 731-732. The "unforeseen side effect" to which Justice Thomas referred was the unanticipated value to plaintiffs of the data collected by states in suits against states for failure to remedy unsafe road conditions of which the state had knowledge. It was these suits that prompted Congress to pass the privilege in the first place.

[5.5] 537 U.S. at 129, 123 S. Ct. at 732.

[6] United States v. Klinzing, 315 F.3d 803, 806-808 (7th Cir. 2003) (rejecting challenge to Deadbeat Parents Punishment Act; interstate child support obligation is a "thing" in interstate commerce, susceptible to congressional regulation); United States v. King, 276 F.3d 109, 113 (2d Cir. 2002) (holding that obligation is a "thing in interstate commerce, and that the failure to meet such an obligation can be regulated and criminalized under the second *Lopez* category"); United States v. Lewko, 269 F.3d 64, 67-68 (1st Cir. 2001) (upholding Child Support Recovery Act; concluding that obligation is either a "thing" in commerce or a valid congressional regulation of the "channels" of interstate commerce); United States v. Faasse, 265 F.3d 475, 481-482 (6th Cir. 2001) (en banc) (divided court) (reversing three-judge panel, upholding Child Support Recovery Act; concluding that the CSRA was valid as either a regulation of the instrumentalities or channels of interstate commerce). Dissenting judges disputed the conclusion that criminalizing the *failure* to put something in interstate commerce could serve as a ground for

congressional regulation under the channels or instrumentalities categories of *Lopez*, and argued the Act should be analyzed under the "affecting commerce" category, whose test, they argued, it failed. *See Faasse*, 265 F.3d at 496-497 (Batchelder, C.J., dissenting); *see also* United States v. Faasse, 227 F.3d 660, 668-669 (6th Cir. 2001), *rev'd* United States v. Faasse, 265 F.3d 475 (6th Cir. 2001) (en banc) (divided court). For other court decisions upholding federal child support enforcement legislation under the affecting commerce rationale, *see, for example,* United States v. Monts, 311 F.3d 993, 996-997 (10th Cir. 2002) (rejecting challenge to Child Support Recovery Act; CSRA contained jurisdictional nexus and explicit findings from Congress; reaffirming prior, pre-*Morrison* case); Harding v. Harding, 121 Cal. Rptr. 2d 450, 454-456 (Ct. App. Cal. 2002) (rejecting Commerce Clause challenge to Full Faith and Credit Child Support Act; child support payments "substantially affect" interstate commerce).

[7] *See, e.g.,* United States v. Ballinger, 395 F.3d 1218, 1228 (11th Cir. 2005) (en banc) (divided court) (holding that federal statute criminalizing church burning could be constitutionally applied to a defendant who used channels and instrumentalities of interstate commerce to accomplish acts prohibited by statute). *Ballinger* overturned a three-judge panel that had reversed the trial judge's decision that the activity in question had a substantial affect on interstate commerce. *See also* Denning & Reynolds, Rulings and Resistance: The New Commerce Clause Encounters the Lower Courts, 55 Ark. L. Rev. 1253, 1298 (2003) (describing this trend).

[B] Regulations "Affecting" Interstate Commerce and the Necessary and Proper Clause

Page 5-12, add new paragraph before "**[C] Proof of Effect on Interstate Commerce**":

In his concurring opinion in *Gonzales v. Raich* (2005), Justice Scalia carefully explained that the power of Congress to reach intrastate, noncommercial production and possession of medical marijuana under the Controlled Substances Act depended upon the combination of the Commerce Clause with the Necessary and Proper Clause.[39.1] "Congress's authority to enact all of these prohibitions of intrastate controlled-substance activity," he wrote, "depends only upon whether they are appropriate means of achieving the legitimate end of eradicating Schedule I substances from interstate commerce."[39.2] Because it was impossible to distinguish intrastate from interstate marijuana, because "Congress need not accept on faith that state law will be effective in maintaining a strict division" between lawful and contraband marijuana, and because there was no otherwise "inappropriate" violation of state sovereignty, he agreed with the majority that "Congress could reasonably conclude that its objective of prohibiting marijuana from the interstate market 'could be undercut' if those activities [permitted by state law] were excepted from its general scheme of regulation."[39.3]

Page 5-12, add to first line of note 39, between "at 421." and "Barber":

In fact, in his dissent from the Court's decision striking down a portion of the Violence Against Women Act, Justice Souter argued that the scope of the commerce power, when joined with the implied power under the Necessary and Proper Clause, gave Congress "plenary" power over commerce, "unsusceptible to categorical exclusions . . . throughout the latter part of the 20th century. . . . " United States v. Morrison, 529 U.S. 598, 640, 120 S. Ct. 1740, 1766 (2000) (Souter, J., dissenting). For interesting arguments that the Court could make use of Chief Justice Marshall's warning, in *McCulloch*, that "pretextual" exercises of power by Congress could not be countenanced by the Court to bolster its recent cases restricting the scope of the Commerce Clause, see Beck, The New Jurisprudence of the Necessary and Proper Clause, 2002 U. Ill. L. Rev. 581; *cf.* Beck, The Heart of Federalism: Pretext Review of Means-Ends Relationships, 36 U.C. Davis L. Rev. 407 (2003) (making similar argument about congressional power under the section 5 of the Fourteenth Amendment). For more on the Necessary and Proper Clause generally, see, for example

Page 5-12, add to second line of note 39, after "but see":

Barnett, *supra* note 1, at 138-139 (arguing that the Necessary and Proper Clause cannot be relied upon to create *carte blanche* power on part of Congress to reach activity that is not "commercial" or that is entirely intrastate);

Page 5-12, add to the end of note 41:

Cf. Board of Trustees v. Garrett, 531 U.S. 356, 390-423, 121 S. Ct. 955, 977-993 (2001) (divided court) (Breyer, J., dissenting) (citing instances of state discrimination against the disabled in dissent from Court decision that Congress had insufficient evidence of such discrimination to abrogate state sovereign immunity under the Americans with Disabilities Act, pursuant to its power under § 5 of the Fourteenth Amendment).

[39.1] Gonzales v. Raich, ___ U.S. ___, ___, 125 S. Ct. 2195, 2215 (2005) (divided court) (Scalia, J., concurring).

[39.2] *Raich*, ___ U.S. at ___, 125 S. Ct. at 2219 (Scalia, J., concurring).
[39.3] ___ U.S. at ___, 125 S. Ct. at 2220 (Scalia, J., concurring).

[C] Proof of Effect on Interstate Commerce

Page 5-13, add to note 42, fourth line from bottom of note, after "See generally":

Buzbee & Schapiro, Legislative Record Review, 54 Stan. L. Rev. 87 (2001); Frickey & Smith, Judicial Review, the Congressional Process, and the Federalism Cases: An Interdisciplinary Critique, 111 Yale L.J. 1707 (2002);

Page 5-13, add to end of note 42:

For doubts about the "law/fact" distinction, *see* Devins, Congressional Factfinding and the Scope of Judicial Review: A Preliminary Analysis, 50 Duke L.J. 1169 (2001).

Page 5-14, insert new paragraph before "**§5.02 THE SUPREME COURT'S ZIG-ZAGS, 1918-1941**":

Despite the skepticism of the Court regarding the sufficiency of congressional findings exhibited in *United States v. Morrison* (2000), the Court appeared to return to a more deferential approach in *Gonzales v. Raich* (2005).[46.1] Upholding the application of the federal Controlled Substances Act (CSA) to those engaged in the noncommercial, intrastate production and possession of marijuana to be used, in accordance with California law, for medical purposes, the majority emphasized how Congress could have rationally believed that all such marijuana needed to be eliminated, lest the federal goal of prohibiting the interstate trade in marijuana be undermined. Writing for the majority, Justice Stevens emphasized that "[w]e need not determine whether respondents' activities, taken in the aggregate, substantially affect interstate commerce in fact, but only whether a "rational basis" exists for so concluding."[46.2]

The Court specifically rejected the argument that since the CSA made no explicit finding regarding the effect of medical marijuana on the interstate marijuana market, such an effect, and the desire to prevent it, could not have served as a rational basis for congressional action. Stevens explained that "[w]hile congressional findings are certainly helpful in reviewing the substance of a congressional statutory scheme particularly when the connection to commerce is not self-evident, and while we will consider congressional findings in the analysis when they are available, the absence of particularized findings does not call into question Congress' ability to regulate."[46.3]

In a dissenting opinion, Justice O'Connor complained that the findings in the CSA were "too vague and unspecific to demonstrate that the federal statutory scheme will be undermined if Congress cannot exert power over individuals like the respondents."[46.4] If the CSA's findings were enough, she reasoned, then *Morrison* should have come out the other way, since the Violence against Women Act, of which the civil-suit provision struck down in that case was a part, came with numerous findings about the impact of gender-motivated violence on the economy.[46.5]

[46.1] *See* United States v. Morrison, 529 U.S. 598, 614, 120 S. Ct. 1740, 1752 (2000) (divided court) (stating that "the existence of congressional findings is not sufficient, by itself, to sustain the constitutionality of Commerce Clause legislation").

[46.2] Gonzales v. Raich, ___ U.S. ___, ___, 125 S. Ct. 2195, ___ (2005) (divided court).

[46.3] ___ U.S. at ___, 125 S. Ct. at 2208 (footnote omitted).

[46.4] ___ U.S. at ___, 125 S. Ct. at 2228 (O'Connor, J., dissenting).

[46.5] ___ U.S. at ___, 125 S. Ct. at 2227 (O'Connor, J., dissenting). For more on *Morrison and Raich see infra* § 5.04.

§ 5.02 THE SUPREME COURT'S ZIG-ZAGS, 1918-1941

Page 5-14, insert new footnote after "were:" and before "1. Hammer v. Dagenhart":

For a lively debate between two constitutional historians over the extent to which the following cases were indeed "zigs and zags," or whether there was a higher degree of continuity in the case law than has heretofore been recognized, see Friedman, The Sometimes-Bumpy Stream of Commerce Clause Doctrine, 55 Ark. L. Rev. 981 (2003) (arguing that "the historical development of the doctrine governing Congress's power under the Commerce Clause in the twentieth century, and especially in the years centering on the New Deal" contained "no discontinuities" and developed through a series of "intellectually undramatic changes that cumulatively caused an enormous transformation"); Cushman, Continuity and Change in Commerce Clause Jurisprudence, 55 Ark. L. Rev. 1009 (2003) (disagreeing with Friedman); Friedman, Charting the Course of Commerce Clause Challenge, 55 Ark. L. Rev. 1055 (2003) (replying to Cushman); Cushman, Small Differences?, 55 Ark. L. Rev. 1097 (2003) (Cushman's surreply).

§5.03 MULTUM IN PARVO: EVERY LITTLE BIT COUNTS

Page 5-22, add to note 72 after "2062." and before "See also":

For a comprehensive overview of the case, the parties, and the legacy of *Filburn*, *see* Chen, *Filburn*'s Legacy, 52 Emory L.J. 1719 (2003).

Page 5-23, add to the end of note 76:

For a contemporary application of *Wickard*, *see* D.A.S. Sand & Gravel, Inc. v. Chao, 2004 WL 1166373 (2d Cir. 2004), at *3 (concluding that federal Mine Act intended to exercise full extent of congressional commerce power and that Act reached mines whose products were sold entirely within the state, citing *Wickard*).

Page 5-24, add to the end of note 77:

For a comprehensive account of the events leading up to the *McClung* and *Heart of Atlanta Motel* cases, including some interesting information about the Court's internal deliberations in those cases, *see* Cortner, Civil Rights and Public Accommodations: The *Heart of Atlanta Motel* and *McClung* Cases (Univ. Press of Kansas, 2001). For an argument that it was *Katzenbach v. McClung* that sounded federalism's death knell, *see* McGoldrick, *Katzenbach v. McClung*: The Abandonment of Federalism in the Name of Rational Basis, 14 B.Y.U. J. Pub. L. 1 (1999).

Page 5-24, add to note 78 before "For lower court cases":

The Court recently cited *McClung* in a decision reversing the Alabama Supreme Court's holding that, in light of *Lopez*, the Federal Arbitration Act required a party seeking to compel arbitration to demonstrate that individual transactions themselves "substantially affect" interstate commerce, as applied to an intrastate loan agreement. Citizens Bank v. Alafabco, Inc., 539 U.S. 52, 123 S. Ct. 2037 (2003) (per curiam). "If the Commerce Clause gives Congress the power to regulate local business establishments purchasing substantial quantities of goods that have moved in interstate commerce . . . it necessarily reaches substantial commercial loan transactions secured by such goods." 539 U.S. at 57, 123 S. Ct. at 2040 (citing Katzenbach v. McClung, 379 U.S. 294, 304-305, 85 S. Ct. 377, 384 (1964)).

Page 5-24, add to the end of note 78:

Professor Cortner, studying the internal deliberation of the Court in the two cases, found that Justice Harlan had circulated a draft opinion upholding Title II with respect to the Heart of Atlanta Motel but invalidating its application to Ollie McClung's restaurant. In language reminiscent of the Court's 1995 *Lopez* opinion, Harlan was concerned that the "framers, once having settled upon its general objective, rummaged in the closet of constitutional powers to find a constitutional peg on which to hang [Title II of the 1969 Act]." Cortner, *supra* note 77, at 160 (quoting Harlan). In particular, Harlan was troubled by the notion that the Court "should look to any theory which might have supported the legislation on any factual basis which Congress could, within the bounds of rationality, have found to be true." Were the Court to "surrender [its] power to determine independently the validity of facts and theories upon which Congress based its exercise of the commerce power . . . [the] result [would be] an essentially limitless power under the Commerce Clause." *Id.* at 162, 163. Eventually, Justice Clark, the author of the opinions, made enough changes to satisfy Justice Harlan, who signed on to the Court's opinion, and did not dissent in *McClung*. *Id.* at 169.

Page 5-24, insert new paragraph before "**§ 5.04 *UNITED STATES V. LOPEZ* (1995): ABOUT-FACE, DETOUR, OR MISSTEP**"?:

Any hopes that the Court's decisions in *United States v. Lopez* (1995) or *United States v. Morrison* (2000) portended the imminent demise of *Wickard v. Filburn* were dashed in *Gonzales v. Raich* (2005), in which the majority went to great lengths to rehabilitate *Wickard.*[78.1] Taking advantage of the fact that *Lopez* — while trying to domesticate *Wickard* — did not overrule it, the majority opinion, written by Justice Stevens, found the application of the federal Controlled Substances Act to plaintiffs engaging in the local, noncommercial production and use of medical marijuana on all fours with the facts of *Wickard*. Stevens wrote, "Our case law firmly establishes Congress' power to regulate purely local activities that are part of an economic 'class of activities' that have a substantial effect on interstate commerce."[78.2]

> In *Wickard*, we had no difficulty concluding that Congress had a rational basis for belief that, when viewed in the aggregate, leaving home-consumed wheat outside the regulatory scheme would have a substantial influence on price and market conditions. Here, too, Congress had a rational basis for concluding that leaving home-consumed marijuana outside federal control would similarly affect price and market conditions.[78.3]

[78.1] Gonzales v. Raich, ___ U.S. ___, 125 S. Ct. 2195 (2005) (divided court).
[78.2] ___ U.S. at ___, 125 S. Ct. at 2205.
[78.3] ___ U.S. at ___, 125 S. Ct. at 2207. For more on *Raich*, *see infra* § 5.04.

§ 5.04 *UNITED STATES V. LOPEZ* (1995): ABOUT-FACE, DETOUR, OR MISSTEP?

[A] *Lopez:* The Court's Ruling

Page 5-26, add to second line of note 83, after "Lopez, see, e.g.,":

1 Tribe, American Constitutional Law (Foundation, 3d ed., 2000), pp. 817-824; Dral & Phillips, Commerce by Another Name: The Impact of *United States v. Lopez* and *United States v. Morrison*, 68 Tenn. L. Rev. 605 (2001); Harsch, *Brzonkala, Lopez,* and the Commerce Clause Canard: A Synthesis of Commerce Clause Jurisprudence, 29 N.M. L. Rev. 321, 362 (1999) (arguing that as the Court again attempts to walk the line between granting Congress sufficient power to deal with "commerce-related exigencies" while "simultaneously tr[ying] to draw a line past which Congress cannot venture," the Court should expressly apply the factors the author argues it has always applied — (i) nexus of regulated activity to commerce power, (ii) seriousness of the exigency, (iii) need for national solution and (iv) sensitivity to the effect of congressional regulation on federal and state relations — instead of "convoluting doctrine in order to meet [a] challenge"); Kramer, Putting the Politics Back into the Political Safeguards of Federalism, 100 Colum. L. Rev. 215 (2000) (criticizing the Court for *Lopez, Printz, Seminole Tribe* and other federalism-regarding decisions); Reynolds & Denning, Lower Court Readings of *Lopez*, or What If the Supreme Court Held a Constitutional Revolution and Nobody Came?,

2000 Wis. L. Rev. 369; Schapiro & Buzbee, Unidimensional Federalism: Power and Perspective in Commerce Clause Adjudication, 88 Cornell L. Rev. 1199 (2003); Badawi, Comment, Unceasing Animosities and the Public Tranquility: Political Market Failure and the Scope of the Commerce Power, 91 Cal. L. Rev. 1331 (2003); Cramer, Note, The Right Result for All the Wrong Reasons: An Historical and Functional Analysis of the Commerce Clause, 53 Vand. L. Rev. 271, 310 (2000) (criticizing *Lopez* for providing inadequate guidance to lower courts and for promulgating criteria that are easily manipulable; proposing a "functional inquiry" that "ask[s] the really important questions of whether the several states can effectively regulate or the realities of the integrated national economy create a functional need for national analysis").

Page 5-27, add to note 83, second paragraph, after "specific laws, see":

Chamberlin, Johnny Can't Read 'Cause Jane's Got a Gun: The Effects of Guns in Schools, and Options After *Lopez*, 8 Cornell J.L. & Pub. Pol'y 281 (1999) (suggesting ways Congress could remedy the fatal defects of the Gun Free School Zones Act invalidated in *Lopez*); Nagle, The Commerce Clause Meets the Delhi Sands Flower-Loving Fly, 97 Mich. L. Rev. 174 (1998); Rokosz, Human Cloning: Is the Reach of FDA Authority Too Far a Stretch?, 30 Seton Hall L. Rev. 464, 491-495 (2000) (discussing the Commerce Clause authority of the FDA to regulate cloning); Shannon, The Jurisdictional Limits of Federal Criminal Child Pornography Law, 21 U. Haw. L. Rev. 73 (1999); VanderMay, The Constitutional Implications of the Federalizations of Child Support Law, 35 Williamette L. Rev. 783 (1999); Adams, Comment, Worship and the Commerce Clause: A Constitutional Combination?, 34 Gonzaga. L. Rev. 471 (1998-1999); Chalis, Comment, Standing Alone in Murky Waters: Evaluating the Fourth Circuit's Solitary Stance on Federal Wetlands Regulation, 34 Wake Forest L. Rev. 1179 (1999); Hong, Note, And "Cloning" Makes Three: A Constitutional Comparison Between Cloning and Other Assisted Reproductive Technologies, 26 Hastings Const. L.Q. 741 (1999); Jaffe, Note, A Federally-Mandated National School Curriculum: Can Congress Act?, 24 Seton Hall Legis. J. 207 (1999); Matthews, Case Comment, Turning the Endangered Species Act Inside Out? 113 Yale L.J. 947 (2004); Moriarty, Comment, Parental Wiretapping: Should Federal Courts Provide a Civil Remedy in a Family Law Matter, 48 U. Kan. L. Rev. 397 (2000); Mason, Comment, Denial of Permission to "Take" an Endangered Species Will Amount to a "Taking" under the Fifth Amendment in Limited Situations,

21 U. Ark. Little Rock L. Rev. 519 (1999); Padget, Comment, Damage Limitations in Medical Malpractice Actions: Necessary Legislation or Unconstitutional Deprivation? 55 S.C. L. Rev. 215 (2003); Pirnot, Note, *United States v. Wilson:* Did Interstate General Substantially Affect Interstate Commerce?, 77 N.C. L. Rev. 361 (1998); Spalding, Note, In the Stream of the Commerce Clause: Revisiting *Asahi* in the Wake of *Lopez* and *Morrison*, 4 Nev. L.J. 141 (2003); White, Comment, The Endangered Species Act's Precarious Perch: A Constitutional Analysis Under the Commerce Clause and the Treaty Power, 27 Ecology L.Q. 215 (2000) (suggesting modifications to the Endangered Species Act to ensure it will pass judicial muster under *Lopez*). The provision of the Violence Against Women Act that granted victims of gender-motivated violence a federal civil remedy against their attackers, subsequently struck down by the U.S. Supreme Court, generated much academic commentary. For a sampling, *see infra* § 5.04[F] (supplement).

Page 5-27, add to the end of note 83:

; *but see* Schwartz & Behrens, A Proposal for Federal Product Liability Reform in the New Millennium, 4 Tex. Rev. L. & Pol. 261, 274-275 (2000) (predicting that federal tort reform would survive Commerce Clause scrutiny); Schwartz, Behrens & Mathews, Federalism and Federal Liability Reform: The United States Constitution Supports Reform, 36 Harv. J. on Legis. 269 (1999). For an informative overview of the federalism issues that surround the debate over federal tort reform, *see* Grey, The New Federalism Jurisprudence and National Tort Reform, 59 Wash. & Lee L. Rev. 475 (2002); *see also* Gasaway, The Problem of Tort Reform: Federalism and the Regulation of Lawyers, 25 Harv. J.L. & Pub. Pol'y 953 (2002); Owen, Federal Preemption of Products Liability Claims, 55 S.C. L. Rev. 411 (2003); Padget, Comment, Damage Limitations in Medical Malpractice Actions: Necessary Legislation or Unconstitutional Deprivation? 55 S.C. L. Rev. 215 (2003).

Page 5-27, add to the end of note 84:

For a defense of *Lopez* and the Court's other federalism cases by a sitting Justice, *see* Thomas, Why Federalism Matters, 48 Drake L. Rev. 231, 235-238 (2000); *see also* Wilkinson, Federalism for the Future, 74 S. Cal. L. Rev. 523 (2001) (defense of *Lopez*, et al., by Fourth Circuit Court of Appeals Judge J. Harvey Wilkinson, III).

[B] *Lopez:* "Substantially Affecting" Interstate Commerce?

Page 5-28, add to the end of note 85:

For more on the "channels" and "instrumentalities" categories, *see supra* § 5.01[A][2].

Page 5-29, add to end of note 90:

The "jurisdictional nexus" requirement mentioned in *Lopez* is a shorthand way of describing one of the essential elements of the offense. Its presence or absence does not affect a court's subject matter jurisdiction. *See* United States v. Krilich, 209 F.3d 968, 972 (7th Cir. 2000) ("Even if the government fails to establish connection to interstate commerce, the district court is not deprived of jurisdiction to hear the case.") (internal quotation marks omitted).

Page 5-31, add to the end of note 100:

; *see also* Symposium, Spending Clause, 4 Chap. L. Rev. 1 (2001) (articles by Epstein, Chemerinsky, Maltz, Smith, Binder and Baker, among others); Choper & Yoo, The Scope of the Commerce Power After *Morrison*, 25 Okla. City Univ. L. Rev. 843, 857 (2001) ("Given the broad sweep of the spending power, as currently construed, the federal government would quite clearly have the ability to evade the direct limits on its Commerce Clause powers."); Mitchell, Comment, Conditional Federal Funding to the States: The New Federalism Demands a Close Examination for Unconstitutional Conditions, 48 U. Kan. L. Rev. 161 (1999).

Despite calls from scholars, *see, e.g.*, Baker, *supra*; Garnett, The New Federalism, the Spending Power, and Federal Criminal Law, 89 Cornell L. Rev. 1 (2003), the Supreme Court recently declined an opportunity to rein in Congress's spending power. In *Sabri v. United States*, ____ U.S. ____, 124 S. Ct. 1941 (2004), the defendant challenged his conviction under 18 U.S.C. § 666(a)(2), which criminalizes bribery of state and local officials of entities that receive at least $10,000 in federal funds. Because the law lacked any requirement that the bribe be linked to the federal money, Sabri claimed that the law was facially unconstitutional. ____ U.S. at ____, 124 S. Ct. at 1945. The Court unanimously rejected that argument; Justice Souter wrote that "Congress has authority under the Spending Clause to appropriate federal monies to promote the general welfare . . . and it has corresponding authority under the Necessary and Proper Clause . . . to see to it that taxpayer dollars are . . . not frittered away in grant or on projects undermined when funds are siphoned off or corrupt public officials are derelict about demanding value for dollars." ____ U.S. at ____, 124 S. Ct. at 1946. *Lopez* and *Morrison* were no aid, continued the Court, because of the difference in the source of congressional power. "The power to keep a watchful eye on expenditures and on the reliability of those who use public money is bound up with congressional authority to spend in the first place. . . . " ____ U.S. at ____, 124 S. Ct. at 1947. Nor did § 666(a)(2) violate *South Dakota v. Dole*, 483 U.S. 203, 107 S. Ct. 2793 (1987) (divided court), because the former statute was "authority to bring federal power to bear directly on individuals who convert public spending into unearned private gain" and not "a means for bringing federal economic might to bear on a State's own choices of public policy." ____ U.S. at ____, 124 S. Ct. at 1947-1948 (footnote omitted).

Page 5-32, add to note 103 before "But see":

Cf. Vermeule, Does Commerce Clause Review Have Perverse Effects?, 46 Vill. L. Rev. 1325 (2001) (arguing that it is plausible that Commerce Clause review "will promote the centralization of public policy at the national level by providing congressional coalitions with *ex ante* incentives to legislate more broadly, and to create national programs that are more comprehensive, than they would otherwise choose").

Page 5-32, add to end of note 103:

Neal Devins, on the other hand, has presented evidence that Congress does not seem to take much heed of recent Supreme Court decisions, like *Lopez*, in crafting legislation, *see* Devins, Congress as Culprit: How Lawmakers Spurred on the Court's Anti-Congress Crusade, 51 Duke L.J. 435, 450-454 (2001); *see also* Sherry, Irresponsibility Breeds Contempt, 6 Green Bag 2d 47, 48 (2002) (suggesting that Congress is not paying sufficient attention to the Court in crafting new legislation). For possible congressional remedies to what some see as an increased (and unwarranted) judicial scrutiny of congressional motives in lawmaking, *see* Buzbee & Schapiro, Legislative Record Review, 54 Stan. L. Rev. 87 (2001).

[C] "Economic" Activity and "Commercial" Transactions

Page 5-34, add to thirteenth line of note 110 after "remain valid)":

; *but see* United States v. Morrison, 529 U.S. 598, 120 S. Ct. 1740 (2000) (striking down civil suit provision of federal Violence Against Women Act; "violence" is not commercial activity whose effects may be aggregated so Congress may regulate under the Commerce Clause); *infra* § 5.04[F][1];

Page 5-34, add to the end of note 111:

Nor have lower federal courts been quick to adopt the differentiation between "economic" and "noneconomic" statutes. *See, e.g.*, Solid Waste Agency of Northern Cook Co. v. United States Army Corps of Engineers, 191 F.3d 845, 849-851 (7th Cir. 1999) (upholding a Corps of Engineers interpretation permitting jurisdiction over intrastate bodies of water used by birds protected by treaty or by migratory birds that cross state lines under *Wickard* aggregation theory without discussing whether the rule served "economic" ends), *rev'd on other grounds*, 531 U.S. 159, 121 S. Ct. 675 (2001) (divided court) (concluding that Congress did not intend to give Corps authority under Clean Water Act to regulate intrastate waters used by migratory birds); *see also* Denning & Reynolds, Rulings and Resistance: The New Commerce Clause Encounters the Lower Courts, 55 Ark. L. Rev. 1253, 1279-1299 (2003) (citing examples of lower courts' generous definitions of what constitutes "economic" or "commercial" activity). Chalis, *supra* note 83. *But see* United States v. Morrison, 529 U.S. 598, 120 S. Ct. 1740 (2000) (explicitly adopting economic/non-economic distinction for purposes of *Wickard* aggregation); *infra* 5.04[F][1]. For a critique of *Lopez* and *Morrison*'s distinction between economic and non-economic activity, *see* Ides, Economic Activity as a Proxy for Federalism: Intuition and Reason in *United States v. Morrison*, 18 Const. Commentary 563 (2001).

Page 5-35, add new paragraph after note 112 and before "**[D] Lopez and Prior Case Law — Stare Decisis**"*:*

Whatever difficulties the Court might have in the future drawing the line between "commercial" or "economic" activity, on the one hand, and "non-commercial" or "non-economic" activity, on the other, *Citizens*

Bank v. Alafabco, Inc. (2003) suggests that the reach of the commerce power regarding commercial or economic activity, however defined, remains great.[112.1] Following the *Lopez* decision, the Alabama Supreme Court ruled that to invoke the jurisdiction of the Federal Arbitration Act (FAA), the party seeking to enforce an arbitration clause under federal law must demonstrate that the transaction embodied in the contract in which the clause was included *itself* substantially affected interstate commerce.[112.2] For the next several years, the Alabama Supreme Court heard dozens of cases in which it applied this standard, over the objection of one of its members, who argued that the Alabama court had misinterpreted *Lopez*.[112.3]

In the *Alafabco* case, the Alabama Supreme Court had refused to order arbitration of a financial dispute between the parties, holding that agreements containing the arbitration clauses did not, themselves, have a sufficient nexus to interstate commerce.[112.4] The Supreme Court, in a brief, per curiam opinion, reversed. The Court first noted that the FAA used the term "in commerce," which the Court took to signal Congress's intent to exercise its power to the broadest possible extent.[112.5] The relevant question, then, became not whether the individual transactions themselves substantially affected interstate commerce, but rather if, in the aggregate, the economic activity in question would have a substantial effect on interstate commerce.[112.6]

Having posed the proper question, the Court answered that "[t]his case is well within our previous pronouncements on the extent of Congress's Commerce Clause power" and criticized the Alabama court's "improperly cramped view of Congress's Commerce Clauses power" that rested on a "misreading" of *Lopez*.[112.7] Specifically, the Court noted that while the transactions at issue were intrastate in nature, they nonetheless satisfied the "substantially affects" test because (i) Alafabco "engaged in business throughout the southeastern United States" using the bank loans; (ii) the debt "was secured by all of Alafabco's business assets, including its inventory of goods assembled from out-of-state parts and raw materials"; and (iii) because of "the broad impact of commercial lending on the national economy," which the Court regarded as obvious or at least as not requiring "elaborate explanation."[112.8] *Lopez*, the Court added, did not "purport to announce a new rule governing Congress' Commerce Clause power over concededly economic activity such as the debt restructuring agreements" between the parties.[112.9]

In *Gonzales v. Raich* (2005), moreover, the majority seemed to adopt a capacious definition of "economic" activity, concluding that, though noncommercial, the intrastate production of medical marijuana was economic activity reachable by Congress because it involved the "production, distribution, and consumption of commodities for which there is an established, and lucrative, interstate market" with which the "local" products might compete.[112.10] In her dissent, Justice O'Connor criticized the majority's definition of economic activity as "breathtaking," and complained that its definition "threatens to sweep all of productive human activity into federal regulatory reach."[112.11] The majority's use of "a dictionary definition of economics" skirted "the real problem of drawing a meaningful line between 'what is national and what is local'. . . . "[112.12] Because commercial goods have a homemade or noncommercial substitute, she argued, "[t]o draw the line wherever private activity affects the demand for market goods is to draw no line at all, and to declare everything economic."[112.13] Justice O'Connor would tie "economic activity" to that which was explicitly "commercial"—a line that would have excluded the medical marijuana at issue from regulation.[112.14] "In *Lopez* and *Morrison*," she noted, "we suggested that economic activity usually relates directly to commercial activity. . . . The homegrown cultivation and personal possession and use of marijuana for medicinal purposes has no apparent commercial character."[112.15]

[112.1] Citizens Bank v. Alafabco, Inc., 539 U.S. 52, 123 S. Ct. 2037 (2003) (per curiam).

[112.2] Sisters of the Visitation v. Cochran Plastering Co., 775 So. 2d 759 (2000) (divided court). *See generally* Brown, State Court Attempts to Limit the Applicability of the Federal Arbitration Act in a Post-*Lopez* World, 56 U. Miami L. Rev. 1051 (2002); Richmond, Comment, *Sisters of the Visitation v. Cochran Plastering Co.*: Earnest Federalism or Reconstructive Defiance to the Federal Arbitration Act?, 25 Am. J. Trial Advoc. 633 (2002).

[112.3] *Alafabco*, 539 U.S. at 54-55, 123 S. Ct. at 2039. For a list of the decisions themselves, see infra § 5.05[C] (supplement).

[112.4] Citizens Bank v. Alafabco, Inc., 2002 WL 1998268 (D. Ala.) (Aug. 30, 2002), at *3, *5.

[112.5] 539 U.S. at 57, 123 S. Ct. at 2040.

[112.6] 539 U.S. at 57, 123 S. Ct. at 2040.

[112.7] 539 U.S. at 57, 58, 123 S. Ct. at 2040, 2041.

[112.8] 539 U.S. at 57-58, 123 S. Ct. at 2040-2041.

[112.9] 539 U.S. at 58, 123 S. Ct. at 2041. For post-*Alafabco* FAA cases, see Legacy Wireless Services, Inc. v. Human Capital, L.L.C., 2004 WL 843706 (D. Oregon) (April 20, 2004) (FAA applied to contract involving employment issues subject to federal law between companies incorporated in different states); Pitchford v. AmSouth Bank, 285 F. Supp. 2d 1286, 1290 (M.D. Ala. 2003) (transaction involving "a commercial loan made by AmSouth, a regional bank, to the Plaintiffs for the purposes of financing the purchase of a truck . . . constitutes interstate commerce" because of the impact of commercial lending on the national economy; FAA applies); McKenzie Check Advance of Mississippi LLC v. Hardy, 866 So. 2d 446, 452 (Miss. 2004) (transaction between citizens of different states sufficient to trigger FAA); Service Corp. Int'l v. Fulmer, 2003 WL 22872183 (Ala. 2003) (contract for intrastate funeral home services involves commerce; FAA applicable); Steele v. Walser, 2003 WL 22463387 (Ala. 2003) (same, as applied to contract involving construction and sale of home); Elizabeth Homes, L.L.C. v. Gantt, 2003 WL 22520218 (Ala. 2003) (same); Edward D. Jones & Co., L.P. v. Wehby, 2003 WL 22753426 (Ala. 2003) (same, involving contract between investment companies trading securities in different states); SouthTrust Corp. v. James, 2003 WL 22463399 (Ala. 2003) (same, involving agreement to arbitrate between bank and bank customer as condition for opening checking account; where initial check used to open account drawn on out-of-state bank and interstate nature of bank's business); Hedges v. Carrigan, 2004 WL 729160 (Ct. App. Cal.) (April 6, 2004), at ___ (residential purchase agreement involving loans obtained from Federal Housing Administration and documents available only to members of the National Association of Realtors sufficient to characterize transaction as "involving commerce" for purposes of the FAA); Thornton v. Trident Medical Center, L.L.C., 2003 WL 22887990 (Ct. App. S.C. 2003) (FAA applies to employment agreement between physicians and medical center involving relocation of Michigan physician to South Carolina; held, agreement involved interstate commerce).

[112.10] Gonzales v. Raich, ___ U.S. ___, ___, 125 S. Ct. 2195, 2211 (2005) (divided court).

[112.11] *Raich*, ___ U.S. at ___, 125 S. Ct. at 2224 (O'Connor, J., dissenting).

[112.12] ___ U.S. at ___, 125 S. Ct. at 2224-2225 (O'Connor, J., dissenting).

[112.13] ___ U.S. at ___, 125 S. Ct. at 2225 (O'Connor, J., dissenting).

[112.14] ___ U.S. at ___, 125 S. Ct. at 2225 (O'Connor, J., dissenting).

[112.15] ___ U.S. at ___, 125 S. Ct. at 2225 (O'Connor, J., dissenting).

[D] *Lopez* and Prior Case Law—Stare Decisis

Page 5-36, add to the end of note 116:

The Court recently confirmed its commitment to *stare decisis* in its Commerce Clause cases when it reversed the Alabama Supreme Court's holding that *Lopez* required that parties seeking arbitration under the Federal Arbitration Act prove that the transaction itself substantially affected interstate commerce. Citizens Bank v. Alafabco, Inc., 539 U.S. 52, 123 S. Ct. 2037 (2003) (per curiam). In 1995, in a pre-*Lopez*, opinion, the Court held that Congress had intended to exercise its commerce power to the fullest extent in passing the FAA. Allied-Bruce Terminix Cos. v. Dobson, 513 U.S. 265, 273, 115 S. Ct. 834, 839 (1995). Criticizing the Alabama court for its "improperly cramped view of Congress' Commerce Clause power," the Court stressed that "*Lopez* did not restrict the reach of the FAA or implicitly overrule *Allied-Bruce Terminix Cos.* — indeed, we did not discuss that case in *Lopez*." 539 U.S. at 58, 123 S. Ct. at 2041. The proper inquiry for ascertaining the reach of the FAA, according to the Court, was not whether individual transactions alone substantially affected interstate commerce, but whether "if in the aggregate the economic activity in question would represent 'a general practice . . . subject to federal control"' by substantially affecting interstate commerce. *See* 539 U.S. at 57, 123 S. Ct. at 2040 (quoting Mandeville Island Farms, Inc. v. American Crystal Sugar Co., 334 U.S. 219, 236, 68 S. Ct. 996, 1006 (1948)). *See also* Gonzales v. Raich, ____ U.S. ____, 125 S. Ct. 2195 (2005) (divided court) (upholding application of federal Controlled Substance Act to intrastate, noncommercial production and possession of marijuana for medical purposes; emphasizing similarity between the Controlled Substances Act and statutes in cases like *Wickard v. Filburn* and *Perez v. United States*). For *Lopez*'s reception in the lower courts, *see infra* § 5.04[E]; for the Supreme Court's post-*Lopez* decisions, *see infra* § 5.04[G].

Page 5-36, add the following new subsections after carryover paragraph:

[E] Intermezzo: *Lopez* in the Lower Courts

If the *Lopez* Court had intended its decision to inaugurate a sweeping reexamination of congressional commerce-based regulation it must have been disappointed: in the five years immediately following the *Lopez* decision, the lower courts refused to take the hint.[116.1] Despite the entreaties of literally hundreds of litigants, lower courts generally declined to read *Lopez* expansively, particularly against statutes that had, pre-*Lopez*, been upheld by the Supreme Court.[116.2] Immediately following *Lopez*, district courts were sometimes more willing to overturn statutes based on *Lopez*, particularly if the statutes were passed following, or contemporaneous with, the *Lopez* decision.[116.3] In fact, only the Fourth Circuit Court of Appeals struck down a federal statute by invoking *Lopez* — the federal civil remedy afforded to victims of gender-motivated violence, a decision which was later upheld by the Supreme Court.[116.4]

The Fourth Circuit's *Brzonkala* decision notwithstanding, the courts of appeals have turned aside, *en masse*, facial challenges to a host of federal statutes: the Federal Access to Clinic Entrances Act;[116.5] the federal carjacking statute;[116.6] a federal "anti-stalking" statute;[116.7] the federal bank robbery statute;[116.8] the Hobbs Act, which prohibits using violence to obstruct interstate commerce;[116.9] the federal racketeering act, known as RICO;[116.10] a federal prohibition on the operation of an "illegal gambling business";[116.11] the federal child pornography statute;[116.12] the federal arson statute;[116.13] federal environmental laws and regulations;[116.14] and a number of federal firearms laws.[116.15] In no small part, the lower court timorousness can be traced to judges' uncertainty about the intended scope of *Lopez*, as well as confusion over how the "substantially affects" test was to be applied prospectively.[116.16]

At their most formalistic, lower courts treated *Lopez* as no more than a command to Congress to say "Simon Says": if it dutifully recited a connection to interstate commerce, the courts would inquire no further.[116.17] Other courts seemed to suspect that the Court intended Congress to do a bit more than comply with certain forms and formalities, but again, confusion over the scope of the ruling encouraged caution. These courts were often more receptive to "as applied" challenges; requiring the government to prove interstate elements of federal criminal statutes, and suspicious of overly-attenuated connections between alleged criminal activity and its effects on interstate commerce.[116.18] Finally, there was the Fourth Circuit's *Brzonkala* decision, which seemed willing to expand the reach of *Lopez*, or at least not confine it to its specific facts.[116.19] Coming nearly five years after *Lopez* itself, the *Brzonkala* decision set the stage for the Supreme Court to clarify whether *Lopez* was a harbinger of further change, or as one commentator quipped, was "destined to be a 'but see' citation."[116.20]

[F] Act Two: *Morrison* and *Jones*

[1] *United States v. Morrison*

In *United States v. Morrison* (2000), the Supreme Court affirmed the Fourth Circuit's earlier decision[116.21] invalidating 42 U.S.C. § 13981, which provided a federal civil remedy against victims of gender-motivated violence.[116.22] This provision of the Violence Against Women Act[116.23] (VAWA) had been passed by Congress as an exercise both of its commerce power, as well as its power to secure equal protection under the Fourteenth Amendment.[116.24] The Court, per Chief Justice Rehnquist, held that Congress exceeded its authority under both, relying on both *United States v. Lopez*[116.25] and *The Civil Rights Cases*.[116.26]

The broad remedy afforded complainants under § 13981 was emphasized by the Court. The statute rendered any person "who commits a crime of violence motivated by gender . . . shall be liable to the party injured" for compensatory and punitive damages, as well as injunctive relief.[116.27] A "crime of violence motivated by gender" was defined as "a crime of violence committed because of gender or on the basis of gender, and due, at least in part, to an animus based on the victim's gender."[116.28] The term "crime of violence," moreover, was defined as an act or acts that would constitute a felony against a person or that would constitute a felony against property, if the acts present a "serious risk of physical injury to another."[116.29] However, no criminal charges need have been filed to take advantage of the remedy.[116.30]

There were some limitations. No cause of action was permitted for "random acts of violence unrelated to gender" or for those acts for which gender animus could not be proven "by a preponderance of the evidence."[116.31] In addition, Congress took pains to state that the act was not intended to confer subject matter jurisdiction on federal courts over divorce or child custody matters.[116.32] Further, in an obvious effort to remedy the deficiencies of the Gun Free School Zones Act (GFSZA) struck down in *Lopez*, the passage of § 13981 was accompanied by copious congressional findings describing the effects that gender violence had on the national economy.[116.33]

The Court, however, was unimpressed. While allowing that acts of Congress are entitled to a "presumption of constitutionality" and acknowledging that, since 1937, "Congress has had considerably greater latitude in regulating conduct and transactions under the Commerce Clause than . . . previous case law permitted," the Court found that § 13981 nevertheless exceeded this latitude.[116.34]

The Court began its analysis with an enunciation of first principles, similar to that with which it began *Lopez*. First, "[e]very law passed by Congress must be based on one or more of its powers enumerated in the Constitution."[116.35] Even under an expansive post–New Deal interpretation, the Commerce Clause, like all powers of Congress "is not without effective bounds."[116.36] Repeating *Lopez*'s three categories under which Congress may properly exercise its commerce power — regulation of the channels of interstate commerce, protection of the instrumentalities of interstate commerce and persons or things in interstate commerce, and, finally, those activities that substantially affect interstate commerce — the Court analyzed § 13981 under the last (Category Three).[116.37]

Category Three cases, the Court continued, are to be analyzed according to the framework set forth in *Lopez*. In striking down the GFSZA, the Court wrote, "[s]everal significant considerations contributed to our decision."[116.38] First, the GFSZA was a criminal statute with little or no connection to commerce, a characteristic that Chief Justice Rehnquist called "central to our decision."[116.39] Second, the Court noted the lack of a jurisdictional element tying the proscribed activity to interstate commerce.[116.40] Third, the Court noted that the GFSZA came with no findings regarding the effects of gun possession in school zones on interstate commerce.[116.41] "Finally," wrote Rehnquist, "our decision in *Lopez* rested in part on the fact that the link between gun possession and a substantial effect on interstate commerce was attenuated."[116.42] The Court noted that it rejected the government's arguments in favor of regulation — that crime is a national problem that the entire population shares because its costs are spread through insurance, that it can harm productivity and hinder travel because of fear of crime, and that guns in schools can affect the educational process and result in a less effective national workforce — because "they would permit Congress to 'regulate not only all violent crime, but all activities that may lead to violent crime, regardless of how tenuously they relate to interstate commerce.' "[116.43]

With such a set up, the rest of the Commerce Clause analysis was a foregone conclusion. "Gender-motivated crimes of violence are not, in any sense of the phrase, economic activity. While we need not adopt a categorical rule against aggregating the effects of any noneconomic activity in order to decide these cases;" the Court stressed that the Commerce Clause has been accorded its furthest reach "only where activity is economic in nature."[116.44] Similar to the GFSZA, § 13981 had no "jurisdictional element establishing that the federal cause of action is in pursuance of Congress' power to regulate interstate commerce. . . . Congress elected to cast § 13981's remedy over a wider, and more purely intrastate, body of violent crime."[116.45]

However, what § 13981 did have — and what the GFSZA lacked — was plenty of congressional findings establishing a connection between gender violence and interstate commerce. However, what the Court hinted in *Lopez* it made explicit in *Morrison*: "[T]he existence of congressional findings is not sufficient, by itself, to sustain the constitutionality of Commerce Clause legislation."[116.46] In the end, the Court declared, questions regarding the scope of Congress's commerce power are judicial, rather than legislative, and are thus for the Court to decide.[116.47]

Further, "Congress' findings are substantially weakened by the fact that they rely so heavily on a method of reasoning that we have already rejected as unworkable if we are to maintain the Constitution's enumeration of powers."[116.48] In doing so, the Court strongly reaffirmed what was another of *Lopez*'s themes, what has been termed the "noninfinity principle":[116.49] that the doctrine of enumerated powers precludes any interpretation of the Commerce Clause that renders it a *de facto* federal police power with no articulable limits save those imposed by Congress itself. Given Congress's findings, that gender-motivated violence deterred victims from travelling in interstate commerce and from transacting business, thus harming national productivity and increasing nationwide medical costs, Chief Justice Rehnquist wrote

> the concern that we expressed in *Lopez* that Congress might use the Commerce Clause to completely obliterate the Constitution's distinction between national and local authority seems well founded. . . . The reasoning that petitioners advance seeks to follow the but-for causal chain from the initial occurrence of a violent crime (the suppression of which has always been the prime object of the States' police powers) to every attenuated effect upon interstate commerce. If accepted, petitioners' reasoning would allow Congress to regulate any crime as long as the nationwide, aggregated impact of that crime has substantial effects on employment, production, transit, or consumption.[116.50]

"Indeed," the Chief Justice continued, "if Congress may regulate gender-motivated violence, it would be able to regulate murder or any other type of violence" since the larger class of violent crime is certain to have a greater impact that the lesser subset that Congress chose to regulate.[116.51] The reasoning employed by the government, moreover, could "be applied equally as well to family law and other areas of traditional state regulation since the aggregate effect of marriage, divorce, and childrearing on the national economy is undoubtedly significant."[116.52] The Court was unimpressed by Congress's self-imposed limitation, which prevented § 13981 from being interpreted to extend the reach of the federal courts into these areas. "Under our written Constitution . . . the limitation of congressional authority is not solely a matter of legislative grace."[116.53] Accordingly, the Court rejected "the argument that Congress may regulate noneconomic, violent criminal conduct based solely on that conduct's aggregate effect on interstate commerce. . . . The regulation and punishment of intrastate violence . . . not directed at the instrumentalities, channels, or goods involved in interstate commerce has always been the province of the states."[116.54]

The majority's opinion was accompanied by a vigorous dissent, penned by Justice Souter, who accused the majority of reviewing the legislation for its "soundness" as opposed to mere "rationality."[116.55] The dissenters would have distinguished *Morrison* from *Lopez* because of the former's "mountain of data assembled by Congress . . . showing the effects of violence against women on interstate commerce."[116.56] In light of the data on which Congress relied in invoking its commerce authority, Justice Souter asked whether Congress's conclusion was "irrational."[116.57] Not only was it not manifestly irrational, according to Justice Souter, but the information amassed was more than that which existed when the Court decided *Heart of Atlanta Motel v. United States* (1964) and *Katzenbach v. McClung* (1964), or even *Wickard v. Filburn* (1942).[116.58] Thus, "[t]he Act would have passed muster at any time between *Wickard* in 1942 and *Lopez* in 1995, a period in which the law enjoyed a stable understanding that congressional power under the Commerce Clause . . . extended to all activity that, when aggregated, has a substantial effect on interstate commerce."[116.59] That the majority had held the Act invalid signaled to Justice Souter that "the Court's nominal adherence to the substantial effects test is merely that."[116.60]

Souter and the dissenters accused the Court of returning to the formalism of an earlier day by drawing a distinction between economic and noneconomic activities for purposes of deciding whether Congress had exceeded its authority.[116.61] Lassiez-faire economic theory was behind earlier decisions, like *Carter Coal*, in which the Court had separated commerce, mining, manufacturing, and the like. The source of the current Court's renewed formalism, wrote Justice Souter, "is not that the majority fails to see causal connections in an integrated economic world."[116.62] Rather, "in the minds of the majority there is a new animating theory that makes the categorical formalism seem useful again. Just as old formalism had value in the service of an economic conception, the new one is useful in serving a conception of federalism."[116.63] Souter then cited the majority's use of "traditional areas of state concern" as a factor in determining whether Congress had overstepped its bounds, and made the following observation: "Again, history seems to be recycling, for the theory of traditional state concern as grounding a limiting principle has been rejected previously, and more than once."[116.64] Souter then argued that the use of judicial review to police the boundaries of federalism was inconsistent not only with the intent of the Framers, who had expected such conflicts to be mediated through the political process, but also with subsequent constitutional developments like the

Seventeenth Amendment, which provided for the direct election of senators.[116.65]

"All of this," Souter concluded, "convinces me that today's ebb of the commerce power rests on error, and at the same time leads me to doubt that the majority's view will prove to be enduring law."[116.66] The Court's experiment, he predicted, will end when the majority's conception of the commerce power, and its larger attempts to judicially enforce its vision of federalism, run up against the dual realities of an "integrated national economy and a political relationship between States and Nation much affected by their respective treasuries and constitutional modifications adopted by the people."[116.67]

[2] *Jones v. United States*

In the second of the two cases that applied *Lopez* in 2000, the Court pruned federal authority to prosecute defendants under the federal arson statute. The defendant in *Jones v. United States* (2000) was convicted of arson under 18 U.S.C. § 844(i), which criminalizes arson of property in or affecting interstate commerce.[116.68] The Court unanimously held that, under *Lopez*, arson of "an owner-occupied residence not used for any commercial purpose does not qualify as property 'used in' commerce or commerce-affecting activity" and was not subject to federal prosecution. The Court rejected the reasoning of the government, which had been accepted by a number of other jurisdictions,[116.69] that a private residence was "used in" interstate commerce by, *inter alia*, using the house as collateral to secure a mortgage from an out-of-state lender; by using the house to obtain insurance from an out-of-state insurer; and by using the house to receive natural gas from outside the state.[116.70] "Were we to adopt the Government's expansive interpretation," wrote Justice Ginsburg, "hardly a building in the land would fall outside the federal statute's domain. Practically every building in our cities, towns, and rural areas is constructed with supplies that have moved in interstate commerce, served by utilities that have an interstate connection . . . or bears some other trace of interstate commerce."[116.71] *Lopez*, the "rule of lenity" that counsels narrow construction of penal statutes, and *Bass*'s reluctance to interpret federal statutes so as to upset the federal-state balance in crime control all counseled a more narrow reading of the statute than that which the government urged upon the Court.[116.72]

The similarity of the arguments used by the government to support this prosecution and those used to defend the civil suit provisions of the

Violence Against Women Act makes the unanimity of the Court somewhat surprising. Even more surprising is the solicitude for the proper balance between federal and state relations evinced in the concurring opinion, written by Justices who dissented in *Morrison*. Here, however, the dissenters could point not only to the rule of construction that counsels against expansive readings of federal criminal statutes, but also to *United States v. Bass* (1971), in which the Court overturned a conviction under a federal firearms statute when the requisite nexus with interstate commerce was not demonstrated, while upholding the statute on its face.[116.73]

[G] What Hath *Raich* Wrought?

The dire commentary in the wake of *Lopez* and *Morrison* to the effect that the Court was out to deprive Congress of its power to do the people's business turned out to be unwarranted.[116.74]

In the aftermath of *Lopez* and *Morrison*, the lower courts proceeded cautiously, preferring the as-applied challenge to facial invalidation of congressional statutes. In the year following *Morrison* and *Jones*, only one statute was struck down; only a handful of convictions—particularly those under federal arson statute—were reversed on the grounds that the government had not presented enough evidence that the property in question was "used in" interstate commerce, as required by the statute.[116.78] Most other challenges to federal criminal statutes concerning robbery, gun possession by felons and those subject to protective orders, drug trafficking, child pornography, racketeering, and illegal gambling were unsuccessful.[116.79]

For its part, the U.S. Supreme Court was equally cautious, denying certiorari in many of the aforementioned cases, thus declining the opportunity to expand *Lopez* and *Morrison* further. One case it did take up, *Solid Waste Agency of Northern Cook County v. United States Army Corps of Engineers* (2001), added nothing to the conversation begun by *Lopez*, but rather was decided on narrow grounds of statutory interpretation.[116.80]

Subsequent cases suggested that the chances the Court would develop robust limitations on the Commerce Clause were slim. In *Pierce Co. v. Guillen* (2003), the Court upheld the power of Congress to regulate the channels and instrumentalities of interstate commerce by, in this case, prohibiting the discovery or disclosure in state and federal lawsuits of certain highway safety data collected by states in order to receive federal highway funds.[116.81] In *Citizens Bank v. Alafabco* (2003), moreover, the Court signaled that the reach of congressional power to regulate activities that "substantially affect" interstate commerce is still quite broad, if the underlying activity is "economic" or "commercial."[116.82] In *Alafabco*, the Court reversed a line of cases from the Alabama Supreme Court that had required parties seeking arbitration to prove that the underlying transaction itself substantially affected interstate commerce.[116.83] The Supreme Court called the Alabama High Court's view of congressional power "improperly cramped" and held that the proper inquiry for ascertaining the reach of the FAA was not whether individual transactions alone substantially affected interstate commerce, but whether "if in the aggregate the economic activity in question would represent 'a general practice . . . subject to federal control' " by substantially affecting interstate commerce.[116.84]

In 2003, the Ninth Circuit held that federal drug laws could not be constitutionally applied to "the intrastate, noncommercial cultivation, possession and use of marijuana for personal medical purposes on the advice of a physician."[116.85] When the Court granted certiorari, the stage was set for a decision explaining how much (or how little) the Court will limit congressional power.

Those who hoped that the Court would expand *Lopez* and *Morrison*—perhaps even overruling cases like *Wickard v. Filburn*—would be disappointed. In *Gonzales v. Raich* (2005), a divided Court reversed the Ninth Circuit and held that if Congress had the authority to eliminate the market in Schedule I drugs, like marijuana, under the Controlled Substances Act (CSA), then it could constitutionally regulate even noncommercial, intrastate instances of the regulated conduct.[116.86] To the surprise of many, the *Raich* majority included Justices Kennedy and Scalia, who had been part of the majority in *Lopez* and *Morrison.*

In his opinion for the Court, Justice Stevens downplayed the significance of *Lopez* and *Morrison*, stating that those opinions needed to be considered in "the larger context of modern-era Commerce Clause jurisprudence preserved by those cases," and warning against reading those cases "too broadly."[116.87] The tone of *Raich* differs substantially from *Lopez* and *Morrison*; the Court adopted a more deferential tone than in either of the prior cases. For example, Justice Stevens emphasized that, as Stevens put it later in the opinion, "[i]n assessing the scope of Congress' authority under the Commerce Clause, we stress that the task before us is a modest one. *We need not determine whether respondents' activities, taken in the aggregate, substantially affect interstate commerce in fact, but only whether a 'rational basis' exists for so concluding*." (emphasis added).

Stevens focused on the similarities between the facts in *Raich* and those in *Wickard* and *Perez*: the *Raich* plaintiffs were, in essence, asking the Court to recognize theirs as a class of activities that could not "substantially affect" interstate commerce and that, since the activity at issue was not "commercial" or "economic"—the marijuana was grown locally, for personal consumption pursuant to state law, and was not sold—Congress's commerce power could not reach that activity.[116.88]

According to the Court, its prior decisions, left undisturbed by *Lopez* and *Morrison*, foreclosed such arguments. "Our case law firmly establishes Congress' power to regulate purely local activities that are part of an economic 'class of activities' that have a substantial effect on interstate commerce."[116.89] Congress could have rationally concluded that the activities engaged in by the respondents undercut its efforts to eliminate the national market in marijuana and thus regulate it.

> In *Wickard*, we had no difficulty concluding that Congress had a rational basis for belief that, when viewed in the aggregate, leaving home-consumed wheat outside the regulatory scheme would have a substantial influence on price and market conditions. Here, too, Congress had a rational basis for concluding that leaving home-consumed marijuana outside federal control would similarly affect price and market conditions.[116.90]

The Court went on to reject attempts by the petitioners to distinguish *Wickard*. They argued that (1) the Agricultural Adjustment Act contained exemptions, not present in the CSA, that excluded small commercial farms from the Act; (2) *Wickard* involved economic activity, production of goods on a commercial farm, not present here; and (3) there were insufficient findings in the CSA, unlike in *Wickard*, establishing that the aggregate production of homegrown, medicinal marijuana had a substantial effect on the interstate market for marijuana regulated by the CSA.[116.91]

As to the first, the Court noted that the decision to exempt small farms in *Wickard* did "not speak to his power to regulate all those whose aggregated production was significant, nor did that fact play any role in the Court's analysis."[116.92] Second, the activity for which *Wickard* was fined, growing wheat in excess of his quota, the Court noted, "was not treated . . . as part of his commercial farming operation."[116.93]

Finally, the Court felt that the findings accompanying the CSA were sufficient to demonstrate a substantial effect on the interstate marijuana market by the class of respondents' activities. The Court specifically rejected the argument that since the CSA made no explicit finding regarding the effect of medical marijuana on the interstate marijuana market, such an effect, and the desire to prevent it, could not have served as a rational basis for congressional action.[116.94] The Court was critical of the dissenters' suggestion that such particularized findings are necessary for congressional regulation: "Such an exacting requirement is not only unprecedented," Stevens wrote, "it is also impractical . . . given that the CSA initially identified 80 other substances subject to regulation as Schedule I drugs. . . . Surely, Congress cannot be expected (and certainly should not be required) to include specific findings on each and every substance contained therein to satisfy the dissenters' unfounded skepticism."[116.95]

Only at the end of the opinion did the majority address *Lopez* and *Morrison*; it had little trouble distinguishing them. First, the challenges in *Lopez* and *Morrison* were facial challenges to, respectively, "a brief, single-subject statute" and a federal civil remedy that "did not regulate economic activity."[116.96] The CSA, in contrast, "was a lengthy and detailed statute creating a comprehensive framework for regulating the production, distribution, and possession of five classes of 'controlled substances.'"[116.97] The CSA, moreover, regulated "economic activity," i.e., the "production, distribution, and consumption of commodities for which there is an established, and lucrative, interstate market."[116.98] It rejected the Court of Appeal's attempt to "isolat[e] a 'separate and distinct' class of activities" in order to make the activity seem less "commercial" or "economic."[116.99] The question for the Court was "whether Congress' . . . decision to include this narrower 'class of activities' within the larger regulatory scheme was constitutionally deficient."[116.100]

The Court answered that it was not. It rejected the argument that marijuana use permitted under California's law could be distinguished from that regulated under the CSA because it was used for medical purposes and prescribed by a doctor. "The CSA," the Court noted, "designates marijuana as contraband for *any* purpose," and its classification as a Schedule I drug under the CSA indicates Congress's judgment that "the drug has no acceptable medical uses."[116.101] Nor was the Court swayed by the argument that the marijuana here was being grown and consumed in accordance with state law: "The Supremacy Clause unambiguously provides that if there is any conflict between federal law and state law, federal law shall prevail."[116.102] The Court also expressed considerable skepticism that California could "surgically excise[] a discrete activity that is hermetically sealed off from the larger interstate market. . . ."[116.103] It argued that "[t]he exemption for cultivation by patients and caregivers can only increase the supply of marijuana in the California market," thus undermining Congress's intent to eliminate the market in marijuana.[116.104] "[T]he case for the exemption," the majority concluded, "comes down to the claim that a locally cultivated product that is used domestically rather than sold on the open market is not subject to federal regulation. Given the findings in the CSA and the undisputed magnitude of the commercial market for marijuana, our decisions in *Wickard v. Filburn* and the later cases endorsing its reasoning foreclose that claim."[116.105]

Justice Scalia concurred, stressing his reliance on the Necessary and Proper Clause to reach the conclusion that the activity at issue in *Raich* could be regulated under the CSA.[116.106] He found the case to be "straightforward."[116.107]

> In the CSA, Congress has undertaken to extinguish the interstate market in Schedule I controlled substances, including marijuana. The Commerce Clause unquestionably permits this. . . . To effectuate its objective, Congress has prohibited almost all intrastate activities related to Schedule I substances — both economic activities (manufacture, distribution, possession with the intent to distribute) and noneconomic (simple possession). . . . That simple possession is a noneconomic activity is immaterial to whether it can be prohibited as a necessary part of a larger regulation. Rather, Congress's authority to enact all of these prohibitions of intrastate controlled-substance activity depends only upon whether they are appropriate means of achieving the legitimate end of eradicating Schedule I substances from interstate commerce.[116.108]

Because it was impossible to distinguish intrastate from interstate marijuana, because "Congress need not accept on faith that state law will be effective in maintaining a strict division" between lawful and contraband marijuana, and because there was no otherwise "inappropriate" violation of state sovereignty, he agreed with the majority that "Congress could reasonably conclude that its objective of prohibiting marijuana from the interstate market 'could be undercut' if those activities [permitted by state law] were excepted from its general scheme of regulation."[116.109]

Justice Scalia distinguished the case from *Lopez* and *Morrison* on the grounds that while they "affirm that Congress may not regulate certain 'purely local' activity . . . based solely on the attenuated effect that such activity may have in the interstate market," neither case held "noneconomic intrastate activities to be categorically beyond the reach of the Federal Government."[116.110] He also noted that neither case "involved the power of Congress to exert control over intrastate activities in connection with a more comprehensive scheme of regulation. . . ."[116.111]

Justice O'Connor wrote the principal dissent, in which Chief Justice Rehnquist and Justice Thomas joined.[116.112] For the dissenters, *Raich* was "materially indistinguishable" from *Lopez* and *Morrison*; the majority's decision "irreconcilable" with those decisions.[116.113] "Today's decision," she wrote, "allows Congress to regulate intrastate activity without check, as long as there is some implication by legislative design that regulating intrastate activity is essential (and the Court appears to equate 'essential' with 'necessary') to the interstate regulatory scheme."[116.114] If this is true, O'Connor continued, "then *Lopez* stands for nothing more than a drafting guide," because Congress could merely have passed a larger regulatory scheme prohibiting the transfer or possession of firearms anywhere, and regulated the possession near a school zone as an incident to that larger scheme.[116.115]

O'Connor argued that the Court should seek "objective markers" that, on the one hand, prevent individual litigants from claiming, in as-applied challenges, that "their personal activities do not have a substantial effect on interstate commerce," while, on the other hand, not permitting Congress to regulate everything by letter it "set the terms of analysis."[116.116] In *Raich*, O'Connor found several such markers present. First was the fact that medical and nonmedical uses of drugs are recognized and distinguished not only in California's law, but in the CSA as well.[116.117] Second, O'Connor regarded it as important that the state law here "involved . . . criminal law and social policy," both areas of traditional state interest.[116.118] The question was whether Congressional interference with California's decision to permit the cultivation, possession, and use of medical marijuana was warranted — that is, whether "the conduct is economic and, in the aggregate, substantially affects interstate commerce."[116.119]

O'Connor criticized the majority's definition of economic activity as "breathtaking," and complained that its definition "threatens to sweep all of productive human activity into federal regulatory reach."[116.120] The majority's use of "a dictionary definition of economics" skirted "the real problem of drawing a meaningful line between 'what is national and what is local'. . . . "[116.121] Saying that Congress could regulate intrastate noncommercial activity because of the effect on demand for commercial goods means that there is no limit at all. Because commercial goods have a homemade or noncommercial substitute, "[t]o draw the line wherever private activity affects the demand for market goods is to draw no line at all, and to declare everything economic."[116.122] O'Connor would have tied "economic activity" to that which was explicitly "commercial" — a line that would have excluded the medical marijuana at issue from regulation.[116.123]

Further, she argued that the government had made no showing that the medical marijuana grown by respondents, even if found to be "economic" and considered in the aggregate, had a substantial effect on interstate commerce.[116.124] Unlike in *Wickard,* where the actual effects of the impact of the homegrown wheat could be evaluated by the Court because the parties had stipulated to that impact, all the Court had here were findings in the CSA itself that O'Connor dismissed as "a legislative insistence that the regulation of controlled substances must be absolute" without "any supporting evidence — descriptive, statistical, or otherwise."[116.125] The CSA's findings were "too vague and unspecific to demonstrate that the federal statutory scheme will be undermined if Congress cannot exert power over individuals like the respondents. The declarations are not even about marijuana," she complained.[116.126] If the CSA's findings were enough, she reasoned, then *Morrison* should have come out the other way, since the Violence Against Women Act, of which the civil-suit provision struck down in that case was a part, came with numerous findings about the impact of gender-motivated violence on the economy.[116.127] While she would not have voted for California's law had she been in its legislature, she concluded with the observation that whatever the wisdom of California's law, "the federalism principles that have drive our Commerce Clause cases require that room for experiment be protected in this case."[116.128]

Justice Thomas also wrote separately in dissent.[116.129] As he had in *Lopez,* Thomas urged a fundamental reconsideration of the scope of congressional power under the Commerce Clause. He argued that (1) the activity regulated here was not "commerce" as that term was understood at the time of the Framing;[116.130] (2) the regulation of the intrastate activity was neither "necessary" nor "proper";[116.131] and (3) the "substantial effects" test itself was so malleable that it should be discarded by the

Court.[116.132] Thomas also argued, as did O'Connor, that the majority's decision was difficult to square with *Lopez* and *Morrison*.[116.133]

* * *

At the very least, it seems that *Raich* spells the end to many as-applied challenges that had been successfully made by defendants to convictions under federal statutes regulating child pornography, machine gun possession, and arson.[116.134] If Congress can eliminate an interstate market in something, then it has authority, according to *Raich*, to regulate every instance of that activity—no matter how local or noncommercial. But *Raich* may mean an end to the raft of Commerce Clause challenges inaugurated by *Lopez* and *Morrison*. Lower courts, which had never rushed to apply those cases vigorously,[116.135] will likely see *Raich* as a confirmation of their earlier caution. Moreover, cases like *Lopez* and *Morrison*, involving statutes like the GFSZA or the civil-suit provision of VAWA, are unlikely to arise again, since Congress apparently has the option of regulating a particular interstate market as broadly as possible, making the appropriate findings, and, as a result being able to sweep within its regulatory scope all manner of intrastate, noncommercial activity. If that is the case, then *Raich* likely marks the end of judicially enforced limits on Congress's commerce power for the foreseeable future.

[116.1] Hundreds of cases cite *Lopez*. For a discussion, by no means exhaustive, of post-*Lopez* cases, *see* United States v. Wall, 92 F.3d 1483-1484 & nn.57-62 (6th Cir. 1996) (Boggs, J., concurring in part and dissenting in part); 1 Tribe, supra note 83, at § 5-4 n.50; Kopel & Reynolds, supra note 83 *passim*; Reynolds & Denning, supra note 83, at 378-391; Stevens, Revolutionary or Aberrational?: The Status of the Supreme Court's Recent Federalism Cases in the Eighth Circuit, 44 St. Louis U. L.J. 529 (2000).

[116.2] The Sixth Circuit noted that "[c]riminal defendants across the country have exploited . . . *Lopez* in hopes that the statutes underlying their convictions will . . . be invalidated," but the judge added that "[m]ost courts have resisted urgings to extend *Lopez* beyond" the Gun Free School Zones Act. United States v. Wall, 92 F.3d 1444, 1448 (6th Cir. 1996); *but see* Jones v. United States, 529 U.S. 848, 859, 120 S. Ct. 1904, 1912 (2000) (relying in part on *Lopez* to reverse a federal arson conviction, where arson was committed against a private residence not otherwise used commercially).

[116.3] *See, e.g.*, Bergerson v. Bergerson, 48 F. Supp. 2d 628, 638 (M.D. La. 1999) (striking down portions of the Violence Against Women Act); Hoffman v. Hunt, 923 F. Supp. 791, 807 (W.D.N.C. 1996) (striking down the federal Freedom of Access to Clinic Entrances Act), *rev'd* 126 F.3d 575 (4th Cir. 1997); United States v. Parker, 911 F. Supp. 830, 834 (E.D. Pa. 1995) (striking down the federal Child Support Recovery Act), *rev'd* 108 F.3d 28 (3d Cir. 1997).

[116.4] Brzonkala v. Virginia Polytechnic Institute, 169 F.3d 820 (4th Cir. 1999) (en banc), *aff'd sub. nom* United States v. Morrison, 529 U.S. 598, 120 S. Ct. 1740 (2000) (divided court). The *Brzonkala* case generated a good deal of commentary, including a defense penned by the ranking minority member on the Senate Judiciary Committee, *see* Biden, The Civil Rights Remedy of the Violence Against Women Act: A Defense, 37 Harv. J. on Legis. 1 (2000); *see also* Kropf, The Failure of *United States v. Lopez*: Analyzing the Violence Against Women Act, 8 S. Cal. Rev. L. & Women's Studies 373 (1999); Recent Cases, Constitutional Law — Commerce Clause — Fourth Circuit Rules That Violence Against Women Act Is an Unauthorized Exercise of Congressional Authority — *Brzonkala v. Virginia Polytechnic Institute and State University*, 169 F.3d 820 (4th Cir. 1999) (en banc), *cert. granted sub nom. United States v. Morrison*, 120 S. Ct. 11 (1999), 113 Harv. L. Rev. 816 (2000); Cain, Comment, The Civil Rights Provisions of the Violence Against Women Act: Its Legacy and Its Future, 34 Tulsa L.J. 367 (1999); Douglas, Note, The Violence Against Women Act and Contemporary Commerce Power: Principled Regulation and the Concerns of Federalism, 1999 Utah L. Rev. 703; Regan, Note, A Whole Lot of Nothing Going On: The Civil Rights "Remedy" of the Violence Against Women Act, 75 Notre Dame L. Rev. 797 (1999); Mincavage, Comment, Title III of the Violence Against Women Act: Can It Survive a Commerce Clause Challenge in the Wake of *United States v. Lopez*?, 102 Dickinson L. Rev. 441 (1998); Hatch, Comment, The Violence Against Women Act: Surviving the Substantial Effects of *United States v. Lopez*, 31 Suffolk U. L. Rev. 423 (1997); Kurtz, Comment, Does the Violence Against Women Act Do Violence to the Limits of Congressional Power?, 34 San Diego L. Rev. 1047 (1997). For a discussion of the *Morrison* opinion, *see* infra § 5.04[F].

[116.5] *See* United States v. Hart, 212 F.3d 1067 (8th Cir. 2000) (upholding Federal Access to Clinic Entrances Act against Commerce Clause challenge); United States v. Dinwiddie, 76 F.3d 913, 920 (8th Cir. 1996), *cert. denied* 519 U.S. 1043, 117 S. Ct. 613 (1996) (holding that conduct prohibited substantially affected interstate commerce).

[116.6] *See, e.g.*, United States v. Taylor, 226 F.3d 593, 599-600 (7th Cir. 2000) (upholding conviction under federal carjacking statute, 18 U.S.C. § 2119; court concluding that (i) carjacking was "economic activity" that Congress could regulate; (ii) the statute was "'an essential part of a larger regulation of economic activity . . . that arise[s] out of or [is] connected with a commercial transaction which viewed in the aggregate, substantially affects interstate commerce"; and (iii) the statute possessed a jurisdictional nexus requirement lacking in the statutes invalidated in *Lopez* and *Morrison*); United States v. Romero, 122 F.3d 1334, 1339 (10th Cir. 1997) (upholding 18 U.S.C. § 2119, the federal carjacking statute, against a commerce clause challenge); *see also* United States v. Martinez-Esparza, 2004 WL 2965508, at *1 (5th Cir. 2004) (rejecting challenge to federal carjacking statute); United States v. Redditt, 2003 WL 21212672 (6th Cir.) (May 21, 2003) (unpublished), at *2-*3 (rejecting Commerce Clause challenge to federal carjacking statute; cars are both "instrumentalities" of interstate commerce, which Congress may constitutionally act to protect and carjacking has the potential to "substantially affect" interstate commerce); United States v. Dixon, 2002 WL 31681805 (10th Cir.) (Nov. 27, 2002) (unpublished), at *1 (rejecting challenge to federal carjacking statute); United States v. Bradley, 2002 WL 31356390 (4th Cir.) (Oct. 21, 2002) (unpublished), at *1 (rejecting challenge to federal carjacking statute); United States v. Cortes, 299 F.3d 1030, 1032-1037 (9th Cir. 2002) (reconsidering, and rejecting, challenge to federal carjacking statute in light of *Morrison* and *Jones*; concluding that carjacking substantially affects interstate commerce).

[116.7] *See, e.g.*, United States v. Young, 202 F.3d 262 (4th Cir. 1999) (upholding 18 U.S.C. § 2261A, which criminalizes interstate stalking; "[b]ecause the interstate stalking statute contains an interstate travel requirement and prohibits the commission of a crime, its constitutionality is firmly established under existing Commerce Clause jurisprudence").

[116.8] *See, e.g.*, United States v. Spinello, 95 F. Supp. 2d 242, 248 (D.N.J. 2000) (upholding federal bank robbery statute, both on its face and as applied to an intrastate robbery of a local bank with no out-of-state branches; *held,* Congress could have rationally concluded "that bank robbery substantially affects interstate commerce" and that "the disruption and threat to the flow of business from bank robbery . . . substantially affects interstate commerce"); *see also* United States v. Rollins, 301 F.3d 511, 520-521 (7th Cir. 2002) (upholding the federal bank robbery statute); United States v. Jones, 2002 WL 1492264 (4th Cir. 2002) (unpublished), at *2 (rejecting challenge to federal bank robbery statute; failure to raise not ineffective assistance of counsel).

[116.9] *See* United States v. Jennings, 195 F.3d 795 (5th Cir. 1999) (allowing unconnected intrastate acts to be aggregated to "substantially affect" interstate commerce and sustain a conviction under the Hobbs Act); United States v. Taylor, 176 F.3d 331 (6th Cir. 1999) (same, upholding Hobbs Act); United States v. Guerra, 164 F.3d 1358 (11th Cir. 1999) (same).

[116.10] *See, e.g.*, United States v. Garcia, 68 F. Supp. 2d 802, 807-812 (E.D. Mich. 1999) (upholding both RICO and the Violence in Aid of Racketeering Acts (VARA) — 18 U.S.C. §§ 1961 and 1959, respectively — against facial constitutional challenges based on presence of jurisdictional element; upholding facial challenge against RICO, *de minimis* impact on interstate commerce all that is required; but sustaining challenge to VARA, as applied against "a street crime committed by a thug as part of a local turf war in southwest Detroit" with a *de minimis* impact on interstate commerce).

[116.11] *See* United States v. Lee, 173 F.3d 809 (11th Cir. 1999) (per curiam); United States v. Threadgill, 172 F.3d 357 (5th Cir. 1999); United States v. Boyd, 149 F.3d 1062 (10th Cir. 1998); United States v. Zizzo, 120 F.3d 1338 (7th Cir. 1997); United States v. Wall, 92 F.3d 1444 (6th Cir. 1996) (divided court).

[116.12] *See, e.g.*, United States v. Rodia, 194 F.3d 465 (3d Cir. 1999) (upholding federal statute criminalizing intrastate, noncommercial possession of child pornography).

[116.13] *See, e.g.*, United States v. Rea, 169 F.3d 1111, 1113 (8th Cir. 1999). For more on the federal arson statute, *see* infra § 5.04[F].

[116.14] *See, e.g.*, United States v. Silverwood Realtors, 2000 WL 631373 (N.D. Ill. 2000), at *3 (slip opinion) (upholding Toxic Substance Control Act and Residential Lead-Based Paint Hazard Reduction Act, as applied against owner of residential rental properties, against commerce clause challenge; "residential rental properties categorically substantially affect interstate commerce").

[116.15] *See, e.g.*, United States v. Fleischli, 119 F.Supp. 2d 819, 821-822 (C.D. Ill. 2000) (*Morrison* does not require reassessment of Seventh Circuit decision approving of 18 U.S.C. § 922(o) (prohibiting possession of a machine gun)); United States v. Hall, 171 F.3d 1133, 1138 (8th Cir. 1999) (upholding conviction for possession of an unregistered silencer); United States v. Luna, 165 F.3d 316 (5th Cir. 1999) (upholding federal law prohibiting knowing possession of a stolen firearm); United States v. Baker, 197 F.3d 211, 218 (6th Cir. 1999) (upholding the constitutionality of § 922(g)(8), which prohibits one subject to a domestic violence protection order from possessing a firearm; jurisdictional element insulates statute from *Lopez* challenge); United States v. Willbern, 2000 WL

554134 (D. Kan. 2000), at *1 (slip opinion) (upholding constitutionality of § 922(g)(9); jurisdictional requirement that firearm traveled in interstate commerce sufficient to sustain statute against *Lopez* challenge).

[116.16] *See, e.g., Wall,* 92 F.3d at 1451-1452 (arguing that *Lopez* did not require invalidation of previous circuit courts of appeals determinations that the prohibition of "illegal gambling businesses" did not exceed congressional commerce power; adding that "[u]ntil the Supreme Court provides a clearer signal or cogent framework to handle ["substantial effects"] legislation, this court is content to heed the concurrence of [Justices Kennedy and O'Connor] that the history of Commerce Clause jurisprudence still 'counsels great restraint'"); *see also, e.g.,* Solid Waste Agency v. United States Army Corps of Eng'rs, 998 F. Supp. 946, 951-952 (N.D. Ill. 1998) ("[W]hile the *Lopez* decision may help define the outer limits of federal commerce clause jurisdiction, it does not signal a retreat from the constitutional principles set forth in *Wickard* and its progeny."). Even fans of *Lopez* expressed some frustration at its Delphic ambiguity. *See Wall,* 92 F.3d at 1456 (Boggs, C.J., dissenting) (expressing disappointment that *Lopez*'s "analytical framework, particularly in relation to subparts of the 'substantial effects' test, is not laid out as clearly . . . as it might have been").

[116.17] *See, e.g.,* United States v. Serang, 156 F.3d 910, 913 (9th Cir. 1998) (upholding federal arson statute; assuming arson was economic activity and if individual acts had only a trivial impact on interstate commerce, aggregation was permitted to allow congressional regulation). Another court upheld the federal arson statute's application to arson of a private residence, holding that the jurisdictional nexus requirement was satisfied by the house's receipt of natural gas and electricity, both of which had traveled in interstate commerce. United States v. Brown, 74 F. Supp. 2d 637, 644 (N.D. W. Va. 1998). Once that jurisdictional nexus was satisfied, the court concluded, a *de minimis* impact would suffice. *See also* Reynolds & Denning, *supra* note 83, at 389-391. *But see* Jones v. United States, 529 U.S. 848, 857, 120 S. Ct. 1904, 1911 (2000) (rejecting such arguments; holding that statute does not reach arson of private residence not otherwise used in interstate commerce).

[116.18] *See, e.g.,* United States v. McGuire, 178 F.3d 203, 205 (3d Cir. 1999) (overturning conviction under federal arson statute where sole nexus between incident and interstate commerce was a single bottle of Tropicana orange juice in truck of victim's car); United States v. Pappadopoulous, 64 F.3d 522 (9th Cir. 1995) (federal arson statute does not apply to arson of a private residence); United States v. Garcia, 68 F. Supp. 2d 802, 807-812 (E.D. Mich. 1999) (sustaining as-applied challenge to indictment under federal Violence in Aid of Racketeering Act against "a street crime committed by a thug as part of a local turf war in southwest Detroit" with a *de minimis* impact on interstate commerce).

[116.19] Brzonkala v. Virginia Polytechnic Institute, 169 F.3d 820 (4th Cir. 1999) (en banc) (divided court), *aff'd sub. nom* United States v. Morrison, 529 U.S. 598, 120 S. Ct. 1740 (2000) (divided court). Individual judges, too, sometimes expressed frustration at their colleagues' unwillingness to apply *Lopez* outside the unique factual circumstances surrounding the Gun Free School Zones Act. *See, e.g.,* Navegar, Inc v. United States, 200 F.3d 868, 869-871 (D.C. Cir. 2000) (per curiam) (Sentelle, C.J., dissenting from denial of petition for rehearing en banc) (arguing that court's refusal reconsider constitutionality of federal ban on "manufacture, transfer, or possess[ion of] a semiautomatic assault rifle" "perpetuate[d] an approach to Commerce Clause jurisprudence hopelessly out of date under contemporary Supreme Court interpretations"); United States v. Hickman, 179 F.3d 230, 231 (5th Cir. 1999) (en banc) (Higginbotham, C.J., dissenting).

[116.20] Nagle, The Commerce Clause Meets the Delhi Sands Flower-Loving Fly, 97 Mich. L. Rev. 174, 176 (1998).

[116.21] Brzonkala v. Virginia Polytechnic Institute and State University, 169 F.3d 820 (4th Cir. 1999) (en banc) (divided court).

[116.22] United States v. Morrison, 529 U.S. 598, 120 S. Ct. 1740 (2000) (divided court).

[116.23] 42 U.S.C. § 13981. There were several other provisions of the VAWA that were not challenged, for example, provisions making it a federal crime to cross state lines to commit domestic violence. *See, e.g.*, 18 U.S.C. § 2262 (prohibiting the crossing of state lines or into Indian country with the intent to violate a protection order).

[116.24] 42 U.S.C. § 13981.

[116.25] United States v. Lopez, 514 U.S. 549, 115 S. Ct. 1624 (1995) (divided court).

[116.26] 109 U.S. 3, 3 S. Ct. 18 (1883) (divided court). Congress had passed § 13981 under both the Commerce Clause and § 5 of the Fourteenth Amendment. The Court rejected both bases for congressional action; the discussion here omits the Court's discussion of congressional authority under the Fourteenth Amendment.

[116.27] 42 U.S.C. § 13981(c).

[116.28] 42 U.S.C. § 13981(d)(1).

[116.29] 42 U.S.C. § 13981(d)(1)(A)-(B).

[116.30] 42 U.S.C. § 13981(e)(2).

[116.31] 42 U.S.C. § 13981(e)(1).

[116.32] 42 U.S.C. § 13981(e)(4).

[116.33] *See, e.g.*, H.R. Conf. Rep. No. 103-711 (1994); S. Rep. No. 103-138 (1993).

[116.34] *Morrison*, 529 U.S. at 608, 120 S. Ct. at 1749.

[116.35] 529 U.S. at 607, 120 S. Ct. at 1748.

[116.36] 529 U.S. at 608, 120 S. Ct. at 1748.

[116.37] Other provisions of VAWA were passed under Categories One or Two, and were not challenged here. 529 U.S. at 608-609, 120 S. Ct. at 1749.

[116.38] 529 U.S. at 609, 120 S. Ct. at 1749.

[116.39] 529 U.S. at 610, 120 S. Ct. at 1750.

[116.40] 529 U.S. at 611-612, 120 S. Ct. at 1750-1751.

[116.41] 529 U.S. at 612, 120 S. Ct. at 1751.

[116.42] *Id.*

[116.43] 529 U.S. at 612-613, 120 S. Ct. at 1751 (quoting *Lopez*, 514 U.S. at 564, 115 S. Ct. at 1632).

[116.44] 529 U.S. at 613, 120 S. Ct. at 1751.

[116.45] 529 U.S. at 613, 120 S. Ct. at 1751, 1752.

[116.46] 529 U.S. at 614, 120 S. Ct. at 1752.

[116.47] *See* 529 U.S. at 614, 120 S. Ct. at 1752.

[116.48] 529 U.S. at 615, 120 S. Ct. at 1752.

[116.49] Kopel & Reynolds, *supra* note 83, at 69.

[116.50] *Morrison*, 529 U.S. at 615, 120 S. Ct. at 1752-1753.

[116.51] 529 U.S. at 615, 120 S. Ct. at 1753.

[116.52] 529 U.S. at 615-616, 120 S. Ct. at 1753.

[116.53] 529 U.S. at 616, 120 S. Ct. at 1753 (footnote omitted).

[116.54] 529 U.S. at 617, 120 S. Ct. at 1754. Justice Thomas wrote separately

> to express my view that the very notion of a 'substantial effects' test under the Commerce Clause is inconsistent with the original understanding of Congress' power and with the Court's early . . . cases. By continuing to apply this rootless and malleable standard, however circumscribed, the Court has encouraged the federal government to persist in its view that the Commerce Clause has virtually no limits.

529 U.S. at 627, 120 S. Ct. at 1759 (Thomas, J., concurring).

[116.55] 529 U.S. at 628, 120 S. Ct. at 1760 (Souter, J., dissenting).

[116.56] 529 U.S. at 628-629, 120 S. Ct. at 1760 (Souter, J., dissenting).

[116.57] 529 U.S. at 634, 120 S. Ct. at 1763 (Souter, J., dissenting).

[116.58] 529 U.S. at 635, 120 S. Ct. at 1763 (Souter, J., dissenting).

[116.59] 529 U.S. at 637, 120 S. Ct. at 1764 (Souter, J., dissenting).

[116.60] 529 U.S. at 637, 120 S. Ct. at 1764 (Souter, J., dissenting).

[116.61] 529 U.S. at 637, 120 S. Ct. at 1764 (Souter, J., dissenting).

[116.62] 529 U.S. at 644, 120 S. Ct. at 1768 (Souter, J., dissenting).

[116.63] 529 U.S. at 644, 120 S. Ct. at 1768 (Souter, J., dissenting). *See also* 528 U.S. at 655, 120 S. Ct. at 1774 (Souter, J., dissenting) ("The federalism of some earlier time is no more adequate to account for those facts today than the theory of laissez-faire was able to govern the national economy 70 years ago.").

[116.64] 529 U.S. at 645, 120 S. Ct. at 1768 (Souter, J., dissenting).

[116.65] 529 U.S. at 652, 120 S. Ct. at 1772 (Souter, J., dissenting).

[116.66] 529 U.S. at 654, 120 S. Ct. at 1773 (Souter, J., dissenting).

[116.67] 529 U.S. at 655, 120 S. Ct. at 1774 (Souter, J., dissenting). Justice Breyer also filed a dissenting opinion, in which he suggested that the Court, instead of attempting to draw fine distinctions such as those proposed by the majority, focus on the process that produced an act that allegedly transgressed federalism principles. In the case of the Violence Against Women Act, Justice Breyer noted, Congress "complied a 'mountain of data' explicitly documenting the interstate commercial effects" of gender-based violence; it "focused the federal law upon documented deficiencies in state legal systems"; and "it tailored the law to prevent its use in certain areas of traditional state concern, such as divorce, alimony, or child custody." 529 U.S. at 662, 120 S. Ct. at 1777 (Breyer, J., dissenting). As a result, "the law before us seems to represent an instance, not of state/federal conflict, but of state/federal efforts to cooperate in order to help solve a mutually acknowledged national problem." 529 U.S. at 662, 120 S. Ct. at 1777 (Breyer, J., dissenting). Though Justices Souter and Ginsburg joined Justice Breyer's complaints about the majority's opinion, only Justice Stevens signed on to Justice Breyer's suggestion that the Court exercise a role in safeguarding the *process* by which legislation like that at issue was passed by Congress. *See* 529 U.S. at 655, 120 S. Ct. at 1774 (Breyer, J., dissenting).

[116.68] Jones v. United States, 529 U.S. 848, 120 S. Ct. 1904 (2000).

[116.69] United States v. Jones, 178 F.3d 479 (7th Cir. 1999) (federal statute covers arson of private residence; such scope is constitutional under *Lopez*); *but see* United States v. Papadopolous, 64 F.3d 522 (9th Cir. 1995) (holding that the federal statute could not reach arson of private residence not otherwise used in interstate commerce); *see also* §3.13[B] supra.

[116.70] *See Jones*, 529 U.S. at 855, 120 S. Ct. at 1910.

[116.71] 529 U.S. at 857, 120 S. Ct. 1911.

116.72 529 U.S. at 857, 120 S. Ct. at 1912. Justice Stevens concurred to emphasize his believe that "we should interpret narrowly federal criminal laws that overlap with state authority unless congressional intention to assert its jurisdiction is plain." 529 U.S. at 860, 120 S. Ct. at 1912-1913 (Stevens, J., concurring). Justice Thomas also concurred to emphasize the fact that he (and Justice Scalia, who joined him) "express no view on the question whether the federal arson statute . . . as there construed, is constitutional in its application to all buildings used for commercial activities." 529 U.S. at 860, 120 S. Ct. at 1913 (Thomas, J., concurring).

116.73 United States v. Bass, 404 U.S. 336, 92 S. Ct. 515 (1971).

116.74 *See, e.g.*, Shane, Federalism's "Old Deal": What's Right and Wrong with Conservative Judicial Activism, 45 Vill. L. Rev. 201 (2000); Kramer, The Arrogance of the Court, Wash. Post, May 23, 2000, at A29; Savage, Endangered Statutes, A.B.A.J., July 2000, at 32-33; Shane, In Whose Best Interest? Not the States, Wash. Post, May 21, 2000, at B5. For an earlier article that accurately predicted the outcome of the *Morrison* decision, but deplored it, *see* Rosen, Hyperactive, New Republic, Jan. 31, 2000, at 20. For scholarly commentary on *Morrison* and *Jones*, pro and con, *see* Bradley, Federalism and Federal Criminal Law, 55 Hastings L.J. 573 (2004); Bork & Troy, Locating the Boundaries: The Scope of Congress's Power to Regulate Interstate Commerce, 25 Harv. J.L. & Pub. Pol'y 849 (2002); Choper, Taming Congress's Power Under the Commerce Clause: What Does the Near Future Portend?, 55 Ark. L. Rev. 731 (2003); Choper & Yoo, The Scope of the Commerce Clause After *Morrison*, 25 Okla. City U. L. Rev. 843 (2000); Dral & Phillips, Commerce by Another Name: The Impact of *United States v. Lopez* and *United States v. Morrison*, 68 Tenn. L. Rev. 605 (2001); Goldfarb, The Supreme Court, the Violence Against Women Act, and the Use and Abuse of Federalism, 71 Fordham L. Rev. 57 (2002); Goldfarb, Violence Against Women and the Persistence of Privacy, 61 Ohio St. L.J. 1, 67-76 (2000); Goldscheid, *United States v. Morrison* and the Civil Rights Remedy of the Violence Against Women Act: A Civil Rights Law Struck Down in the Name of Federalism, 86 Cornell L. Rev. 109 (2000); Ides, Economic Activity as a Proxy for Federalism: Intuition and Reason in *United States v. Morrison*, 18 Const. Commentary 563 (2001); Jennings & Razook, *United States v. Morrison*: Where the Commerce Clause Meets Civil Rights and Reasonable Minds Part Ways: A Point and Counterpoint from a Constitutional and Social Perspective, 35 New England L. Rev. 23 (2000); Killenbeck, The Physics of Federalism, 51 U. Kan. L. Rev. 1 (2002); MacKinnon, Disputing Male Sovereignty: On *United States v. Morrison*, 114 Harv. L. Rev. 135 (2000); Rotunda, The Implications of the New Commerce Clause Jurisprudence: An Evolutionary or Revolutionary Court?, 55 Ark. L. Rev. 795 (2003); Rotunda, The Commerce Clause, the Political Question Doctrine, and *Morrison*, 18 Const. Commentary 319 (2001); Rotunda, The New States' Rights, the New Federalism, the New Commerce Clause, and the Proposed New Abdication, 25 Okla. City U. L. Rev. 869 (2001); Sungaila, *United States v. Morrison*: The United States Supreme Court, the Violence Against Women Act and the "New Federalism," 9 S. Cal. Rev. L. & Women's Stud. 301 (2000); Valauri, The Clothes Have No Emperor, or, Cabining the Commerce Clause, 41 San Diego L. Rev. 405 (2004); Goldberg, Comment, Substantial Activity and Non-Economic Commerce: Toward a New Theory of the Commerce Clause, 9 J.L. & Pol'y 563 (2001); Jost, Note, The Commerce Clause in the New Millennium: Enumeration Still Presupposes Something Not Enumerated, 1 Wyo. L. Rev. 195 (2001); McGimsley, Comment, The Commerce Clause and Federalism After *Lopez* and *Morrison*: The Case for Closing the Jurisdictional Element

Loophole, 90 Cal. L. Rev. 1675 (2002); Mark, Casenote, *United States v. Morrison*, the Commerce Clause and the Substantial Effects Test: No Substantial Limit on Federal Power, 34 Creighton L. Rev. 675 (2001); Martin, Note, *United States v. Morrison*: Federalism Against the Will of the States, 32 Loy. U. Chi. L.J. 243 (2000); Vaughn, Casenote, The Civil Rights Remedy of the Violence Against Women Act as Litigated in *United States v. Morrison*: The Supreme Court's Sacrificial Lamb to Reinforce *United States v. Lopez*, 24 Hamline L. Rev. 163 (2000).

[116.74a] *See, e.g.*, Citizens Bank v. Alafabco, Inc., 539 U.S. 52, 123 S. Ct. 2037 (2003) (per curiam) (holding Federal Arbitration Act applies to instrastate commercial transactions "if in the aggregate the economic activity i question would represent 'a general practice . . . subject to federal control' " by substantially affecting interstate commerce); *see also* Pierce Co. v. Guillen, 537 U.S. 129, 123 S. Ct. 720, 731-732 (2003) (upholding, as regulation of channels and instrumentalities of interstate of commerce, federal law prohibiting the use of certain highway safety data collected by states pursuant to federal law in federal or state trials).

[116.75] For a discussion of the Court's expansive preemption decisions, *see infra* §§ 5.06[D]-[E].

[116.76] *See Morrison*, 529 U.S. at 613, 120 S. Ct. at 1751-1752 ("Like the Gun-Free School Zones Act . . . § 13981 contains no jurisdictional element establishing that the federal cause of action is in pursuance of Congress' power to regulate interstate commerce. Although *Lopez* makes clear that such a jurisdictional element would lend support to the argument that § 13981 is sufficiently tied to interstate commerce, Congress elected to cast § 13981's remedy over a wider, and more purely intrastate, body of violent crime.").

[116.77] Reynolds & Denning, supra note 83, at 399 (footnote omitted).

[116.78] *See* United States v. Rea, 300 F.3d 952, 960-963 (8th Cir. 2002) (reversing federal arson conviction for arson of church annex; insufficient facts presented to permit conclusion annex either used in or affected interstate or foreign commerce); United States v. Odom, 252 F.3d 1289, 1296-1297 (11th Cir. 2001) (reversing conviction under federal arson statute for destruction of church; government evidence of connection with interstate commerce "too passive, too minimal and too indirect to substantively affect interstate commerce"); United States v. Johnson, 246 F.3d 749, 752 (5th Cir. 2001) (per curiam) (reconsideration of decision vacating guilty plea of defendant under federal arson statute for burning down one-story church building on grounds that government had furnished insufficient factual basis for the plea; concluding that "nothing in the Court's *Jones* opinion or in its holding there, is inconsistent with or suggests error in . . . vacating Johnson's plea and remanding case for further proceedings"); United States v. Ramey, 227 F.3d 1058, 1063-1064 (4th Cir. 2000) (vacating sentence under federal arson statute in light of *Jones*); United States v. Ryan, 227 F.3d 1058, 1063-1064 (8th Cir. 2000) (reversing arson conviction for destruction of abandoned fitness center; center "was not being 'used in' an activity affecting commerce"; rejecting "government's contention that because *Jones* involved residential rather than commercial property, its holding is inapplicable"); United States v. Rayborn, 138 F Supp 2d 1029 (W.D. Tenn. 2001) (denying motion to reconsider dismissal of federal indictment for arson; finding that church was not actively used in interstate commerce); *but see* United States v. Grassie, 237 F.3d 1199, 1208-1209 (10th Cir. 2001) (sustaining arson conviction for burning of a church; church "used in" interstate commerce; government need only prove *de minimis* effect on commerce to sustain conviction once church shown to be "used in" interstate commerce);

United States v. Tush, 151 F. Supp. 2d 1246 (D. Kan. 2001) (upholding guilty plea of defendant charged with arson of a church under federal arson statute; relying, in part, on reasoning in *Grassie*); United States v. Sawyer, 133 F. Supp. 2d 969, 970-971 (E.D. Mich. 2001) (upholding conviction for arson of rental property).

As was true following *Lopez, Morrison* has furnished legal commentators with new material for speculating on the viability of existing statutes or of recent particular congressional initiatives. For a sampling, *see* Gerhardt, On Revolution and Wetland Regulations, 90 Geo. L.J. 2143 (2002); Klinck, Recent Development, The Pain Relief Promotion Act, 38 Harv. J. on Legis. 103 (2001) (expressing constitutional doubts, suggesting possible congressional fixes); Moiseyev, *Solid Waste Agency of Northern Cook County v. United States Army Corps of Engineers*: The Clean Water Act Bypasses a Commerce Clause Challenge, But Can the Endangered Species Act?, 7 Hastings W.-N.W.J. Envtl. L. & Pol'y 191 (2001); Post, Equal Protection by Law: Federal Antidiscrimination Legislation After *Morrison* and *Kimel*, 110 Yale L.J. 441 (2000); Saylor, Federalism and the Family After *Morrison*: An Examination of the Child Support Recovery Act, the Freedom of Access to Clinic Entrances Act, and a Federal Law Outlawing Gun Possession by Domestic Violence Abusers, 25 Harv. Women's L.J. 57 (2002); Tiefer, After *Morrison*, Can Congress Preserve Environmental Laws from Commerce Clause Challenge?, 20 Envtl. L. Rep. 10888 (2000) (concluding that it can); Varona & Layton, Anchoring Justice: The Constitutionality of the Local Law Enforcement Enhancement Act in *United States v. Morrison*'s Shifting Seas, 12 Stan. J.L. & Pol'y Rev. 9 (2001); Walston, The Federal Commerce and Navigation Powers: *Solid Waste Agency of Northern Cook County*'s Undecided Constitutional Issue, 42 Santa Clara L. Rev. 699 (2002). *Morrison*, like *Lopez*, has also been a boon for law students eager for a "hot" comment or note topic. *See, e.g.*, Brignac, Recent Development, The Commerce Clause Justification of Endangered Species Protection: *Gibbs v. Babbitt*, 79 N.C. L. Rev. 873 (2001); Curtis, Note, Does the Commerce Clause Provide Constitutional Refuge for the Child Support Recovery Act of 1992: *United States v. Faasse*, 46 How. L.J. 147 (2002); Fallek, Recent Development, The Pain Relief Promotion Act: Will It Spell "Death with Dignity" or Is It Unconstitutional?, 27 Fordham Urb. L.J. 1739 (2000); Fischer, Comment, Deadbeat Dads as Champions of Federalism? *Lopez*'s Dramatic (Unintended?) Effect on Commerce Clause Jurisprudence, as Illustrated by the Child Support Recovery Act, 86 Marq. L. Rev. 107 (2002); Kohnke, Comment, Can Congress Do That?: An Analysis of the Federal Prohibition on Marijuana Possession, 19 Miss. C. L. Rev. 381 (1999) (concluding that it cannot, under recent Commerce Clause cases); Matthews, Case Comment, Turning the Endangered Species Act Inside Out? 113 Yale L.J. 947 (2004); Neusch, Comment, Medical Marijuana's State in the Aftermath of the Supreme Court's New Commerce Clause Jursiprudence, 72 U. Colo. L. Rev. 201 (2001); Newbern, Comment, Good Cop, Bad Cop: Federal Prosecutions of State-Legalized Medical Marijuana Use After *United States v. Lopez*, 88 Calif. L. Rev. 1575 (2000); Safra, Note, The Amended Gun-Free School Zones Act: Doubt as to Its Constitutionality Remains, 50 Duke L.J. 637 (2000); Scalero, Note, The Endangered Species Act's Application to Isolated Species: A Substantial Effect on Interstate Commerce?, 3 Chap. L. Rev. 317 (2000); Seman, Comment, *United States v. Corp*: Where to Draw the Interstate Line on Congress' Commerce Clause Authority to Regulate Intrastate Possession of Child Pornography, 9 Vill. Sports & Ent. L. J. 181 (2002); Spalding, Note, In the Stream of the Commerce Clause: Revisiting *Asahi* in the Wake of *Lopez* and *Morrison*, 4 Nev. L.J. 141 (2003).

116.79 For more discussion of challenges to specific federal statutes, see *infra* § 5.04[H].

116.80 Solid Waste Agency of Northern Cook County v. United States Army Corps of Engineers, 531 U.S. 159, 121 S. Ct. 675 (2001) (divided court). At issue in *SWANCC* was the validity of a rule promulgated by the Corps of Engineers under a Clean Water Act provision regulating the discharge of fill material into "navigable waters." Under its regulations, the Corps had defined navigable waters to include all waters that are or might be used by certain types of birds, such as those protected by treaty, which cross state lines, or which are endangered. *SWANCC*, 531 U.S. at 164-165, 121 S. Ct. at 678. In the case at hand, the rule was being applied by the Corps to prevent the filling of a 533-acre site to be used by suburban Chicago cities as a disposal site for non-hazardous waste. 531 U.S. at 162-163, 121 S. Ct. at 678. SWANCC had challenged the rule and the statute as having exceeded Congress's power under the Commerce Clause. Applying the canon of statutory construction that holds constitutional questions in abeyance if there is another means of disposing of the case, the Court concluded that it would be premature to address the Commerce Clause question, in the absence of a clear signal from Congress that it approved and intended the expansive definition of "navigable waters" promulgated by the Corps of Engineers. In the Court's opinion, written by Chief Justice Rehnquist, the Court found "nothing approaching a clear statement from Congress that it intended [the Clean Water Act] to read an abandoned sand and gravel pit such as we have here. Permitting respondents to claim federal jurisdiction over ponds and mudflats . . . would result in a significant impingement of the States' traditional and primary power over land and water use." 531 U.S. at 174, 121 S. Ct. at 684. Four members of the Court dissented. In an opinion written by Justice Stevens, the dissenters disputed the Court's characterization of the Clean Water Act as not evincing sufficient congressional intent to support the Corps's expansive definition of navigable waters, then found that such a definition is well within Congress's commerce power, even after *Lopez* and *Morrison*. 531 U.S. at 184-197, 121 S. Ct. at 684-696 (Stevens, J., dissenting). As to the second question, Justice Stevens concluded that "the discharge of fill into 'isolated' wetlands that serve as migratory bird habitat will, in the aggregate, adversely affect migratory bird populations." 531 U.S. at 194, 121 S. Ct. at 694. This would, in turn, affect "literally millions of people [who] regularly participate in birdwatching and hunting [which] generate a host of commercial activities of great value. The causal connection between the filling of wetlands and the decline of commercial activities associated with migratory birds is not 'attenuated.'" 531 U.S. at 194-195, 121 S. Ct. at 695 (footnote omitted). Finally, Justice Stevens concluded that the Corps's rule did not unduly blur the line between national and local activity: "The destruction of aquatic migratory bird habitat . . . is an action in which the benefits . . . are disproportionately local, while many of the costs . . . are widely dispersed and often borne by citizens living in other states. In such situations . . . federal regulation is both appropriate and necessary." 531 U.S. at 195, 121 S. Ct. at 695. Moreover, the Corps's focus on birds that travel across interstate lines also satisfied (for Justice Stevens and the dissenters) "this Court's expressed desire for some 'jurisdictional element' that limits federal activity to its proper scope." 531 U.S. at 196, 121 S. Ct. at 695. On the Court's reluctance to take up a number of Commerce Clause challenges to environmental laws, *see* Eastman, A Fistful of Denials: The Supreme Court Takes a Pass on Commerce Clause Challenges to Environmental Laws, 2004 Cato Sup. Ct. Rev. 469. For speculation whether an amended act would survive scrutiny after *Morrison, see* Johnson, Federal Regulation of Isolated

Wetlands After *SWANCC*, 31 Envtl. L. Rep. 10669 (2001); *see also* Gerhardt, On Revolution and Wetland Regulations, 90 Geo. L.J. 2143 (2002); Gerhardt, The Curious Flight of the Migratory Bird Rule, 31 Envt'l L. Rep. 11079 (2001); McAllister & Glicksman, Federal Environmental Law in the "New" Federalism Era, 30 Envtl. L. Rep. 11122 (2000); Walston, The Federal Commerce and Navigation Powers: *Solid Waste Agency of Northern Cook County*'s Undecided Constitutional Issue, 42 Santa Clara L. Rev. 699 (2002); Lowenberg, Comment, The Texas Cave Bug and the Arroyo Toad "Take" On the Constitution's Commerce Clause, 36 St. Mary's L.J. 149 (2004); Van Balen, Note, Clearing the Muddy Waters?: An Examination of *SWANCC* and the Implications for Wetlands Protection and the Administrative State, 36 Wake Forest L. Rev. 845 (2001).

[116.81] Pierce Co. v. Guillen, 537 U.S. 129, 123 S. Ct. 720, 731-732 (2003). For an argument that *Guillen* was a much more difficult Commerce Clause case than the Court's decision made it out to be, *see* Berman, *Guillen* and Guillibility: Piercing the Surface of Commerce Clause Doctrine, 89 Iowa L. Rev. 1487 (2004).

[116.82] Citizens Bank v. Alafabco, Inc., 539 U.S. 52, 123 S. Ct. 2037 (2003) (per curiam).

[116.83] *See generally* Brown, State Court Attempts to Limit the Applicability of the Federal Arbitration Act in a Post-*Lopez* World, 56 U. Miami L. Rev. 1051 (2002); Richmond, Comment, *Sisters of the Visitation v. Cochran Plastering Co.*: Earnest Federalism or Reconstructive Defiance to the Federal Arbitration Act?, 25 Am. J. Trial Advoc. 633 (2002).

[116.84] 539 U.S. at 52, 123 S. Ct. at 2040 (quoting Mandeville Island Farms, Inc. v. American Crystal Sugar Co., 334 U.S. 219, 236, 68 S. Ct. 996, 1006 (1948)).

[116.85] Raich v. Ashcroft, 353 F.3d 1222, 1228 (9th Cir. 2003) (divided court), *cert. granted* 2004 WL 875062 (June 28, 2004).

[116.86] Gonzales v. Raich, ___ U.S. ___, 125 S. Ct. 2195 (2005) (divided court).

[116.87] *Raich*, ___ U.S. at ___, 125 S. Ct. at 2209; *see also* ___ U.S. at ___, 125 S. Ct. at 2209 (calling respondents' reliance on *Lopez* and *Morrison* "myopic" and chiding them adopting a "narrow prism" that resulted in their reading the cases "far too broadly").

[116.88] ___ U.S. at ___, 125 S. Ct. at 2208.

[116.89] ___ U.S. at ___, 125 S. Ct. at 2205.

[116.90] ___ U.S. at ___, 125 S. Ct. at 2207.

[116.91] ___ U.S. at ___, 125 S. Ct. at 2207.

[116.92] ___ U.S. at ___, 125 S. Ct. at 2207.

[116.93] ___ U.S. at ___, 125 S. Ct. at 2207.

[116.94] ___ U.S. at ___, 125 S. Ct. at 2208 ("While congressional findings are certainly helpful in reviewing the substance of a congressional statutory scheme, particularly when the connection to commerce is not self-evident, and while we will consider congressional findings in the analysis when they are available, the absence of particularized findings does not call into question Congress' ability to regulate.") (footnote omitted).

[116.95] ___ U.S. at ___ n.32, 125 S. Ct. at 2208 n.32.

[116.96] ___ U.S. at ___, ___, 125 S. Ct. at 2209, 2210.

[116.97] ___ U.S. at ___, 125 S. Ct. at 2210.

[116.98] ___ U.S. at ___, 125 S. Ct. at 2211.

[116.99] ___ U.S. at ___, 125 S. Ct. at 2211.

[116.100] ___ U.S. at ___, 125 S. Ct. at 2211.

[116.101] ___ U.S. at ___, 125 S. Ct. at 2211.

116.102 ___ U.S. at ___, 125 S. Ct. at 2212.

116.103 ___ U.S. at ___, 125 S. Ct. at 2213.

116.104 ___ U.S. at ___, 125 S. Ct. at 2214.

116.105 ___ U.S. at ___, 125 S. Ct. at 2215.

116.106 ___ U.S. at ___, 125 S. Ct. at 2215 (Scalia, J., concurring). In contrast to Justice Scalia, Justice Kennedy left unexplained his reasons for joining the majority.

116.107 ___ U.S. at ___, 125 S. Ct. at 2219 (Scalia, J., concurring).

116.108 ___ U.S. at ___, 125 S. Ct. at 2219 (Scalia, J., concurring).

116.109 ___ U.S. at ___, 125 S. Ct. at 2220 (Scalia, J., concurring).

116.110 ___ U.S. at ___, 125 S. Ct. at 2218 (Scalia, J., concurring).

116.111 ___ U.S. at ___, 125 S. Ct. at 2218 (Scalia, J., concurring).

116.112 ___ U.S. at ___, 125 S. Ct. at 2220 (O'Connor, J., concurring).

116.113 ___ U.S. at ___, 125 S. Ct. at 2221, 2222 (O'Connor, J., dissenting).

116.114 ___ U.S. at ___, 125 S. Ct. at 2222-2223 (O'Connor, J., dissenting).

116.115 ___ U.S. at ___, 125 S. Ct. at 2223 (O'Connor, J., dissenting).

116.116 ___ U.S. at ___, 125 S. Ct. at 2223 (O'Connor, J., dissenting).

116.117 ___ U.S. at ___, 125 S. Ct. at 2224 (O'Connor, J., dissenting).

116.118 ___ U.S. at ___, 125 S. Ct. at 2224 (O'Connor, J., dissenting).

116.119 ___ U.S. at ___, 125 S. Ct. at 2224 (O'Connor, J., dissenting).

116.120 ___ U.S. at ___, 125 S. Ct. at 2224 (O'Connor, J., dissenting).

116.121 ___ U.S. at ___, 125 S. Ct. at 2224-2225 (O'Connor, J., dissenting).

116.122 ___ U.S. at ___, 125 S. Ct. at 2225 (O'Connor, J., dissenting).

116.123 ___ U.S. at ___, 125 S. Ct. at 2225 (O'Connor, J., dissenting) ("In Lopez and Morrison, we suggested that economic activity usually relates directly to commercial activity . . . . The homegrown cultivation and personal possession and use of marijuana for medicinal purposes has no apparent commercial character.").

116.124 ___ U.S. at ___, 125 S. Ct. at 2226 (O'Connor, J., dissenting) ("There is simply no evidence that homegrown medical marijuana users constitute, in the aggregate, a sizeable enough class to have a discernable, let alone a substantial, impact on the national illicit drug market—or otherwise to threaten the CSA regime.").

116.125 ___ U.S. at ___, 125 S. Ct. at 2227 (O'Connor, J., dissenting).

116.126 ___ U.S. at ___, 125 S. Ct. at 2228 (O'Connor, J., dissenting).

116.127 ___ U.S. at ___, 125 S. Ct. at 2227 (O'Connor, J., dissenting).

116.128 ___ U.S. at ___, 125 S. Ct. at 2229 (O'Connor, J., dissenting).

116.129 ___ U.S. at ___, 125 S. Ct. at 2229 (Thomas, J., dissenting).

116.130 ___ U.S. at ___, 125 S. Ct. at 2230 (Thomas, J., dissenting) ("In the early days of the Republic, it would have been unthinkable that Congress could prohibit the local cultivation, possession, and consumption of marijuana.").

116.131 ___ U.S. at ___, ___, 125 S. Ct. at 2233, 2233-2234 (Thomas, J., dissenting) (arguing that control of intrastate medical marijuana is not "necessary" because regulation was not "plainly adapted" to end of stopping interstate drug traffic; and that regulation, even if necessary, was not "proper," because "Congress may not use its incidental authority to subvert basic principles of federalism and dual sovereignty").

116.132 ___ U.S. at ___, 125 S. Ct. at 2235 (Thomas, J., dissenting) ("The majority's decision is further proof that the 'substantial effects' test is a 'rootless and malleable standard' at odds with the constitutional design.").

116.133 ___ U.S. at ___, 125 S. Ct. at 2235-2236, 2237 (Thomas, J., dissenting).

116.134 *See infra* § 5.04[H].

116.135 *See* Denning & Reynolds, *supra* note 83.

[H] *Lopez* and *Morrison* in the Lower Courts: Specific Statutes

As noted above, *Lopez*, and later *Morrison* and *Jones*, spawned a host of lawsuits whose variety offers a compelling illustration of the extent to which the federal government relies on the Commerce Clause for its authority to enact a plethora of laws—especially those creating new categories of federal crimes.[8] What was true prior to *Morrison* and *Jones*, however, is still true after those decisions: lower federal courts have not invalidated congressional statutes *en masse*. To the contrary, even after *Morrison* and *Jones*, courts have repeatedly upheld most federal criminal statutes against facial challenges to statutes' constitutionality as they did following *Lopez*. The most common challenges are briefly described below, with accompanying citations. It remains to be seen whether, in the wake of *Raich*, as-applied challenges to specific applications of federal criminal statutes will continue to be entertained by courts.

[1] Federal Gun Laws

[a] Felon-in-Possession Statute

Under federal law, persons convicted of a felony are prohibited from possessing firearms "in or affecting interstate commerce."[9] In *Scarborough v. United States*,[10] the Supreme Court held that to satisfy the statute, the government need only prove that, at some point in the past, the firearm possessed by the felon had moved in interstate commerce.[11] After *Lopez* struck down a statute criminalizing simple gun possession in a school zone, persons convicted under the federal statute challenged their convictions with gusto. These challenges have all failed, despite one thoughtful district court opinion demonstrating that *Scarborough's* reasoning is at least called into question by the Court's recent tacks in *Lopez* and *Morrison*.[12] Most courts conclude that the presence of the jurisdictional nexus requiring proof that the gun had traveled in interstate commerce was sufficient, and that though simple possession might, in a single case, have a *de minimis* effect on interstate commerce, Congress could rationally conclude that the net effect had a substantial effect on interstate commerce.[13] So united is the opinion in the lower courts that few recent opinions rejecting the challenges are designated for publication.[14] And, one suspects in an effort to stanch the flow of such cases onto their dockets, a few courts have announced that failure to challenge the statute's constitutionality on appeal does not constitute ineffective assistance of counsel, in light of the virtual unanimity of the circuits.[15]

Federal law also criminalizes possession of firearms by those who have either been convicted of domestic violence offenses or who are subject to orders of protection.[16] Here, too, the presence of the words "in or affecting interstate commerce" has been deemed sufficient to sustain the statute against a facial challenge.[17]

[b] Federal Ban on Machine Gun Possession

Federal law, with a few enumerated exceptions, prohibits individuals from "transfer[ing] or possess[ing] a machine gun."[18] This law, too, garnered a number of challenges following *Lopez*. But despite many similarities between the Gun Free School Zones Act struck down in *Lopez* and §922(o) (the latter has no jurisdictional nexus and it arguably regulates non-economic activity, simple possession), it has been upheld by eight courts of appeals.[19] A common defense of the statute holds that Congress could have concluded that a ban on possession would curb illicit interstate traffic in machine guns by curbing demand.[20]

However, in *United States v. Stewart* (2003), a divided panel of the Ninth Circuit reversed the conviction of a man charged with unlawful possession of machine guns.[20.1] During a search of his premises on other gun charges, federal agents discovered five machine guns that had been made and assembled by the defendant.[20.2] Stewart challenged his conviction under 18 U.S.C. §922(o)—prohibiting transfer or possession of a machine gun—on the grounds that it exceeded Congress's power under the Commerce Clause.[20.3] Because the defendant had assembled the machine guns himself and had not received them through an illicit transfer, the court concluded that the prosecution under the statute had to satisfy *Lopez*'s Category Three ("substantially affects") test.[20.4] Judge Alex Kozinski concluded that it could not.

Possession of a machine gun, he noted, was noneconomic activity.[20.5] Further, he found that the links between Stewart's possession and interstate commerce were attenuated, noting that *Lopez* and *Morrison* had "already rejected the reasoning that, because the cost of violent crimes is spread through insurance, regulations intended to prevent violent crimes significantly affect the national economy."[20.6] The court further noted the similarity between the statutes struck in *Lopez* and *Morrison* and § 922(o), *viz.*, all lacked a jurisdictional nexus.[20.7] Finally, despite the fact that other courts had relied upon findings included with earlier federal firearms statutes, Kozinski noted all of those findings dealt with "*transactions, sales or deliveries* of firearms" as opposed to the simple possession criminalized by § 922(o).[20.8] Moreover, "nothing in the legislative history of the earlier firearms statutes speaks to the relationship between mere possession of firearms and interstate commerce."[20.9] A dissenting judge would have found that "regulation of possession, as well as transfer, of machine guns is part of Congress's long standing efforts to regulate the whole of the economic activity of trade in machine guns."[20.10] Though Judge Kozinski's argument scrupulously follows the analysis apparently prescribed by *Lopez* and *Morrison*, it appears that the dissenting judge's approach was prescient in light of *Gonzales v. Raich* (2005). For if Congress can reach all activities, no matter how local or noncommercial, in seeking to eliminate the interstate traffic in illicit drugs, then it seems to follow that Congress might also reach the homemade machine gun, if it might rationally conclude that not reaching such activities would undermine its overarching regulatory objectives.

[c] Miscellaneous Firearms Statutes

Federal courts have upheld federal laws that criminalize the knowing possession of a stolen firearm,[21] unregistered silencers,[22] and laws that prohibit the use of firearms in connection with other federal crimes, like drug trafficking.[23]

[2] Federal Drug Laws

Numerous detainees in the federal "war on drugs" have attempted to employ the Supreme Court's new thinking on the Commerce Clause to set aside their convictions under federal drug laws. Like the challenges to the federal gun laws, these are notable only for the swiftness with which they are dispatched by federal judges who conclude, as did the Eighth Circuit recently, that despite the intrastate nature of many drug transactions, when aggregated, they substantially affect interstate commerce.[24] A few courts have also held that failure to raise a Commerce Clause challenge to a drug conviction does not constitute ineffective assistance of counsel.[25] The Supreme Court's recent decision in *Gonzales v. Raich* (2005) confirms the breadth of congressional power to combat drug trafficking.[25.1] In *Raich* the Court held that the federal Controlled Substances Act could be applied to the noncommercial, local production of marijuana for medicinal purposes. To hold otherwise would risk undermining Congress's goal of eliminating the interstate market in illicit drugs like marijuana.

[3] Federal Gambling and Racketeering Laws

Before the federal war on drugs, there was the war against organized crime. Here again, the Commerce Clause was the rock on which Congress built a number of laws aimed at the "rackets" and their illegal proceeds. While the Racketeering Influenced and Corrupt Practicing Act (RICO) is the most famous, there are others, like 18 U.S.C. § 1955, which prohibits the operation of an "illegal gambling business," and 18 U.S.C. § 1959, which punishes the use of violence in furtherance of racketeering. As in the cases involving drug trafficking, courts have treated the substantial effects of such activity on interstate commerce—even if each instance occurs entirely within the boundaries of a single state and, alone, has only a *de minimis* effect on interstate commerce—as almost self-evident.[26] With regard to the federal gambling statute, many courts have distinguished *Lopez* on the ground that the statute refers to a "business," thus restricting its scope, by definition, to "commercial" activities.[27]

[4] Federal Child Pornography Laws

The federal criminal code contains a number of provisions prohibiting the production, shipment, and possession of material depicting sexual activity involving minors.[28] While courts have had little trouble upholding the shipment of material in interstate commerce—*Lopez* and *Morrison* recognized the ability of Congress to close the channels of interstate commerce to harmful or injurious uses[29]—the ban on intrastate, noncommercial possession where the only nexus to interstate commerce is that the materials used to produce the pornography themselves traveled in interstate commerce has given some courts pause.

In a thoughtful Third Circuit opinion, Judge Becker acknowledged that though 18 U.S.C. § 2252(a)(4)(B), which prohibits possession of child pornography made using material that had traveled in interstate commerce, did have a jurisdictional nexus, but he also noted that nearly everything had, at some point, traveled in interstate commerce and that if pressed too far, the jurisdictional nexus would become useless.[30] However, the court held that Congress could have concluded that to combat the demand for interstate traffic, it had to ban purely intrastate, noncommercial possession.[31] Other courts have upheld the ban on possession on similar grounds.[32]

The Sixth Circuit, however, recently reversed a defendant's conviction under the same statute after concluding that the defendant's activity "was not of a type demonstrated *substantially* to be connected or related to interstate commerce on the facts of this case. . . . [The defendant] was not involved, nor intended to be involved, in the distribution or sharing with others of the pictures in question."[33] Similarly, the Ninth Circuit reversed the federal child pornography conviction of a parent who had pictures taken of her children and herself partially clothed and with their genitals exposed.[33.1] For the panel, Judge Stephen Reinhardt held that applying the federal child pornography statute that criminalizes possession of child pornography with materials that had traveled in interstate commerce to "simple intrastate possession of a visual depiction . . . that has not been mailed, shipped, or transported interstate and is not intended for intrastate distribution, or for any economic or commercial use, including the exchange of the prohibited material for other prohibited material" was unconstitutional.[33.2] The court did not, however, strike down the statute on its face, a move that drew a dissent from Judge Trott, who concluded that "because McCoy's conduct clearly falls within the language of the statute . . . precedent requires us to take the statute head on, not carve pieces out of it."[33.3]

Perhaps influenced by these courts of appeals decisions, recent district court decisions have reversed child pornography charges against defendants where the connection to interstate commerce was deemed slight.[33.4] The future of these as-applied challenges, however, is uncertain in light of *Gonzales v. Raich* (2005).[33.5] If Congress may seek to eliminate the interstate and foreign market for child pornography — as it surely may — then *Raich* would appear to permit it to reach *all* such activity, regardless of how noncommercial or local it seems.

[5] The Hobbs Act

Section 1951 of Title 18 subjects to imprisonment anyone who "in any way or degree obstructs, delays, or affects commerce or the movement of any article or commodity in commerce, by robbery or extortion. . . ."[34] Following *Lopez, Morrison*, and *Jones*, the salient question is whether ordinary street crime, like robbery, has the constitutionally required effect on interstate commerce to come within the scope of the Hobbs Act. For the most part, when robbery is committed against a commercial business, courts have upheld both facial and as-applied challenges to the Act's application on the theory that even if the immediate effect of the act has but a *de minimis* effect on interstate commerce, such activity when aggregated meets *Lopez*'s "substantially affects" test.[35]

Robbery of an individual, however, presents a different situation, because allowing federal prosecution for robbery of an individual on the theory that, when aggregated, all such crime "substantially affects" interstate commerce seems to be the sort of reasoning that the Supreme Court dismissed in *Lopez* and *Morrison*.[36] Courts are divided on the proper approach. Some courts have allowed Hobbs Act prosecutions for robbery of an individual on the theory that when a person is robbed of money, that person has less money to spend on goods in interstate commerce, and therefore, in the aggregate, interstate commerce is substantially affected.[37] Other courts, however, have required a more exacting demonstration that the robbery victim was actually engaged in interstate commerce, and that the robbery of that person actually affected interstate commerce in some way.[38] When the government either fails to produce evidence that a particular business operates in interstate commerce, or otherwise fails to establish a nexus with interstate commerce, courts have reversed Hobbs Act convictions.[39] It remains to be seen what effect, if any, *Raich* has on these cases.

[6] The Child Support Recovery Act

In an effort to aid parents collect child support from ex-spouses who resided in other states, Congress passed the Child Support Recovery Act (CSRA), which made it a federal crime to fail to make a court-ordered child support payment when the parent and child live in different states.[40] Earlier court decisions upheld the act on the theory that Congress was merely regulating the channels of interstate commerce and things therein.[41] Following the Court's decision in *Morrison*, two federal courts found that the statute exceeded the limits of Congress's commerce power; both were eventually reversed.[42]

According to the Sixth Circuit panel, "the CSRA is not about recovery of child support payments avoided by interstate flight. Rather, the Act regulates, through the criminal law, obligations owed by one family member to another, using diversity of residence as a jurisdictional 'hook.' "[43] The court rejected the notion that the CSRA regulated the channels of interstate commerce, as *Lopez* and *Morrison* permitted, and then found that it failed to meet the requirements of *Lopez*'s third category of cases, *viz.*, those that "substantially affect" interstate commerce. The court found that the CSRA did not regulate economic activity, and did not contain, in the statute, a jurisdictional nexus.[44] Despite findings that unpaid child support totaled $1.6 billion, these did "not amount to a congressional finding that unpaid child support substantially affects interstate commerce . . . and we would not accept that conclusion based on findings in any event" because "the mere fact that the aggregate social costs of an activity come to a large dollar figure cannot, without more, satisfy the jurisdictional requirement that the activity have a substantial relationship with interstate commerce."[45] Because child support orders are noncommercial, the court noted, the government could not seek to regulate the aggregate effects of nonpayment by relying on *Wickard*.[46] A New York district court agreed, finding the Sixth Circuit's reasoning persuasive and "in accordance with the Supreme Court's federalism jurisprudence as articulated in *Lopez* and further clarified in *Morrison*. . . ."[47]

The Second Circuit and the Sixth Circuit sitting en banc, disagreed. The Sixth Circuit, sitting *en banc*, reversed the three-judge panel and upheld the Child Support Recovery Act.[48] Writing for eight members of the twelve member court, Judge Moore concluded that the CSRA "regulates exclusively interstate cases involving a debtor parent's obligation to send court-ordered payments through interstate channels of commerce for a child residing in another state. We believe that, at the very least, the CSRA falls within Congress's power to regulate a 'thing' in interstate commerce."[49] The court noted that it was following nine of the ten other circuits in so holding.[50]

The Second Circuit's decision closely tracked the Sixth Circuit's, concluding that the Act regulated channels and things in interstate commerce.[51] In the court's view, "*Morrison* did not in any way alter the *Lopez* tripartite framework or otherwise refine the analysis of when something qualifies as a 'thing in interstate commerce' and thus may be permissibly regulated under *Lopez*'s second category."[52]

[7] The Endangered Species Act

In a closely-watched case, the Fourth Circuit Court of Appeals (the Court in which the *Morrison* case originated) upheld a rule of the Fish and

Wildlife Service, passed under the authority of the Endangered Species Act, prohibiting the trapping or killing, on private land, of red wolves that had been reintroduced into North Carolina.[53] Stressing the need to defer to Congress, the panel concluded that the regulations concerned "economic activity" and that they were "reasonable."[54] The taking of red wolves, the court concluded, "implicates a variety of commercial activities and is closely connected to several interstate markets. The regulation in question is also an integral part of the overall federal scheme to protect, preserve, and rehabilitate endangered species, thereby conserving valuable wildlife resources important to the welfare of the country."[55] The court found that preventing takings of the red wolves strengthened an interstate tourist economy, promoted scientific research, and possibly preserved an interstate market for wolf pelts.[56] It also found that the preservation of endangered species was part of a larger regulatory scheme whose efficacy would be undermined if intrastate activity was not reached.[57] Other federal courts have agreed, and have upheld the Endangered Species Act against constitutional challenge in other contexts.[58] As with many of the other statutes discussed in this section, definitive resolution must await the Supreme Court, which declined to review the Fourth Circuit's decision.[59]

[8] The Federal Access to Clinic Entrances Act

Another fairly recent statute whose constitutionality was called into question following *Lopez* was the Federal Access to Clinic Entrances Act ("FACE"), which prohibits interference "with any person because that person is or has been . . . obtaining or providing reproductive health services. . . . "[60] In a case that the Supreme Court declined to review, the Third Circuit upheld the civil suit provision of FACE, concluding that Congress could have concluded that, insofar as the provision of reproductive services was "commerce," interference with them had a substantial effect on interstate commerce.[61] The court wrote that "the physical obstruction and destruction of reproductive health clinics and the intentional interference and intimidation of persons obtaining and providing reproductive health services [are activities] with . . . effect[s] that [are] economic in nature" and that "Congress had a rational basis upon which to conclude that the activities governed by FACE have a substantial effect on interstate commerce."[62]

In his dissent, Circuit Judge Weis argued that the majority gave *Lopez* and *Morrison* short shrift. Calling *Morrison*'s holding "expansive," he wrote that "[t]ogether, *Lopez* and *Morrison* mandate limits to the federalization of local crime under the aegis of the Commerce Clause. FACE . . . is an example of congressional intrusion into criminal law traditionally within the province of the States."[63] While agreeing that the "services provided by abortion clinics are clearly commercial in nature," he noted that FACE was "directed against the conduct of those external to a clinic's operation. . . . [A] protester's conduct does not involve a purchase, sale, or any exchange of value in return for the rendering of a service, and cannot in any sense be deemed economic or commercial in character."[64] He also noted FACE's lack of a jurisdictional nexus, seemingly required by *Morrison*, particularly where Congress attempts to regulate non-economic activity.[65]

A Texas district court recently agreed with Judge Weis. Striking FACE, the court wrote that "the FACE Act does not relate to the prohibition of interstate transportation of persons, items or services incident to some crime. It does not relate to possession or use of any item transported at any time in interstate commerce. And it does not relate to an act of violence that may be used to financially support other illegal conduct that touches on interstate commerce. . . . [T]here is no intrastate commercial activity generated by the anti-abortion activities that arguably generates funds for other criminal activity that is interstate in nature."[65.1] A three-judge panel of the Fifth Circuit, however, vacated the district court's decision.[65.2]

[9] Federal Arson Statutes

Following the Supreme Court's decision in *Jones v. United States* (2000), which required that property be "used in" interstate commerce in a fairly direct way to come within the scope of the statute, a number of defendants have challenged their arson convictions.[66] Particularly where the facts involve arson of churches, the lower courts have wrestled with the question of what is sufficient for churches (and other property) to meet the statutory requirement.[67]

* * *

The discussion in this section is by no means comprehensive. Challenges to a number of other statutes are currently working their way through the federal courts, but, as is true of the challenges described above, they have largely been unsuccessful.[68] The lower court cases can be criticized for their sometimes thin analysis, their unwillingness to reconsider their post-*Lopez* decisions in light of *Morrison* and *Jones*, and their sometimes fine distinctions between the challenged statutes and those struck down in *Lopez* and *Morrison*.[69] On the other hand, given the Supreme Court's denial of certiorari in cases following *Morrison*, and the Court's recent decision in *Raich*, the lower courts' go-slow approach appears to have been prescient.

[8] *See supra* §§ 3.13 & 5.04[E].

[9] 18 U.S.C. § 922(g)(1).

[10] Scarborough v. United States, 431 U.S. 563, 97 S. Ct. 1963 (1977) (divided court).

[11] *Id.* at 568. An earlier case, *United States v. Bass*, 404 U.S. 336, 349, 92 S. Ct. 515, 523 (1971) (divided court), had held that the government must prove that a firearm had, in fact, moved in or otherwise affected commerce to secure a conviction under § 922(g)(1)'s predecessor. This construction was applied in part to avoid constitutional questions raised by congressional criminalization of mere possession. *See* 404 U.S. at 349-350, 92 S. Ct. at 523-524.

[12] United States v. Coward, 151 F. Supp.2d 544 (E.D. Pa. 2001) (Dalzell, J.). Judge Dalzell's opinion, and the Third Circuit's subsequent reconsideration (and reaffirmation) of its prior decision in upholding the statute in a separate case can be found in Denning & Reynolds, *supra* note 111, at 1266-1274; *see also* Young, The Significance of Border Crossings: *Lopez, Morrison*, and the Fate of Congressional Power to Regulate Goods, and Transactions Connected with Them, Based on Prior Passage Through Interstate Commerce, 61 Md. L. Rev. 177 (2002) (critically analyzing *Scarborough.*)

[13] United States v. Olson, 2005 WL 1163676 (7th Cir. 2005), at * ___ (rejecting Commerce Clause challenge to felon-in-possession statute); United States v. Williams, 2005 WL 859427 (10th Cir. 2005), at *7 (same); United States v. Leuschen, 395 F.3d 155, 160-161 (unpublished), at *1 (same); United States v. Harris, 394 F.3d 543, 551 (7th Cir. 2005); United States v. Bateman, 2004 WL 2940814 (8th Cir. 2004), at *1 n.1 (per curiam) (unpublished) (same); United States v. Wilson, 2004 WL 2924180 (7th Cir. 2004), at *2 (unpublished) (same); United States v. Davis, 2004 WL 2368392 (5th Cir. 2003), at *1 (per curiam) (unpublished) (same); United States v. Hill, 386 F.3d 855, 859 (8th Cir. 2004) (same); United States v. Vallejo, 373 F.3d 855, 860-861 (7th Cir. 2004) (same); United States v. Keller, 376 F.3d 713, 716-717 (7th Cir. 2004) (same); United States v. Smith, 2004 WL 1147061 (3d Cir.) (May 19, 2004), at *3 n.1 (same); United States v. Everist, 368 F.3d 517, 519 (5th Cir. 2004) (same); United States v. Peppers, 2004 WL 857096 (3d Cir.) (April 21, 2004) (unpublished) (same); United States v. Thompson, 359 F.3d 470, 480 (7th Cir. 2004) (same, involving possession of ammunition); United States v. Thompson, 361 F.3d 918, 922-923 (6th Cir. 2004) (same); United States v. Haire, 2004 WL 406141 (6th Cir.) (March 2, 2004) (unpublished), at *4-*5 (same); United States v. Jackson, 2004 WL 326857 (5th Cir.) (Feb. 18, 2004) (unpublished) (same); United States v. Shepherd, 2004 WL 326865 (5th Cir.) (Feb. 18, 2004) (unpublished) (same); United States v. Lastraps, 2004 WL 316011 (5th Cir.) (Feb. 18, 2004) (unpublished) (same); United States v. Criston, 2004 WL 304278 (5th Cir.) (Feb. 18, 2004) (unpublished) (same); United States v. Underwood, 2004 WL 306027 (5th Cir.) (Feb. 18, 2004) (unpublished) (same); United States v. Perales, 2004 WL 307307 (5th Cir.) (Feb. 18, 2004)

(unpublished) (same); United States v. Burgess, 2004 WL 96781 (5th Cir.) (Jan. 21, 2004) (unpublished) (same); United States v. Gillaum, 355 F.3d 982, 994 (7th Cir. 2004) (same); United States v. Lewis, 2004 WL 97884 (5th Cir.) (Jan. 19, 2004) (unpublished) (same); United States v. Leathers, 354 F.3d 955, 959 (8th Cir. 2004) (same); United States v. Harris, 2004 WL 49096 (5th Cir.) (Jan. 8, 2004) (unpublished) (same); United States v. Harris, 2003 WL 22965593 (5th Cir.) (Dec. 10, 2003) (unpublished) (same); United States v. Lopez, 2003 WL 22849825 (5th Cir.) (Dec. 1, 2003) (unpublished) (same); United States v. Darrington, 351 F.3d 632, 634 (5th Cir. 2003) (unpublished) (same); United States v. Brown, 2003 WL 22478164 (5th Cir.) (Nov. 3, 2003) (unpublished) (same); United States v. Valencia, 2003 WL 22427953 (5th Cir.) (Oct. 24, 2003) (unpublished) (same); United States v. Dunn, 2003 WL 22158086, at ___ (11th Cir. 2003) (divided court) (same); United States v. Fernandez, 2003 WL 22146118 (6th Cir.) (Sept. 11, 2003) (unpublished) (same); United States v. Gary, 341 F.3d 829, 835 (8th Cir. 2003) (same); United States v. Florence, 2003 WL 22048202 (5th Cir.) (Sept. 3, 2003) (unpublished) (same); United States v. Graham, 2003 WL 21640383 (4th Cir.) (July 14, 2003) (unpublished) (same); United States v. Smith, 2003 WL 21508242 (9th Cir.) (June 30, 2003) (unpublished) (same); United States v. Loney, 331 F.3d 516, 524 (6th Cir. 2003) (same); United States v. Massie, 2003 WL 21321234 (7th Cir.) (June 5, 2003) (unpublished) (same); United States v. Bell, 2003 WL 21267477 (3d Cir.) (June 3, 2003) (unpublished) (same); United States v. Ayers, 2003 WL 21259963 (4th Cir.) (June 2, 2003) (unpublished) (same); United States v. Thornton, 327 F.3d 268, 272-273 (3d Cir. 2003) (same); United States v. Jackubowski, 2003 WL 2013054 (7th Cir.) (Apr. 30, 2003) (unpublished) (same), United States v. Bass, 2003 WL 1793125 (7th Cir.) (Apr. 7, 2003) (same); Singer v. Waco, 2003 WL 1796009 (7th Cir.) (Mar. 27, 2003) (unpublished) (same); United States v. Wolvin, 2003 WL 1796011 (7th Cir.) (Mar. 27, 2003) (unpublished) (same); United States v. Sarvey, 2003 WL 1269403 (3d Cir.) (Mar. 19, 2003) (unpublished) (same); United States v. Wilkerson, 2003 WL 1154136 (4th Cir.) (Mar. 14, 2003) (unpublished) (same); United States v. Zemba, 2003 WL 567121 (3d Cir.) (Feb. 28, 2003) (unpublished), at *7 (same); United States v. Brown, 314 F.3d 1216, 1220-1221 (10th Cir. 2003) (same); United States v. Binion, 2002 WL 31898231 (7th Cir.) (Dec. 27, 2002) (same); United States v. Fleischli, 305 F.3d 643, 652-653 (7th Cir. 2002) (same); United States v. Gonzales, 307 F.3d 906, 914 (9th Cir. 2002) (same); United States v. Shuford, 2002 WL 31245957 (7th Cir.) (Sept. 24, 2002) (same) (unpublished); United States v. Dill, 2002 WL 31761706 (9th Cir.) (Dec. 9, 2002) (unpublished), at *1 (same); United States v. Carter, 2002 WL 31729909 (9th Cir.) (Dec. 5, 2002) (unpublished) (same); United States v. Banyavong, 2002 WL 31728815 (9th Cir.) (Dec. 4, 2002) (unpublished), at *1 (same); United States v. Warren, 2002 WL 31667968 (10th Cir.) (Nov. 27, 2002) (unpublished), at *1 (same); United States v. Liverman, 2002 WL 31513271 (4th Cir.) (Nov. 13, 2002) (same); United States v. Brown, 2002 WL 31474527 (3d Cir.) (Nov. 6, 2002) (unpublished) (same); United States v. Lee, 310 F.3d 787, 788-789 (5th Cir. 2002) (same); United States v. Gonzales, 307 F.3d 906, (9th Cir. 2002) (same); United States v. Robinson, 2002 WL 31116062 (4th Cir.) (Sept. 25, 2002) (unpublished), at *1 (same); United States v. Hall, 2002 WL 31098422 (9th Cir.) (Sept. 9, 2002) (unpublished) (same); United States v. Street, 2002 WL 31085286 (9th Cir.) (Sept. 18, 2002) (unpublished) (same); United States v. Davis, 2002 WL 31056543 (9th Cir.) (Sept. 9, 2002) (unpublished) (same); United States v. Kendricks, 2002 WL 31056549 (9th Cir.) (Sept. 9, 2002) (unpublished) (same); United States v. Lemons, 302 F.3d 769, 770-772, 773 (7th Cir. 2002) (same; jurisdictional nexus sufficient to distinguish statute from those struck down in *Lopez* and *Morrison*; "If . . . *Lopez*'s rationale calls into doubt our construction and application of [the felon-in-possession statute] it is for the Supreme Court to so hold."); United States v. Mitchell, 299 F.3d 632, 633-635 (7th Cir. 2002) (rejecting felon-in-possession challenge brought in light of *Jones* and *Morrison*, but relying on *Bass*); United States v. Gaines, 295 F.3d 293, 302 (2d Cir. 2002) (same); United States v. Coward, 296 F.3d 176, 183-184 (3d Cir. 2002) (same); United States v. Coleman, 2002 WL 1337842 (3d Cir.) (June 18, 2002) (unpublished), at *1 (same); United States v. Rowland, 2002 WL 1301768 (9th Cir.) (June 13, 2002) (unpublished), at *1 (same); United States v. Shorter, 2002 WL 1283933 (3d Cir.) (May 3, 2002) (unpublished), at *1 (same); United States v. Connor, 2002 WL 731018 (3rd Cir.) (April 24, 2002) (unpublished) (rejecting Commerce Clause challenge to 18 U.S.C. §922(g) based on prior circuit precedent); United States v. Powell, 2002 WL 700931 (10th Cir.) (April 24, 2002) (unpublished) (same); United States v. Dixon, 2002 WL 654441 (3rd Cir.) (April 22, 2002) (unpublished) (same); United States v. Blocker, 2002 WL 661717 (9th Cir.) (April 22, 2002) (unpublished) (same); United States v. Wilson, 2002 WL 596841 (3rd Cir.) (April 18, 2002) (unpublished) (same); United States v. Easterling, 2002 WL 568189 (10th Cir.) (April 17, 2002) (unpublished) (same); United States v. Cavazos, 288 F.3d 706, 712-713 (5th Cir. 2002) (same); United States v. Wilkerson, 286 F.3d 1324, 1325 n.1 (11th Cir. 2002) (per curiam) (same); United States v. Shepherd, 284 F.3d 965, 969 (8th Cir. 2002) (same); United States v. Clark, 2002 WL 461718 (9th Cir.) (March 18, 2002) (unpublished) (same); United States v. Williams, 2002 WL 538735 (3rd Cir.) (March 15, 2002) (unpublished) (same); United States v. Marshall, 2002 WL 214537 (4th Cir.) (Feb. 12, 2002) (unpublished) (same); United States v. Stover, 2002 WL 919093 (4th Cir.) (Jan. 24, 2002) (unpublished) (per curiam) (same); United States v. Wynne, 2002 WL 90984 (3rd Cir.) (Jan. 24, 2002) (unpublished) (same); United States v. Malloy, 2002 WL 460322 (9th Cir.) (Jan. 8, 2002) (unpublished) (same); United States v. Estrada, 2002 WL 93136 (10th Cir.) (Jan. 25, 2002) (unpublished) (same); United States v. Davis, 2001 WL 1662485 (6th Cir.) (Dec. 27, 2001) (same); United States v. Singletary, 268 F.3d 196, 200-204 (3rd Cir. 2001) (same); United States v. Gardner, 2001 WL 1048552 (10th Cir.) (Sept. 13, 2001) (unpublished) (same); United States v. Gallimore, 247 F.3d 134 (4th Cir. 2001) (upholding felon-in-possession statute, 18 U.S.C. §922(g)); United States v. Davis, 242 F.3d 1162, 1162 (9th Cir. 2001) (per curiam) (same); United States v. Santiago, 238 F.3d 213 (2nd Cir. 2001) (per curiam) (same); United States v. Boles, 2001 WL 22985 (4th Cir. 2001), at *1 ("We agree with our sister circuits that §922(g) does not offend the Commerce Clause because it requires a particularized finding of a link to interstate commerce."); United States v. Dorris, 236 F.3d 582, 584-586 (10th Cir. 2000) (same); United States v. Baer, 235 F.3d 561 (10th Cir. 2000) (same); United States v. Fowler, 2005 WL 757595 (D. Me.) (March 3, 2005), at *1 (same); United States v. Baker, 2005 WL 283358 (E.D. La.) (Feb. 3, 2005), at *1 (same); United States v. Bradford, 2004 WL 2496136 (E.D. La.) (Nov. 4, 2004), at *8 (same); United States v. Yeley, 2004 WL 2750265 (S.D. Ind.) (Oct. 18, 2004), at *2 (same); Powell v. United States, 2004 WL 1576633 (E.D. Pa.) (July 1, 2004), at *3 (same); United States v. Harrellson, 2004 WL 1447781 (W.D. Wisc.) (June 23, 2004) (same); United States v. Kitsch, 2004 WL 442868 (E.D. Pa.) (Mar. 2, 2004), at ___ (same); United States v. Mackey, 2004 WL 95756 (E.D. La.) (Jan. 15, 2004), at *5 (same); Jones v. United States, 2003 WL 34075804 (E.D. Pa.) (Oct. 23, 2003) (unpublished) (same); United States v. Goodwin, 2003 WL 21266681 (N.D. Ill.) (June 2, 2003) (same); Davis v. United States,

2003 WL 21056988 (E.D.N.Y.) (Mar. 17, 2003) (same); United States v. Wilson, 2002 WL 31387011 (N.D. Ill.) (Oct. 18, 2002), at *1-*2 (same); United States v. Tucker, 2002 WL 31005915 (N.D. Ill.) (Sept. 6, 2002), at *1-*3 (same, also upholding proscribing possession of firearm with obliterated serial number 922(k)); United States v. Peeples, 2002 WL 1483898 (N.D. Ill.) (July 11, 2002) (rejecting challenge to federal law prohibiting possession of firearm with obliterated serial number); United States v. Richardson, 2002 WL 1000297 (N.D. Ill.) (May 16, 2002) (unpublished) (same); United States v. Quintana, 2000 WL 1855130 (S.D.N.Y. 2000) (same); United States v. Holmes, 2002 WL 122306 (D. Neb.) (Jan. 31, 2002), at *5 (same); United States v. Merritt, ___ F. Supp. 2d ___, ___ (S.D. Ind. 2001) (same); United States v. Torres, 149 F. Supp. 2d 199, 201-204 (E.D. Pa. 2001) (same); United States v. Coward, 151 F. Supp. 2d 544 (E.D. Pa. 2001) (Dalzell, J., grudgingly refusing to dismiss charge on felon-in-possession of firearm; urging reconsideration in light of *Morrison, Jones*, and *Lopez*); United States v. Carnes, 113 F. Supp. 2d 1145, 1150 (E.D. Mich. 2000) (upholding felon-in-possession charge against Commerce Clause Challenge). *Cf.* United States v. Kitsch, 2004 WL 442868 (E.D. Pa.) (March 2, 2004), at ___ (rejecting Commerce Clause challenge to 18 U.S.C. § 931(a), prohibiting felons from being in possession of body armor).

[14] *See supra* note 13.

[15] *See* United States v. Hernandez, 190 F. Supp. 2d 773, 774 (E.D. Pa. 2002) (holding that defense counsel not ineffective for failure to raise constitutional challenge to felon-in-possession law); Beamon v. United States, 189 F. Supp. 2d 350, 358 (E.D. Va. 2002) (failure to challenge federal felon-in-possession statute at trial in light of circuit court precedents rejecting such challenges not ineffective).

[16] 18 U.S.C. § 922(g)(8)-(9).

[17] *See* United States v. Morse, 2004 WL 1094491 (4th Cir.) (May 18, 2004) (unpublished) (rejecting Commerce Clause challenge to 18 U.S.C. § 922(g)(9), prohibiting possession of a firearm by one convicted of a misdemeanor crime of domestic violence); United States v. Mills, 2003 WL 22794538 (4th Cir.) (Nov. 21, 2003) (unpublished), at *3 (same); United States v. Ayers, 2003 WL 21259963 (4th Cir.) (June 2, 2003) (unpublished) (same); United States v. Bayles, 310 F.3d 1302, 1307-1308 (10th Cir. 2002) (same); United States v. Gill, 2002 WL 661718 (9th Cir.) (March 8, 2002) (unpublished) (rejecting Commerce Clause challenge to 18 U.S.C. § 922(g)(8), which prohibits possession of a firearm by one under a domestic violence restraining order; "the presence of the defendant's firearm in interstate commerce at some time in the past continues to be a sufficient connection to interstate commerce to pass constitutional muster"); United States v. Ball, 2001 WL 324624 (4th Cir.) (April 4, 2001) (unpublished) (upholding 18 U.S.C. § 922(g)(9), prohibiting possession of firearms by those convicted of domestic violence crimes); United States v. Lewis, 236 F.3d 948, 950 (8th Cir. 2001) (same; "specific interstate-commerce connection [in statute] suffices to validate the statute"); United States v. Brown, 2001 WL 285210 (4th Cir.) (May 23, 2001) (unpublished) (concluding that the statute "contains a specific jurisdictional requirement that the possession be 'in or affecting interstate commerce'"); United States v. Napier, 233 F.3d 394, 399-402 (6th Cir. 2000) (upholding 18 U.S.C. § 922(g)(8), which prohibits gun possession by those subject to certain protection orders; statute requires only that gun have traveled in interstate commerce at some point in the past); United States v. Baker, 197 F.3d 211, 218 (6th Cir. 1999) (upholding the constitutionality of § 922(g)(8), which prohibits one subject to a domestic violence protection order from possessing a firearm; jurisdictional element in-

sulates statute from *Lopez* challenge); United States v. Brown, 2002 WL 31242235 (S.D. Ind.) (Aug. 15, 2002) (unpublished), at *2 (possession of firearm by one convicted of domestic violence crime); United States v. Willbern, 2000 WL 554134 (D. Kan. 2000), at *1 (upholding constitutionality of §922(g)(9); jurisdictional requirement that firearm traveled in interstate commerce sufficient to sustain statute against *Lopez* challenge).

[18] 18 U.S.C. §922(o)(1).

[19] *See* United States v. Rybar, 103 F.3d 273 (3rd Cir. 1996). For a succinct explanation of the *Rybar* decision, *see* Vermeule, Does Commerce Clause Review Have Perverse Effects?, 46 Vill. L. Rev. 1325, 1334-36 (2001). For the pre-*Lopez* cases, *see* United States v. Swida, 2002 WL 54658 (M.D. Pa.) (Jan. 15, 2002), at *1 n.1; *see also* United States v. Burget, 2004 WL 2580922 (9th Cir.) (Nov. 15, 2004) (unpublished), at *1 (upholding conviction for possession of machine gun where defendant purchased a kit that converted a semi-automatic rifle into a machine gun); United States v. Fleischli, 119 F. Supp. 2d 819, 821-822 (C.D. Ill. 2000) (concluding that *Morrison* did not require reassessment of Seventh Circuit decision upholding federal machine gun ban).

[20] *See, e.g., Rybar*, 103 F.3d at 282. The court also concluded that the statute could be upheld because it was part of a national regulatory scheme of the sort approved by *Lopez*—in this case, a scheme to curb illicit arms sales. *Id.* at 283. The rationale for the decision is criticized in Denning & Reynolds, *supra* note 111, at 1274-1279.

[20.1] United States v. Stewart, 348 F.3d 1132 (9th Cir. 2003) (divided court).

[20.2] 348 F.3d at 1134.

[20.3] *Id.*

[20.4] *Id.* at 1135, 1136. An earlier case, *United States v. Rambo*, 74 F.3d 948 (9th Cir. 1996), held that §922(o) was valid because "a transfer or sale must have preceded the criminalized possession." *Stewart*, 348 F.3d at 1134. The court noted that the present case "reveals the limits of Rambo's logic. . . . Stewart did not acquire his machineguns from someone else: He fabricated them himself. The government has never contested Stewart's claim that the machineguns were entirely homemade. . . ." *Id.* at 1135.

[20.5] *Id.* at 1137.

[20.6] *Id.*

[20.7] *Id.* at 1138.

[20.8] *Id.* at 1138-1139.

[20.9] *Id.* at 1139.

[20.10] *Id.* at 1143 (Restani, J., dissenting).

[21] United States v. Pritchett, 327 F.3d 1183 (11th Cir. 2003) (rejecting challenge to §922(j) prohibiting receipt of stolen firearm that previously moved in interstate commerce); United States v. Luna, 165 F.3d 316 (5th Cir. 1999). *See also* United States v. Tucker, 2002 WL 31005915 (N.D. Ill.) (Sept. 6, 2002), at *1-*3 (upholding proscribing possession of firearm with obliterated serial number 922(k)); United States v. Peeples, 2002 WL 1483898 (N.D. Ill.) (July 11, 2002) (rejecting challenge to federal law prohibiting possession of firearm with obliterated serial number); United States v. Richardson, 2002 WL 1000297 (N.D. Ill.) (May 16, 2002) (unpublished) (same).

[22] United States v. Hall, 171 F.3d 1133, 1138 (8th Cir. 1999).

[23] *See* United States v. Peters, 2005 WL 673987 (11th Cir. 2005), at *8-*15 (upholding conviction for selling firearms to felons; "[b]y targeting the available supply of firearms to felons (the ban on sales), as well as the lawful demand for firearms among

felons (the ban on possession) Congress has created a mutually reinforcing framework."); United States v. Britt, 2004 WL 2381271 (5th Cir.) (Oct. 25, 2004) (unpublished), at *3 (upholding conviction under statute punishing murder using a firearm in relation to a drug trafficking crime, 18 U.S.C. §§ 924(c), 924(j); "[m]urder relating to or in furtherance of [drug trafficking] can clearly be proscribed by the federal government."); United States v. Houston, 2004 WL 1465776 (10th Cir.) (June 30, 2004), at *2 (upholding conviction for failure to register a firearm); United States v. Cruz-Rivera, 357 F.3d 10, 14 (1st Cir. 2004) (rejecting Commerce Clause challenge to guilty plea under federal law prohibiting carrying of firearm during and in relation to robbery affecting interstate commerce where defendant killed owner of small business in his home, robbed him of business proceeds, and where business — as a result of owner's death — had to close; "[t]here are significant and interesting questions about whether mere robbery from a private house of monies derived from the owner's interstate business would be sufficient to create a federal crime. . . . We doubt that there is any serious claim of a constitutionally insufficient interstate commerce connection where a robbery directly results in the shutting down of an interstate business."); United States v. Hatches, 2003 WL 22138553 (4th Cir.) (Sept. 17, 2003) (unpublished) (rejecting challenges to laws prohibiting felony possession of a firearm, firearm possession by a drug user, and possessing a firearm in relation to or in furtherance of a drug trafficking crime); United States v. Manna, 2004 WL 491873 (3d Cir.) (Mar 11, 2004) (unpublished), at *4 (rejecting Commerce Clause challenge to 18 U.S.C. § 924(c), criminalizing the use of a firearm during and in relation to a crime of violence, because predicate offense — violation of bank robbery statute — satisfied Commerce Clause); United States v. Ricketts, 317 F.3d 540, 543 (6th Cir. 2003) (rejecting challenge to federal law criminalizing use of firearm and murder connected with drug conspiracy); United States v. Winston, 2003 WL 173046 (6th Cir.) (Jan. 23, 2003) (unpublished), at *12 (rejecting challenge to conviction for use of a firearm in connection with a drug-related murder, 18 U.S.C. § 924 (c), (j)); United States v. Arocho, 305 F.3d 627, 641 (7th Cir. 2002) (upholding 18 U.S.C. § 924(c), prohibiting the use of a firearm during a drug offense, and 21 U.S.C. § 856(a)(1), prohibiting the maintenance of a drug house, against *Lopez* challenge; requirement that gun has been transported in interstate commerce unnecessary since federal crime already requires connection to commerce; "Congress acted within its authority to regulate interstate commerce in criminalizing the maintaining of a drug house because drug dealing is an activity that affects interstate commerce"); Tse v. United States, 290 F.3d 462, 465-466 (1st Cir. 2002) (upholding conviction for violence in aid of racketeering conviction; de minimis effect on interstate commerce sufficient); United States v. Miller, 283 F.3d 907, 913-914 (8th Cir. 2002) (upholding federal statute punishing the use of a firearm during a drug trafficking crime, 18 U.S.C. § 924(o); felon-in-possession statute; and causing the death of a person by firearm during a drug trafficking crime, 18 U.S.C. § 924(j); "[b]ecause Congress may regulate drug trafficking, it may also regulate the use of firearms connected with that trafficking" under its commerce power); United States v. Ferreira, 275 F.3d 1020, 1028 (11th Cir. 2001) (rejecting Commerce Clause challenge to 18 U.S.C. § 924(c), which makes it a federal crime to use a weapon during a crime of violence; noting that neither *Jones* nor *Morrison* suggests that post-*Lopez* decision upholding statute should be revisited); United States v. Castillias, 351 F. Supp. 2d 1045, 1048 (D. Haw. 2004) (rejecting challenge to statute prohibiting drug user from possessing firearms that moved in interstate commerce); Williams v. United States, 2002 WL 1832828 (E.D. Pa.) (Aug. 7, 2002) (unpublished), at *1 (upholding challenge to federal bank robbery statute and statute making it crime to brandish a weapon during bank robbery).

[24] Hays v. United States, 397 F.3d 564, 567-568 (7th Cir. 2005) (holding that prescribing, then stealing, OxyContin from patients' homes satisfied statutory "affects commerce" requirement of 18 U.S.C. § 1365(a), prohibiting tampering with consumer products; "[b]ecause of the prescriptions he wrote to facilitate the use of the drug, pharmacies in Illinois were required to order more OxyContin from Minnesota and to replenish their supply."); United States v. Brown, 2004 WL 243491 (5th Cir.) (Feb. 11, 2004), at *6 (rejecting Commerce Clause challenge to prosecution under federal drug laws); United States v. Mason, 2003 WL 22871696 (4th Cir.) (Dec. 5, 2003) (per curiam) (same); United States v. Jackson, 2003 WL 21153300 (4th Cir.) (May 20, 2003) (unpublished) (same); United States v. Davis, 288 F.3d 359, 362 (8th Cir. 2002) (rejecting Commerce Clause challenge to Controlled Substances Act of 1970); United States v. Jones, 2002 WL 337535 (4th Cir.) (March 4, 2002) (unpublished) (per curiam) (upholding conviction for violating federal statute prohibiting possession and distribution of cocaine against Commerce Clause challenge relying on previous decision concluding that "intrastate drug activity had a substantial effect on interstate commerce"); *see also* United States v. Chapman, 2003 WL 175052 (4th Cir.) (Jan. 28, 2003) (unpublished), at *2 (rejecting challenge to federal drug law); United States v. Harris, 313 F.3d 1228, 1241 (10th Cir. 2002) (rejecting challenge to federal statute prohibiting possession of illegal drugs with intent to distribute within 1000 feet of a school); United States v. Sprofera, 299 F.3d 725, 727-728 (8th Cir. 2002) (rejecting challenge to federal drug statutes); United States v. Mercado, 2002 WL 1732614 (7th Cir. 2002) (unpublished), at *1 (rejecting challenge to federal drug statutes; pronouncing claim that Congress lacked authority to outlaw cocaine distribution "frivolous" because of previous decisions); United States v. Carter, 294 F.3d 978, 981 (8th Cir. 2002) (per curiam) (rejecting challenge to federal drug laws; "*Lopez* is inapposite because there the Court held that Congress did not make findings that the statute substantially affected interstate commerce."); United States v. Brown, 276 F.3d 211, 214 (6th Cir. 2002) (rejecting Commerce Clause challenge to federal drug trafficking statutes because crimes occurred intrastate; noting that "[t]his view has been soundly rejected by this circuit as well as every other circuit to address the issue"); United States v. Brown, 2000 WL 876382 (6th Cir.) (June 20, 2000), at *13 (unpublished) (same); Cirineo v. United States, 2005 WL 1214320 (S.D.N.Y. 2005), at *7 (rejecting Commerce Clause challenge to conviction for conspiracy to distribute and possession with intent to distribute crack cocaine); Shafer v. United States, 2004 WL 1115916 (E.D. Tenn. 2005), at *2 (same); Locke v. United States, 2005 WL 356947 (W.D. Tex. 2005), at *2 (same); Puello v. United States, 2004 WL 42282 (S.D.N.Y.) (Jan. 7, 2004) (same); Caicedo v. United States, 2003 WL 22681437 (S.D.N.Y.) (Nov. 12, 2003) (same); United States v. Rhoiney, 2002 WL 31987473 (D. Kansas) (Dec. 17, 2002) (rejecting Commerce Clause challenge to indictment for possession of crack cocaine with intent to distribute); United States v. Wheat, 2002 WL 31094824 (N.D. Iowa) (Sept. 16, 2002), at *4 (upholding federal drug law against Commerce Clause challenge; failure to raise not ineffective assistance of counsel); United States v. Handschu, 2001 WL 641078 (D. Del.) (June 1, 2001), at *6-*7 (rejecting Commerce Clause challenge to federal drug statues); Pearson v. McCaffrey, 139 F. Supp. 2d 113, 122 (D.D.C. 2001) (same); United States v. Anderson, 1999 WL 477234 (D. Kan.) (May 25, 1999), at *1 (observing that "federal courts have uniformly rejected [constitutional] challenges" to federal drug laws); Dover v. United States, 1999

WL 239281 (E.D. Pa.) (Apr. 8, 1999), at *3 (upholding challenges to federal drug laws and felon-in-possession statute); United States v. Ayala, 47 F. Supp. 2d 196, 197 (D.P.R. 1999) (upholding federal drug trafficking laws against Commerce Clause challenge); Kuromiya v. United States, 37 F. Supp. 2d 717, 723-724 (E.D. Pa. 1999) (upholding federal Controlled Substances Act); *see also* United States v. Real Property Located at 5300 Lights Creek Lane, 2004 WL 2569289 (9th Cir.) (Nov. 12, 2004) (unpublished), at *1 (upholding forfeiture of land used to grow marijuana; growth of marijuana for "private distribution" "commerce" in statutory sense of the word); United States v. Koons, 300 F.3d 985, 992 (8th Cir. 2002) (divided court) (rejecting challenge to conviction under federal law enhancing sentence for drug trafficking within 1000 feet of a school or playground); United States v. Meshack, 225 F.3d 556, 572 (5th Cir. 2000) (upholding conviction under federal money laundering statute as applied to purchase of pickup truck with drug proceeds, which truck was subsequently used drug sales, and as applied to payment of apartment rent with drug money; *de minimis* effect on interstate commerce all that is necessary).

For arguments that *Lopez* and *Morrison* should affect how courts analyze federal drug laws, *see* Hussein, Comment, The Growing Debate on Medical Marijuana: Federal Power vs. States Rights, 37 Cal. W. L. Rev. 369 (2001); Kohnke, Comment, Can Congress Do That?: An Analysis of the Federal Prohibition on Marijuana Possession, 19 Miss. C. L. Rev. 381 (1999) (concluding that it cannot, under recent Commerce Clause cases); Neusch, Comment, Medical Marijuana's State in the Aftermath of the Supreme Court's New Commerce Clause Jurisprudence, 72 U. Colo. L. Rev. 201 (2001); Newbern, Comment, Good Cop, Bad Cop: Federal Prosecutions of State-Legalized Marijuana Use After *United States v. Lopez*, 88 Calif. L. Rev. 1575 (2000).

[25] Caicedo v. United States, 2003 WL 22681437 (S.D.N.Y.) (Nov. 12, 2003) (failure to raise constitutional challenges to federal drug laws not ineffective assistance of counsel); United States v. Handschu, 2001 WL 641078 (D. Del.) (June 1, 2001), at *7 n.4 (rejecting argument that failure to challenge constitutionality of drug statutes constituted ineffective assistance of counsel "[g]iven the abundance of case law upholding . . . these laws under the Commerce Clause"); United States v. Butler, 2001 WL 311209 (E.D. Pa. 2000), at *4 (failure to raise constitutional challenge not ineffective assistance of counsel because such challenges "fruitless" in light of unanimity of courts in rejecting them).

[25.1] Gonzales v. Raich, _____ U.S. _____, 125 S. Ct. 2195 (2005) (divided court).

[26] United States v. Crenshaw, 359 F.3d 977, 983-987 (8th Cir. 2004) (rejecting Commerce Clause challenge to 18 U.S.C. § 1959, the federal murder-in-aid-of-racketeering statute; only activity regulated by statute must "substantially affect" interstate commerce, and murder have been committed to advance within the racketeering enterprise itself); United States v. Shryock, 342 F.3d 948, 984 (9th Cir. 2003) (holding that "de minimis affect [sic] on interstate commerce was sufficient to establish jurisdiction under RICO"); *See* United States v. Riddle, 249 F.3d 529 (6th Cir. 2001) (affirming convictions under 18 U.S.C. §§ 1962 (RICO conspiracy), 1955 (conducting illegal gambling business), and 1959 (violence in furtherance of racketering); *de minimis* effect on interstate commerce sufficient); United States v. Adorno, 2001 WL 253119 (2nd Cir.) (March 12, 2001) (unpublished), at *1 (upholding conviction under 18 U.S.C. § 1951(a)(1), prohibiting murder in aid of racketering; "drug trafficking, even if primarily local in character, is an economic activity with a substantial effect on interstate commerce"); United States v. Brieno, 2001 WL 290618 (N.D. Ill. 2001), at *2 (upholding conviction for running an

illegal gambling business); United States v. Garcia, 68 F. Supp. 2d 802, 807-812 (E.D. Mich. 1999) (upholding both RICO and Violence in Aid of Racketeering Acts (VARA)—18 U.S.C. §§ 1961 and 1959, respectively—against facial constitutional challenges based on the presence of jurisdictional element; upholding facial challenge against RICO, *de minimis* impact on interstate commerce all that is required; but sustaining challenge to VARA, as applied against "a street crime committed by a thug as part of a local turf war in southwest Detroit" with a *de minimis* effect on interstate commerce).

In the same term the Supreme Court decided the *Lopez* case, the Court upheld a conviction under the RICO statute, which reaches enterprises "engaged in, or the activities of which affect, interstate or foreign commerce," 18 U.S.C. § 1962(a), as applied to a company operating a gold mine in Alaska that purchased out-of-state equipment and supplies. United States v. Robertson, 514 U.S. 669, 671, 115S. Ct. 1732, 1733 (1995) (per curiam). That activity, the Court concluded, obviated the need to ascertain the extent to which the activity of the mine "substantially affected" interstate commerce, as required by *Lopez. Robertson*, 514 U.S. at 671-672, 115 S. Ct. at 1733. *See also infra* § 5.05[B] (discussing *Robertson*).

[27] *See, e.g.*, United States v. Vlanich, 2003 WL 22213951 (3d Cir.) (Sept. 24, 2003), at *2 (rejecting Commerce Clause arguments challenging constitutionality of 18 U.S.C. § 1955; noting that "[a]ll of the circuit courts of appeal which have considered the issue since *Lopez* have concluded that Section 1955 continues to be valid under the Commerce Clause"); United States v. Threadgill, 172 F.3d 357, 372-73 (5th Cir. 1999) (distinguishing Lopez's regulation of non-commercial activity and 18 U.S.C. § 1955); United States v. Abels, 167 F.3d 1021, 1027 (6th Cir. 1999) (stating that Lopez is inapplicable to 18 U.S.C. § 1955, in part, because statute in question is "commercial," prohibiting as it does the maintenance of an illegal gambling business); United States v. Zizzo, 120 F.3d 1338, 1350 (7th Cir. 1997) (stating that Lopez is inapplicable to 18 U.S.C. § 1955; latter "prohibits illegal gambling businesses"); United States v. Wall, 92 F.3d 1444 (6th Cir. 1996) (divided court); United States v. Cozzo, 2004 WL 421725 (N.D. Ill.) (March 4, 2002), at *1 (affirming that 18 U.S.C. § 1955, the federal statute governing illegal gambling businesses, constitutionally encompasses local, purely intrastate gambling operations). *But see Wall*, 92 F.3d at 1456-1485 (Boggs, C.J., concurring in part and dissenting in part) (arguing that the absence of a jurisdictional nexus and evidence of "substantial effects" on interstate commerce rendered the statute constitutionally infirm). *See also* United States v. Ables, 167 F.3d 1021 (6th Cir. 1999) (affirming *Wall*); United States v. Owens, 159 F.3d 221, 226 (6th Cir. 1998) (refusing to revisit *Wall*).

[28] *See, e.g.*, 18 U.S.C. § 2251(a) (prohibiting use of minors to produce sexually explicit material to be shipped in interstate or foreign commerce, or using material that has traveled in interstate commerce), § 2252(a)(4) (prohibiting possession of sexually explicit material involving minors that has either traveled in interstate commerce, or the material with which it was produced had so traveled), § 2252A (expanding § 2251 to include transmission of material by computer).

[29] *See, e.g.*, United States v. Riccardi, 2005 WL 896430 (10th Cir. 2005), at *13 (upholding conviction under federal child pornography statute of defendant who both transported his victims across state lines and paid them to pose for him); United States v. Bredimus, 352 F.3d 200, 204–208 (5th Cir. 2003) (upholding 18 U.S.C. § 2423(b), prohibiting traveling in interstate or foreign commerce for the purpose of engaging in sexual act with person under 18 years of age; statute regulates channels of interstate

commerce, "substantially affects" test inapplicable; *Lopez*'s three categories are analytically distinct); United States v. Griffith, 284 F.3d 338, 345-358 (2d Cir. 2002) (upholding conviction under federal statute prohibiting use of minors to perform sexual acts when the depiction will be transported in interstate commerce; where the depiction was produced using materials that had traveled in interstate commerce or the depiction itself had traveled in interstate commerce, 18 U.S.C. § 2251(a), and where proven that videotape defendant had made had traveled between New York and New Jersey, no requirement that the tape was produced for economic purposes); United States v. Butler, 151 F. Supp. 2d 82, 85-86 (D. Me. 2001) (concluding that 18 U.S.C. § 2252A(a)(2)(A), which prohibits knowingly receiving child pornography over the Internet, involved regulation of the channels of interstate commerce and did not exceed Congress's commerce powers).

[30] United States v. Rodia, 194 F.3d 465, 472 (3rd Cir. 1999) ("A hard and fast rule that the presence of a jurisdictional element [guarantees constitutionality] ignores the fact that . . . the jurisdictional hook may be so attenuated as to fail to guarantee that the activity regulated has a substantial effect on interstate commerce."); *cf.* United States v. Kitsch, 2004 WL 442868 (E.D. Pa. 2004), at___ ("Congress's mere inclusion of a jurisdictional element in a statute will not necessarily make all applications of the statute constitutional. If *Morrison* makes anything clear, it is that the judiciary will not elevate form over substance and uncritically uphold every statute where Congress declares that conduct has an attenuated effect on interstate commerce.").

A couple of district courts recently dismissed child pornography convictions against defendants where the only connection to interstate commerce was that the camera, film, or electronic medium had been shipped in interstate commerce. *See* United States v. Selseth, 2004 WL 603461 (N.D. Ill. 2004) (dismissing child pornography indictment against defendant alleged to have possessed five images of minor where only connection to interstate commerce was that the scan card or computer disk at some point had traveled in interstate commerce); United States v. Jeronimo-Bautista, 2004 WL 1219663 (D. Utah 2004) (refusing to apply federal child pornography statute where only connection to interstate commerce was film and camera that was manufactured out of state and had crossed state lines into Utah at some point). *But see* United States v. Mugan, 394 F.3d 1016, 1024 (8th Cir. 2005) (upholding child pornography conviction of defendant whose pictures were stored on a digital memory card that had traveled via interstate commerce; images placed on a medium "which would permit their immediate and widespread dissemination over the internet"); United States v. Colburn, 2004 WL 2943373 (5th Cir.) (Dec. 17, 2004) (rejecting constitutional challenge to federal child pornography statute conviction based on out-of-state manufacture of camera and film); United States v. Andrews, 2004 WL 1944137 (6th Cir. 2004), at *4 (evidence in record establishing nexus between activity and interstate commerce sufficient to support conviction where pen camera purchased to take pornographic pictures was made in China and computer on which pornographic pictures displayed purchased in New Jersey).

[31] *Rodia*, 194 F.3d at 477 (noting that Congress could have concluded that "the possession of 'home grown' pornography may well stimulate a further interest in pornography that immediately or eventually animates demand for interstate pornography").

[32] United States v. Randolph, 2004 WL 736867 (3d Cir. 2004) (reaffirming previous holding that Congress could have rationally concluded that intrastate possession of child pornography has substantial effects on interstate commerce); United States v. Harris, 358

F.3d 221, 223 (2d Cir. 2004) (rejecting Commerce Clause challenge to 18 U.S.C. §2252A(a)(5)(b), criminalizing possession of child pornography); United States v. McBarron, 2003 WL 22533194 (5th Cir.) (Nov. 7, 2003) (unpublished) (rejecting challenge to convictions for conspiracy to produce and possessing child pornography); United States v. Holston, 343 F.3d 83 (2d Cir. 2003) (concluding, following application of *Lopez* and *Morrison* factors, that federal statute prohibiting production of child pornography was permissible under congressional commerce power, both on its face and as applied to the defendant); United States v. Adams, 343 F.3d 1024, 1027-1034 (9th Cir. 2003) (upholding, against facial challenge, federal statute criminalizing intrastate possession of child pornography); United States v. Galo, 239 F.3d 572 (3rd Cir. 2001) (upholding 18 U.S.C. §2252(a)(4)(B), which criminalizes intrastate possession of child pornography); United States v. White, 2001 WL 51014 (4th Cir.) (Jan. 22, 2001) (unpublished) (same); United States v. Kallestad, 236 F.3d 225, 226 (5th Cir. 2000) (divided court) (same; "Congress could rationally conclude that to regulate a national market in child pornography it was necessary to regulate its local possession"); United States v. Angle, 234 F.3d 326, 337-338 (7th Cir. 2000) (same; concluding that Congress could have had a rational basis for concluding that "intrastate possession of child pornography has a substantial effect on interstate commerce"; counterarguments ignored the "interstate demand for child pornography that Congress took into consideration in enacting the statutory scheme"); *see also* United States v. Morales-de Jesus, 372 F.3d 6, 8-21 (1st Cir. 2004) (upholding federal child pornography statute against both facial and as-applied challenges); United States v. Wyatt, 2003 WL 1605799 (4th Cir.) (Mar. 28, 2003) (unpublished) (rejecting challenge to federal child pornography statute); United States v. Harden, 2002 WL 2004854 (4th Cir.) (Sept. 3, 2002) (unpublished), at *3 (rejecting challenge to federal child pornography statute; rejecting as-applied challenge as well); United States v. Riccardi, 258 F. Supp. 2d 1212 (Kan. 2003) (rejecting challenge to child pornography conviction; *Wickard* aggregation applicable to intrastate possession of child pornography); *but see* United States v. McCoy, 232 F.3d 1114, 1132-33 (9th Cir. 2003) (divided court) (finding that federal child-pornography statute could not constitutionally be applied to intrastate possession of pictures of parent and children with genitals exposed); *Kallestad*, 236 F.3d 233 (Jolly, C.J., dissenting) ("In the facts before us, Kallestad's non-commercial, local possession of child pornography, where no interstate transportation or commercial transacting occurred, had at most an insubstantial affect [*sic*] on the interstate market for child pornography.").

[33] United States v. Corp, 236 F.3d 325, 332 (6th Cir. 2001). The "pictures in question" were of a seventeen-year-old girl and the defendant's wife; the court was persuaded on the facts that the activity was consensual and that the defendant had not intended to sell or distribute them. *Corp*, 236 F.3d at 333.

[33.1] United States v. McCoy, 323 F.3d 1114 (9th Cir. 2003) (divided court).

[33.2] *McCoy*, 323 F.3d at 1115.

[33.3] *Id.* at 1133 (Trott, C.J., dissenting). *See also* United States v. Smith, 2005 WL 628686 (11th Cir. 2005), at * ___ (reversing child pornography conviction of defendant whose "noneconmic, purely intrastate criminal activity" had no demonstrable substantial effect on interstate commerce).

[33.4] United States v. Selseth, 2004 WL 603461 (N.D. Ill. 2004) (dismissing child pornography indictment against defendant alleged to have possessed five images of minor where only connection to interstate commerce was that the scan card or computer disk at some point had traveled in interstate commerce); United States v. Matthews, 2004 WL

199298 (N.D. Ala. 2004) (dismissing indictment of defendant who produced video with 16-year-old girlfriend, for noncommercial purposes and without intention to sell or distribute the tape; federal child pornography statutes unconstitutional "*as applied to* simple *intra*-state production and possession of child pornography, or visual depictions of a minor engaging in sexually explicit conduct, when such images and visual depictions were not mailed, shipped, or transported in interstate or foreign commerce"); United States v. Jeronimo-Bautista, 2004 WL 1219663 (D. Utah 2004) (refusing to apply federal child pornography statute where only connection to interstate commerce was film and camera that was manufactured out of state and had crossed state lines into Utah at some point). *But see* United States v. Mugan, 394 F.3d 1016, 1024 (8th Cir. 2005) (upholding child pornography conviction of defendant whose pictures were stored on a digital memory card that had traveled via interstate commerce; images placed on a medium "which would permit their immediate and widespread dissemination over the internet"); United States v. Colburn, 2004 WL 2943373 (5th Cir.) (Dec. 17, 2004) (rejecting constitutional challenge to federal child pornography statute conviction based on out-of-state manufacture of camera and film); United States v. Andrews, 2004 WL 1944137 (6th Cir. 2004), at *4 (evidence in record establishing nexus between activity and interstate commerce sufficient to support conviction where pen camera purchased to take pornographic pictures was made in China and computer on which pornographic pictures displayed purchased in New Jersey). *See generally* Fischer, Between Scylla and Charybdis: The Disagreement Among the Federal Circuits Over Whether Federal Law Criminalizing the Intrastate Possession of Child Pornography Violates the Commerce Clause, 10 Nexus 99 (2005).

[33.5] Gonzales v. Raich, _____ U.S. _____, 125 S. Ct. 2195 (2005) (divided court).

[34] 18 U.S.C. § 1951.

[35] *See, e.g.*, United States v. Wiley, 2005 WL 1285712 (6th Cir.) (May 26, 2005) (unpublished), *5 (robbery of businesses selling goods in interstate commerce sufficient to sustain conviction); United States v. Urban, 404 F.3d 754, 768-769 (3d Cir. 2005) (rejecting constitutional challenge to Hobbs Act conviction); United States v. Hopson, 2004 WL 1147257 (6th Cir.) (May 20, 2004) (unpublished), at *11 (*de minimis* effect on interstate commerce sufficient to sustain Hobbs Act conviction for robbery of a business); United States v. Lynch, 367 F.3d 1148, 1158 (9th Cir. 2004) (per curiam) (sustaining Hobbs Act conviction of defendants who participated in an illegal drug-trafficking business and lured robbery victim across state lines to rob him of drugs and money; held, actions had a direct effect on interstate commerce); United States v. Moore, 2004 WL 758435 (7th Cir. 2004), at *3 ("no more than a *de minimis* effect on interstate commerce need be shown so long as the entity itself belongs to a class of businesses that in the aggregate has a substantial effect on interstate commerce"); *id.* at *3 ("Although we have recognized the irony in applying the Hobbs Act effectively to protect unlawful businesses, insofar as it bars acts of extortion against interstate criminal enterprises like drug trafficking, we have upheld its application in those situations nonetheless" despite "recent trend away from the federalization of crimes that are also subject to state prosecution"); United States v. Rodriquez, 360 F.3d 949, 956-57 (9th Cir. 2004) (holding that robbery of drug traffickers equivalent to robbery of an interstate business and thus did not have to satisfy heightened circuit requirement for Hobbs Act when robbery of individual occurred; "Because the trafficking of narcotics is a federally-regulated activity implicating interstate commerce, we conclude that federal jurisdiction exists to apply the Hobbs Act to conspiracies involving the theft of cocaine from narcotics traffickers"); United States v. Capozzi, 347 F.3d 327, 334-337 (1st Cir. 2003) (Hobbs Act conviction valid as applied to defendant who attempted to extort

price of recently purchased used car from car dealer); United States v. Curtis, 344 F.3d 1057,1069-1071 (10th Cir. 2003) (evidence that businesses robbed by defendant received most of their merchandise from interstate commerce sufficient to sustain Hobbs Act conviction on "depletion-of-assets" theory); United States v. Williams, 342 F.3d 350, 353-355 (4th Cir. 2003) (concluding that robbery of drug dealer of $1,000 was sufficient to sustain Hobbs Act conviction; "the Hobbs Act's jurisdictional predicate . . . requires only a minimal effect on commerce"); United States v. Clausen, 2003 WL 1550717 (3d Cir.) (Mar. 26, 2003) (unpublished) (rejecting challenge to Hobbs Act conviction of retail businesses and massage parlors); United States v. Dupree, 323 F.3d 480, 485-86 (6th Cir. 2003) (rejecting challenge to Hobbs Act conviction for robbery of armored car); United States v. Rubio, 321 F.3d 517, 523-524 (5th Cir. 2003) (rejecting challenge to Hobbs Act conviction for scheme to bribe state officials for favorable disposition of criminal cases); United States v. Taniguchi, 2002 WL 31371978 (6th Cir.) (Oct. 11, 2002) (unpublished), at *5 (rejecting challenge to Hobbs Act convictions; robbery of business engaged in interstate commerce sufficient to meet *de minimis* effect on interstate required under statute); United States v. Rodriguez, ___ F.3d ___, 2002 WL 31732265 (3d Cir.) (Dec. 6, 2002) (unpublished), at *9 (rejecting challenges to federal carjacking and Hobbs Act convictions; evidence car moved in interstate commerce sufficient; potential depletion of armored car companies assets sufficient to sustain robbery conviction); United States v. Fabian, 312 F.3d 550 (2d Cir. 2002) (divided court) (planned robbery of alleged loan shark and drug dealer sufficient to trigger Hobbs Act where alleged "drug proceeds" the target of robbery); *but see id.* (Parker, C.J., dissenting in part) (finding evidence insufficient to sustain Hobbs Act conviction; "evidence at trial showed the goal of the robbery was not to obtain drug proceeds at all"); United States v. McFarland, 311 F.3d 376 (5th Cir. 2002) (en banc) (affirming, by an equally divided court, Hobbs Act conviction of man convicted of robbing convenience stores); *but see id.* at 376 (Garwood, C.J., dissenting); *id.* at 410 (Higginbotham, C.J., dissenting); United States v. Jamison, 299 F.3d 114, 117-121 (2d Cir. 2002) (divided court) (sustaining Hobbs Act conviction of home invasion robbery of drug dealer who commingled funds from retail store owned by victim with proceeds from victim's cocaine sales; depletion of assets theory); *but see id.* (Jacobs, C.J., dissenting) (would reverse the conviction because robbery of individual, as opposed to that of business, involved; would hold that Hobbs Act jurisdiction cannot be sustained on the *de minimis* on interstate commerce caused by robbery of individual at his home); United States v. Elias, 285 F.3d 183, 188 (2d Cir. 2002) (holding that in Hobbs Act prosecutions, government need only prove *de minimis*; fact that neighborhood grocery store bought and sold goods produced in interstate commerce sufficient); United States v. Morris, 247 F.3d 1084, 1085-1086 (10th Cir. 2001) (*de minimis* effect sufficient to sustain Hobbs Act conviction); United States v. Malone, 222 F.3d 1286, 1294 (10th Cir. 2000) (upholding Hobbs Act conviction of defendants charged with robbing gas station; *de minimis* impact on interstate commerce sufficient to sustain conviction); United States v. Jennings, 195 F.3d 795 (5th Cir. 1999) (allowing unconnected intrastate acts to be aggregated to "substantially affect" interstate commerce and sustain a conviction under the Hobbs Act); United States v. Taylor, 176 F.3d 331 (6th Cir. 1999) (same, upholding Hobbs Act); United States v. Guerra, 164 F.3d 1358 (11th Cir. 1999) (same). Given the weight of precedent, courts are beginning to hold that failure to raise constitutional challenges to Hobbs Act convictions does not constitute ineffective assistance of counsel. *See* United States v. Fields, 2004 WL 3037960 (D. Kan. 2004), at *5 (failure to raise challenge to

Hobbs Act conviction and to urge plea of guilty in light of "well-established law . . . that drug trafficking affects interstate commerce and that robbing a drug dealer satisfies" the Hobbs Act not ineffective assistance of counsel); Meeks v. United States, 2003 WL 1989653 (N.D. Ill.) (April 30, 2002) (failure to raise constitutional challenge to Hobbs Act not ineffective assistance of counsel given circuit precedent); United States v. Stewart, 2002 WL 1162419 (D. Kan.) (April 23, 2002) (unpublished) (no ineffective assistance of counsel for failure to raise argument that Hobbs Act didn't apply due to insufficient nexus between activity and interstate commerce where circuit had rejected such an argument previously); *cf.* §§ 5.04[H][1][a] (discussing felon-in-possession challenges) & 5.04[H][2] (challenges to federal drug laws). *But see* United States v. Chance, 306 F.3d 356, 373-376 (6th Cir. 2002) (upholding as applied challenge to RICO conviction, reversing one count of Hobbs Act conviction; insufficient evidence connecting activity to interstate commerce); United States v. Hickman, 179 F.3d 230, 231 (5th Cir. 1999) (en banc) (Higginbotham, C.J., dissenting) (dissenting from the decision of equally divided en banc panel affirming Hobbs Act convictions of defendants who committed several robberies in Texas; arguing that *Lopez* does not permit aggregation of unrelated crimes in order to meet "substantially affects" test). For an extensive discussion of post- *Lopez* Hobbs Act challenges, *see* McGrail, Note, The Hobbs Act After *Lopez*, 41 B.C. L. Rev. 941, 959-966 (2000).

[36] *See* Brown, Constitutionalizing the Federal Criminal Law Debate: *Morrison, Jones*, and the ABA, 2001 U. Ill. L. J. 983, 1019 ("Although many courts have rejected *Lopez* based attacks on the de minimis approach, it is clearly at variance with the spirit of that case. Moreover, it also seems at variance with the notion that one of the potential advantages of jurisdictional elements is that they can serve as a means of identifying the cases where federal intervention is necessary."). For more insightful commentary on Hobbs Act cases, and Commerce Clause challenges to many of the federal statutes discussed here, *see* Bradley, Federalism and the Federal Criminal Law, 55 Hastings L.J. 573 (2004).

[37] This is known as the "depletion of assets" theory. Its application can result in some surprising convictions. *See, e.g.*, United States v. Marrero, 299 F.3d 653, 654-656 (7th Cir. 2002) (Posner, C.J.) (upholding Hobbs Act conviction of drug dealers convicted of robbing others of other dealers by offering to sell them flour; "there is an element of paradox in a prosecution for obstructing *illegal* commerce . . . [b]ut . . . any argument that the Hobbs Act, or Congress's commerce power . . . does not reach robberies that disrupt rather than promote illegal trafficking in drugs is foreclosed by the case law . . ."; had defendants not robbed dealers of money, dealers would have used money to buy drugs elsewhere); United States v. Bailey, 227 F.3d 792, 797-798 (7th Cir. 2000) (upholding conviction for robbery of cocaine dealer under "depletion of assets theory," *viz.*, "the government asserts that cocaine must enter Illinois through interstate commerce. The result is . . . that the robbery of cocaine dealers depleted the assets available to purchase cocaine through interstate commerce, thereby creating the requisite effect on interstate commerce"); United States v. Jackson, 2000 WL 1745284 (N.D. Ill.) (Nov. 28, 2000) (unpublished), at *5 (prosecution of police officers for extortion of drug dealers under Hobbs Act permissible under "depletion of assets" theory; "[d]efendants' extortion of cocaine dealers depleted assets available to purchase cocaine through interstate commerce"). Similar reasoning has been employed to uphold the federal bank robbery statute, 18 U.S.C. § 2113. *See* United States v. Spinello, 265 F.3d 150, (3d Cir. 2001). The court

found that bank robbery was "economic activity" because the bank robber is motivated "by his or her own economic gain." *Spinello*, 265 F.3d at 156. Moreover, it continued, "wholly aside from whether FDIC insurance will ultimately kick in, the victim bank and its depositor suffer immediate economic losses as well as the disruption to their . . . abilities to engage in commerce, interstate or otherwise . . ." *Id.*

[38] United States v. Lynch, 282 F.3d 1049, 1055 (9th Cir. 2002) (holding that, to secure conviction of defendant under the Hobbs Act for robbery of individual, as opposed to a business, government must prove (1) that defendant stole from person "directly and customarily engaged in interstate commerce"; (2) that defendant thereby created a likelihood that the assets of an entity engaged in interstate commerce would be depleted; or (3) that defendants either victimized a large number of persons or took a large enough sum that there could be cumulative effect on interstate commerce). *But see* United States v. Liburd, 291 F. Supp. 2d 383, 365-386 (D.V.I. 2003) (attempted extortion of individual sufficient to support Hobbs Act conviction if attempt depleted the victim's assets and would have "some *de minimis* effect on interstate commerce"); *see also* United States v. McCormack, 371 F.3d 22, 28 (1st Cir. 2004) (robbery of individual where individual kidnapped and $100,000 extorted from him with instructions to liquidate assets to evade federal reporting requirements sufficient to support Hobbs Act conviction; "[a] reasonable jury could have concluded that there was a 'realistic probability' that the kidnapping would have a de minimis effect on interstate commerce.").

[39] United States v. Chance, 306 F.3d 356, 373-376 (6th Cir. 2002) (upholding as applied challenge to RICO conviction; reversing one count of Hobbs Act conviction; insufficient evidence connecting activity to interstate commerce); United States v. Peterson, 236 F.3d 848, 854-855 (7th Cir. 2001) (reversing Hobbs Act conviction; government failed to produce evidence that illegal drug business was "interstate business" to bring within scope of federal statute); United States v. Wang, 222 F.3d 234, 238-239 (6th Cir. 2000) (reversing Hobbs Act conviction of defendant convicted of robbing individual, noting attenuated connection to interstate commerce where criminal act directed not toward *businesses* but merely individuals; "upholding federal jurisdiction over [defendant's] offense would . . . acknowledge a general police power with respect to the crimes of robbery and extortion," contrary to the admonitions in *Morrison*). *But see* United States v. Jamison, 299 F.3d 114, 117-121 (2d Cir. 2002) (divided court) (sustaining Hobbs Act conviction of home invasion robbery of drug dealer who commingled funds from retail store owned by victim with proceeds from victim's cocaine sales; depletion of assets theory); *but see id.* (Jacobs, C.J., dissenting) (would reverse the conviction because robbery of individual, as opposed to that of business, involved; would hold that Hobbs Act jurisdiction cannot be sustained on the *de minimis* on interstate commerce caused by robbery of individual at his home).

[40] 18 U.S.C. §228.

[41] *See, e.g.*, United States v. Bailey, 115 F.3d 1222, 1226 (5th Cir. 1997); United States v. Sage, 92 F.3d 101 (2d Cir. 1996); United States v. MacSweeney, 2000 WL 1634400 (S.D.N.Y.) (Oct. 31, 2000); *see also* United States v. Klinzing, 315 F.3d 803, 806-808 (7th Cir. 2003) (rejecting challenge to Deadbeat Parents Punishment Act; interstate child support obligation is a "thing" in interstate commerce, susceptible to congressional regulation).

[42] United States v. Faasse, 227 F.3d 660 (6th Cir. 2000), *rev'd* 265 F.3d 475 (6th Cir. 2001) (en banc) (divided court); United States v. King, 2001 WL 111278 (S.D.N.Y.) (Feb. 8, 2001), *rev'd* 276 F.3d 109 (2d Cir. 2002).

[43] *Faasse*, 227 F.3d at 664.

[44] *Id.* at 669-671.

[45] *Id.* at 671.

[46] *Id.* The court did note that the Full Faith and Credit Clause of the Constitution meant that Congress could otherwise assist states in the collection of their own enforcement orders. *Id.* at 672.

[47] *King*, 2001 WL 111278, at *5.

[48] United States v. Faasse, 265 F.3d 475 (6th Cir. 2001) (en banc) (divided court).

[49] *Id.* at 481.

[50] *See id.* at 481-482 & n.5. Judge Batchelder, who wrote the original *Faasse* opinion, filed a dissent in which three other judges joined. She reiterated her analysis, concluding that the Commerce Clause did not authorize the passage of the CSRA. *Id.* at 494 (Batchelder, C.J., dissenting).

[51] United States v. King, 276 F.3d 109 (2d Cir. 2002).

[52] *Id.* at 113. *See also* United States v. Rich, 336 F.3d 293 (4th Cir. 2003) (per curiam) (declining to revisit prior decision upholding Child Support Recovery Act in light of *Morrison*); United States v. Monts, 311 F.3d 993, 996-997 (10th Cir. 2002) (rejecting challenge to Child Support Recovery Act; CSRA contained jurisdictional nexus and explicit findings from Congress; reaffirming prior, pre-*Morrison* case); United States v. Pillor, 2005 WL 1126791 (N.D. Cal. 2005), at *1 (rejecting Commerce Clause challenge to CSRA); Harding v. Harding, 121 Cal. Rptr.2d 450, 454-456 (Ct. App. Cal. 2002) (rejecting Commerce Clause challenge to Full Faith and Credit Child Support Act; child support payments "substantially affect" interstate commerce).

[53] Gibbs v. Babbitt, 214 F.3d 483 (4th Cir. 2000) (divided court), *cert. denied sub nom.* Gibbs v. Norton, 121 S. Ct. 1081 (2001).

[54] *Gibbs*, 214 F.3d at 492.

[55] *Id.*

[56] *See id.* at 493-495.

[57] *Id.* at 497. Judge Luttig, the author of the appeals court opinion in *Brzonkala*, dissented. He complained that the majority's conclusions [of substantial effect on tourism, scientific research, and possible resurgence of the fur trade] are not even arguably sustainable under *Lopez*, *Morrison*, and *Brzonkala*, much less for the reasons cobbled together by the majority. . . . " *Id.* at 507 (Luttig, C.J., dissenting). He further accused the majority of actually adopting the views of those in the dissent in *Lopez* and *Morrison*, and for treating those cases as aberrations. *Id.* at 508-510 (Luttig, C.J., dissenting).

[58] *See, e.g.*, GDF Realty Investments Ltd. v. Norton, 169 F. Supp. 2d 648, 660 (S.D. Tex. 2001) (rejecting argument that provisions of Endangered Species Act prohibiting the taking of protected species, which interferes with plan to develop property, violates the Commerce Clause because endangered species on property did not affect interstate commerce), *aff'd* 326 F.3d 622, 627-641 (5th Cir. 2003) (rejecting challenge to ESA taking provision); Rancho Viejo, LLC v. Norton, 2001 WL 1223502 (D.D.C.) (Aug. 20, 2001), at *6-*10 (concluding that Endangered Species Act provision as applied to halt housing development did not violate the Commerce Clause), *aff'd* 323 F.3d 1062, 1068-1077 (D.C. Cir. 2003). For rejections of challenges to other federal environmental statutes, *see* Nebraska v. Environmental Protection Agency, 331 F.3d 995, 998 (D.C. Cir. 2003) (rejecting facial Commerce Clause challenge to EPA order regarding arsenic levels in drinking water; fact that EPA regulation applies to water that is sold in interstate

commerce sufficient to defeat facial attack); United States v. Deaton, 2003 WL 21357305 (4th Cir.) (June 12, 2003), at *6 (rejecting challenge to EPA jurisdiction over wetlands ditch that flowed into navigable waterway; regulation of navigable waterways permissible under congressional power to regulate channels of interstate commerce); Freier v. Westinghouse Elec. Corp., 303 F.3d 176, 200-203 (2d Cir. 2002) (upholding portion of federal environmental clean-up statute, CERCLA, against Commerce Clause challenge); United States v. Ho, 311 F.3d 589, 596-604 (5th Cir. 2002) (upholding Clean Air Act and regulations related to asbestos removal as applied to removal company that failed to comply with both; extensive analysis of *Lopez/Morrison*); United States v. Domenic Lombardi Realty, Inc., 204 F. Supp. 2d 318, 325-329 (D.R.I. 2002) (upholding CERCLA against Commerce Clause challenge; intrastate disposal of hazardous wastes substantially affects interstate commerce); FD & P Enterprises, Inc. v. United States Army Corps of Engineers, 239 F. Supp. 2d 509, 518 (D.N.J. 2003) (rejecting Commerce Clause challenge to Corps assertion of jurisdiction over wetlands fed by nonnavigable waterway).

[59] ?*See supra note* 53. For commentary on *Gibbs*, *see* Fitzgerald, Seeing Red: *Gibbs v. Babbitt*, 13 Vill. Envt'l L.J. 1 (2002); Bowlin & Brewer, Note, *Gibbs v. Babbitt*: Red Wolf Protection Under the Endangered Species Act Leaps Beyond the "Outer Boundaries" of the Commerce Clause, 23 Pub. Land & Res. L. Rev. 221 (2002). For their part, scholars argue that Congress still has plenty of room to protect endangered species under the Commerce Clause. *See, e.g.*, Mank, Protecting Intrastate Threatened Species: Does the Endangered Species Act Encroach on Traditional State Authority and Exceed the Outer Limits of the Commerce Clause?, 36 Ga. L. Rev. 723 (2002) (arguing that *Lopez* and *Morrison* allow for extensive congressional protection of endangered species, even if located intrastate); Nagle, The Commerce Clause Meets the Dehli Sands Flower-Loving Fly, 97 Mich. L. Rev. 174 (1998); Brignac, Recent Development, The Commerce Clause Justification of Endangered Species Protection: *Gibbs v. Babbitt*, 79 N.C. L. Rev. 873 (2001); Scalero, Note, The Endangered Species Act's Application to Isolated Species: A Substantial Effect on Interstate Commerce?, 3 Chap. L. Rev. 317 (2000); White, Comment, The Endangered Species Act's Precarious Perch: A Constitutional Analysis Under the Commerce Clause and the Treaty Power, 27 Ecology L.Q. 215 (2000).

[60] 18 U.S.C. §248(a)(1). *See, e.g.*, Hoffman v. Hunt, 923 F. Supp. 2d 791, 807 (W.D.N.C. 1996) (striking down FACE under the Commerce Clause), *rev'd* 126 F.3d 575 (4th Cir. 1997).

[61] United States v. Gregg, 226 F.3d 253 (3d Cir. 2000) (divided court), *cert. denied* 121 S. Ct. 1600 (2001). Section 248(c)(1) authorizes civil suits for injunctive relief and damages against parties that violate the Act. *See also* United States v. Kopp, 2005 WL 839672 (W.D.N.Y. 2005), at *12 (rejecting Commerce Clause challenge to FACE); Norton v. Reno, 2000 WL 1769580 (W.D. Mich. 2000), at *5 (upholding FACE; concluding that the activity regulated was "economic" and that "[r]eproductive health facilities have a direct and substantial affect [*sic*] on interstate commerce"), *aff'd sub nom.* Norton v. Ashcroft, 298 F.3d 547, 555-559 (6th Cir. 2002).

[62] *Gregg*, 226 F.3d at 262, 263.

[63] *Id.* at 268-269 (Weis, C.J., dissenting).

[64] *Id.* at 269-270.

[65] *See id.* at 270-271 (Weis, C.J., dissenting). For a similar argument that the use of RICO to prosecute anti-abortion activists exceeds Congress's commerce power, *see*

Oestreicher, *Scheidler* Meets *Morrison* (at the Entrance to a Health Clinic), 35 Creighton L. Rev. 693 (2002).

[65.1] United States v. Bird, 279 F. Supp. 2d 827, 837-838 (S.D. Tex. 2003).

[66] 18 U.S.C. § 844(i); Jones v. United States, 529 U.S. 848, 120 S. Ct. 1904 (2000).

[67] For a discussion of *Jones* and citations to subsequent lower court cases, *see supra* § 3.13[B].

[68] *See, e.g.*, Westchester Day School v. Mamaroneck, 280 F. Supp. 2d 230, 237-238 (S.D.N.Y. 2003) (rejecting Commerce Clause challenge to RLUIPA); Johnson v. Martin, 223 F. Supp. 2d 820, 827-830 (W.D. Mich. 2002) (upholding portions of the Religious Land Use and Institutionalized Persons Act, 42 U.S.C. §§ 2000cc-2000cc-5 that limit state and local land use policies affecting religious organizations against a Commerce Clause challenge); Freedom Baptist Church of Delaware Co. v. Middletown, 204 F. Supp. 2d 857 (E.D. Pa. 2002) (upholding RLUIPA against a Commerce Clause challenge; holding that "insofar as state or local authorities 'substantially burden' the economic activity of religious organizations, Congress has ample authority to act under the Commerce Clause"); Mayweathers v. Terhune, 2001 WL 804140 (E.D. Cal.) (July 2, 2001), at *8 (upholding Religious Land Use and Institutionalized Persons Act against, *inter alia*, Commerce Clause challenge; statute possessed jurisdictional nexus that statutes in *Lopez* and *Morrison* lacked), *aff'd* 314 F.3d 1062 (9th Cir. 2002) (upholding RLUIPA against, *inter alia*, Spending Clause and Establishment Clause challenges). *But see* Elsinore Christian Center v. Lake Elsinore, 291 F. Supp. 2d 1083, 1103–1104 (C.D. Cal. 2003) (holding RLUIPA to be unconstitutional exercise of congressional commerce power because it "regulates the way States regulate private parties"); Madison v. Riter, 240 F. Supp. 2d 566, 582 (W.D. Va. 2003) (striking down RLUIPA as violation of Establishment Clause); *see also* United States v. Johnson, 2001 WL 1313789 (N.D. Ill.) (Oct. 25, 2001), at *2 (rejecting constitutional challenge to federal statute prohibiting production and transfer of false identification documents; holding that presence of jurisdictional nexus insulated statute from challenge under *Lopez* and *Morrison*). *See generally* Guidry, Comment, If At First You Don't Succeed . . . : Can the Commerce and Spending Clauses Support Congress's Latest Attempt at Religious Freedom Legislation?, 32 Cumb. L. Rev. 419 (2001-2002). Doubts are still raised about new or proposed federal legislation. *See, e.g.*, Virelli, "Federalism Whether They Want It or Not": The New Commerce Clause Doctrine and the Future of Federal Civil Rights Legislation After *United States v. Morrison*, 3 U. Pa. J. Const. L. 926 (2001); Hasenstab, Comment, Is Hate a Form of Commerce?: The Questionable Constitutionality of Federal "Hate Crime" Legislation, 45 St. Louis U. L. J. 973 (2001); Hussein, Comment, The Growing Debate on Medical Marijuana: Federal Power vs. States Rights, 37 Cal. W. L. Rev. 369 (2001).

For recent — and rejected — constitutional challenges to a mixed grill of congressional statutes not discussed above, *see* United States v. Martinez-Esparza, 2004 WL 2965508, at *1 (5th Cir. 2004) (rejecting challenge to federal carjacking statute); United States v. Robinson, 389 F.3d 582, 593-594 (6th Cir. 2004) (rejecting Commerce Clause challenge to federal bank robbery statute); United States v. Bruce, 405 F.3d 145, 147-148 (3d Cir. 2005) (upholding federal loan-sharking statute as applied to persons who, in the course of attempting to recover money loaned to individuals for purpose of purchasing drugs, beat and tortured one of the individuals; "the statute will reach individuals such as Bruce and Mussare, who act solely in an intrastate context and are not members of organized crime or loan sharks in the traditional sense."); United

States v. Manna, 2004 WL 491873 (3d Cir.) (March 11, 2004) (unpublished), at *4 (rejecting Commerce Clause challenge to federal bank robbery statute); United States v. Khilchenko, 324 F.3d 917 (7th Cir. 2003) (rejecting challenge to federal loan sharking statute); United States v. Mississippi Dept. Pub. Safety, 321 F.3d 495, 499-501 (5th Cir. 2003) (rejecting argument that the Americans with Disabilities Act, as applied to states, exceeded congressional commerce power); Freilich v. Upper Chesapeake Health, Inc., 313 F.3d 205, 213 (4th Cir. 2002) (rejecting Commerce Clause challenge to federal Health Care Quality Improvement Act; finding that hospitals "are regularly engaged in interstate commerce, performing services for out-of-state patients, and generating revenues from out-of-state sources"); United States v. Whited, 311 F.3d 259, 268-272 (3d Cir. 2002) (rejecting challenge to 18 U.S.C. §669, which prohibits embezzling from a health care provider; theft in connection with health care "is economic in nature," jurisdictional nexus present, presence of findings describing effect support conclusion "that Congress [had] a rational basis for" criminalizing "even seemingly minor local thefts or embezzlements in connection with health care"; in addition, statute did not create risk of eliminating distinction between what is national and what is local); United States v. Turner, 301 F.3d 541, 547-548 (7th Cir. 2002) (rejecting challenge to federal statute criminalizing embezzlement from insurance company affecting interstate commerce; defendant's conduct "impeded the channels of interstate commerce and the statute properly reached his conduct").

[69] *See, e.g.*, Denning & Reynolds, *supra* note 111; Reynolds & Denning, Lower Court Readings of Lopez, or What If the Supreme Court Held a Constitutional Revolution and No One Came?, 2000 Wis. L. Rev. 369.

§5.05 FEDERAL FORBEARANCE: INTRODUCTION

[B] Statutory Use of Term "Commerce" in Restricted Sense

Page 5-38, add to the end of note 122:

For a case dismissing a claim brought under the FLSA on the ground that the business against which the complaint was lodged did not fall within the statute's scope, *see* Lamont v. Frank Soup Bowl, Inc., 2001 WL 521815 (S.D.N.Y. 2001), at *4 ("Neither Plaintiff nor his employer engaged in the type of commercial activity Congress chose to regulate [under the FLSA].").

Page 5-38, add to the end of note 124:

The federal arson statute 18 U.S.C. §844(i) requires that structures destroyed be "used in" interstate commerce. Following the Supreme Court's decision in *Jones*, lower courts have seized upon this congressionally imposed limitation to distinguish the arson statute from other, more broadly worded federal criminal statutes. *See, e.g.*, United States v. Malone, 222 F.3d 1286, 1294 (10th Cir. 2000) (distinguishing arson statute in *Jones* from Hobbs Act, which does not require that property subject to extortion or robbery be "used in" interstate commerce); United States v. Napier, 233 F.3d 394, 399-402 (6th Cir. 2000) (rejecting challenge to 18 U.S.C. § 922(g)(8), which prohibits person subject to certain court orders from possessing any firearm "in or affecting" interstate commerce; *Jones* in-applicable because statute does not require "use" of gun in interstate commerce).

Page 5-41, add to the end of note 130:

The Court has, however, developed certain canons of construction to aid it in interpreting statutes in an effort to strike the proper balance between state and federal power. For a recent application of these presumptions to reverse an application of the federal arson statute to a private, owner-occupied residence, not otherwise used in interstate commerce, *see* Jones v. United States, 529 U.S. 848, 120 S. Ct. 1904 (2000).

[C] Static or Dynamic Chronological Coverage?

Page 5-41, add text and note to the end of section [C]:

At least one state supreme court has interpreted the *Lopez* decision to restrict the reach of the Federal Arbitration Act, whose language the U.S. Supreme Court had interpreted to apply to transactions "affecting" interstate commerce.[133.1] In *Citizens Bank v. Alafabco* (2003), however, the Court rejected this "improperly cramped" view of congressional power — which required individual transactions standing alone to substantially affected interstate commerce — and held that the proper inquiry for ascertaining the reach of the FAA was whether "if in the aggregate the economic activity in question would represent 'a general practice . . . subject to federal control'" by substantially affecting interstate commerce.[133.2]

[133.1] *See* Sisters of the Visitation v. Cochran Plastering Co., 775 So. 2d 759 (Ala. 2000) (divided court) (holding that the FAA did not apply to a contract between in-state residents for work performed entirely within the bounds of the state). For commentary on *Sisters of the Visitation, see* Brown, State Court Attempts to Limit the Applicability of the Federal Arbitration Act in a Post-*Lopez* World, 56 U. Miami L. Rev. 1051 (2002); Richmond, Comment, *Sisters of the Visitation v. Cochran Plastering Co.:* Earnest Federalism or Reconstructive Defiance to the Federal Arbitration Act?, 25 Am. J. Trial Advoc. 633 (2002).

[133.2] Citizens Bank v. Alafabco, Inc., 539 U.S. 52, 56, 123 S. Ct. 2037, 2040 (2003) (per curiam) (quoting Mandeville Island Farms, Inc. v. American Crystal Sugar Co., 334 U.S. 219, 236, 68 S. Ct. 996, 1006 (1948)).

[D] Excluded Persons, Facilities, or Services

Page 5-42, insert at end of note 135:

Cf. Johnson v. Apna Ghar, Inc., 330 F.3d 999, 1004 (7th Cir. 2003) (employer with extensive out-of-state commercial contacts satisfies Title VII's definition of "employer" where defined as "person engaged in an industry affecting interstate commerce").

§5.06 FEDERAL PREEMPTION: INTRODUCTION

[A] The Birth of Preemption

Page 5-44, add to the end of note 144:

; Spence & Murray, The Law, Economics, and Politics of Federal Preemption Jurisprudence: A Quantitative Analysis, 87 Cal. L. Rev. 1125, 1127-1134 (1999) (discussing *Gibbons* and the birth of preemption).

[B] Preemption Today

Page 5-45, add to the end of note 148:

; Crosby v. Nat'l Foreign Trade Council, 530 U.S. 363, 120 S. Ct. 2288 (2000) (striking down state law restricting state business opportunities of entities that do business, directly or indirectly, with Burma because state law goes farther than federal sanctions); Miami Light Project v. Miami-Dade Co., 97 F. Supp. 2d 1174, 1180-1181 (S.D. Fla. 2000) (granting preliminary injunction against local ordinance restricting the transaction of county business with persons or entities that do business with Cuba on, *inter alia*, likelihood that plaintiffs could prevail on merits of claim that because ordinance goes farther than federal embargo, and federal action preempts local action); *see* Puentes, Comment, The Politics of Music and Film: The Validity of a Local Government's Cultural Embargo on Cuba, 31 U. Miami Inter-Am. L. Rev. 235 (2000) (concluding that the ordinance violates the Commerce Clause, is preempted by federal law, and offends the First Amendment).

Page 5-46, add to the end of note 149:

A helpful schematic illustrating the different forms of express and implied preemption can be found in Weiland, Comment, Federal and State Preemption of Environmental Law: A Critical Analysis, 24 Harv. Envt'l L. Rev. 237 (2000). For a critique of the Supreme Court's recent approaches to preemption, *see* Nelson, Preemption, 86 Va. L. Rev. 225 (2000).

Page 5-46, add to the end of note 151:

For other recent discussions of preemption, *see, for example*, Dinh, Reassessing the Law of Preemption, 88 Geo. L.J. 2085 (2000); Donze, Legislating Comity: Can Congress Enforce Federalism Constraints Through Restrictions on Preemption Doctrine?, 4 N.Y.U. J. Legisl. & Pub. Pol'y 239 (2001); Goldsmith, Statutory Foreign Affairs Preemption, 2000 Sup. Ct. Rev. 175. For judicial acknowledgement of the preemption classifications' fluidity, *see* Geier v. American Honda Motor Co., Inc., 529 U.S. 861, 873, 120 S. Ct. 1913, 1921 (2000) (divided court) ("The Court has not previously driven a legal wedge — only a terminological one — between 'conflicts' that prevent or frustrate the accomplishment of a federal objective and 'conflicts' that make it 'impossible' for private parties to comply with both state and federal law. . . . [I]t has said that both forms of conflicting state law are 'nullified' by the Supremacy Clause . . . and it has assumed that Congress would not want either kind of conflict.").

[C] Express Preemption

Page 5-47, add to the end of note 155:

For a similar example, involving the Federal Food, Drug, and Cosmetic Act, *see* Goya de Puerto Rico, Inc. v. Santiago, 59 F. Supp. 2d 274, 279-280 (D.P.R. 1999) (express terms of federal statute preempted Puerto Rico regulations regarding labeling of imported pigeon peas); *see also* A.G.G. Enterprises, Inc. v. Washington Co., 2000 WL 361892 (D. Or. 2000), at *5-*8 (slip opinion) (concluding that portions of local regulation of solid waste disposal were preempted by portion of the Federal Aviation Administration Authorization Act of 1994), *rev'd*, 281 F.3d 1324 (9th Cir. 2001); CSX Transportation, Inc. v. Plymouth, 92 F. Supp. 2d 643 (E.D. Mich. 2000) (local regulation limiting the amount of time that a train could block a grade crossing preempted by Federal Railway Safety Act and the Interstate Commerce Commission Termination Act).

Note, too, that express preemption does not necessarily have to clear the way for a federal regulatory regime. In *Reno v. Condon*, 528 U.S. 141, 120 S. Ct. 666 (2000), a unanimous Court upheld the federal Driver's Privacy Protection Act, which prohibited states from selling driver's license data in interstate commerce. *See generally* Preiser, Note, Staking Out the Border Between Comandeering and Conditional Preemption: Is the Driver's Privacy Protection Act Constitutional Under the Tenth Amendment?, 98 Mich. L. Rev. 514 (1999).

Page 5-49, add to the end of note 160:

See also Lindsey v. Tacoma Pierce Co. Health Dept., 195 F.3d 1065 (9th Cir. 1999) (Federal Cigarette Labeling and Advertising Act preempts local ban on outdoor tobacco advertising); *but see* Greater New York Metro. Food Council, Inc. v. Guiliani, 195 F.3d 100 (2d Cir. 1999); Federation of Advertising Indust. Representatives, Inc. v. Chicago, 189 F.3d 633 (7th Cir. 1999) (both holding that federal statute did not ban *all* regulation of outdoor tobacco advertising).

[D] Conflict or Impossibility Preemption

Page 5-50, add to the end of note 163:

More recently, the Court invoked conflict preemption in striking down certain Washington State regulations governing the operation of oil tankers in state water. In *United States v. Locke* (2000), a unanimous Court found that state regulations relating to navigation watch procedures, English language skills, training and casualty reporting were preempted by similar Coast Guard regulations promulgated under the authority of a 1972 Act. United States v. Locke, 529 U.S. 89, 120 S. Ct. 1135 (2000). *Locke* was a sequel of sorts to the Court's 1978 decision in *Ray v. Atlantic Richfield Co.*, 435 U.S. 151, 98 S. Ct. 988 (1978) (divided court) (holding that Washington State's regulations regarding tanker design and construction preempted; requirements failed under "field preemption" analysis). While many of the regulations were invalidated under a "field preemption" analysis, the Court found that at least one state requirement directly conflicted with Coast Guard regulations. *Locke*, 529 U.S. at 116, 120 S. Ct. at 1152. Shortly after *Locke*, the Court struck down a state boycott aimed at the government of Myanmar (Burma), finding that scope of the restrictions conflicted with a less expansive and more flexible federal sanctions regime. *See* Crosby v. Nat'l Foreign Trade Council, 530 U.S. 363, 120 S. Ct. 2288 (2000). *Crosby* is discussed below; *Locke* is discussed more fully in the following section on field preemption, *see infra* § 5.06[E]. In *Geier v. American Honda Motor Company, Inc.*, 529 U.S. 861, 120 S. Ct. 1913 (2000) (divided court), the Supreme Court held that ordinary conflict preemption principles precluded a state tort action against an automobile manufacturer for failing to equip its automobiles with driver's side airbags, where the manufacturer had complied with a federal vehicle safety standard issued by the Department of Transportation pursuant to the statute. *See Geier*, 529 U.S. at 867, 120 S. Ct. at 1917-1918. For more on *Geier, see infra* § 5.06[D].

See also Bioganic Safety Brands, Inc. v. Ament, 174 F. Supp. 2d 1168, 1175-1178 (D. Colo. 2001) (federal act exempting pesticide from regulation preempted state law regulating labeling of pesticides where exemption from federal regulation contingent upon satisfying requirement regarding label); Algonquin LNG v. Loqa, 79 F. Supp. 2d 49 (D.R.I. 2000) (local zoning ordinance in conflict with federal Natural Gas Act must give way to federal law); *but see* Jones v. Union Pacific Railroad, 79 Cal. App. 4th 1053 (Ct. App. Cal. 1999) (holding that the Interstate Commerce Commission Termination Act and the federal Noise Control Act did not preempt a lawsuit in state court by plaintiff living near a Union Pacific railyard who claimed that employees of the company left diesel engines idling in front of his property, blew train whistles unnecessarily, and engaged in both activities more frequently after plaintiff complained).

Page 5-51, add the following text and notes to the end of section [D]:

More recently, the Supreme Court recently struck down a Massachusetts law aimed at punishing the government of Myanmar (formerly Burma) by preventing companies that did business with Myanmar from doing business with the State.[170.1] The State had lost both in the district court and in the First Circuit Court of Appeals, which held that the

Massachusetts statute was invalid under both the "dormant" foreign affairs power and the dormant Foreign Commerce Clause doctrine.[170.2] A unanimous Supreme Court, by contrast, rested its decision in *Crosby v. National Foreign Trade Council* (2000) on preemption: it held that the State statute was incompatible with the federal sanctions against Myanmar, which had been promulgated just a few months after Massachusetts's.[170.3]

Starting with the proposition that Congress may preempt state law explicitly or implicitly, and a brief explanation of "field" and "impossibility" preemption, Justice Souter settled on "conflict" preemption to bolster the conclusion that "the state Burma law [was] an obstacle to the accomplishment of Congress's full objectives under the federal act" by: (i) interfering with the delegation of discretion to the President necessary to maintain flexibility in the sanctions regime; (ii) sweeping more broadly than the federal sanctions in its scope, both in terms of the parties covered and the range of actions prohibited; and (iii) interfering with the congressional directive to the President "to proceed diplomatically in developing a comprehensive, multilateral strategy towards Burma."[170.4]

Justice Souter noted that "Congress clearly intended the federal act to provide the President with flexible and effective authority over economic sanctions against Burma."[170.5] He characterized as "implausible" the suggestion that Congress would have so empowered the President only "to compromise his effectiveness by deference to every provision of state statute or local ordinance," like that of Massachusetts's, which "impos[ed] a different, state system of economic pressure."[170.6] Different, because "the state statute penalizes some private action that the federal Act . . . may allow, and pulls levers of influence that the federal Act does not reach."[170.7] Congress restricted its sanctions to "United States persons" and imposed a limited sanction against "new investment"; the State statute, on the other hand, "conflicts with federal law at a number of points by penalizing individuals and conduct that Congress . . . explicitly exempted or excluded from sanctions."[170.8]

Finally, the Court found that the State sanctions prevented the President from carrying out Congress's directive, set forth in the federal statute, that he use diplomacy to promote human rights and democracy in Myanmar. The Court found particularly persuasive the fact that "the Executive has consistently represented that the state Act has complicated its dealing with foreign sovereigns and proven an impediment to accomplishing objectives assigned to it by Congress."[170.9] As a result of the

Massachusetts law, formal protests were lodged by Japan, the European Union, and other Asian nations.[170.10]

Two aspects of the *Crosby* case are interesting in light of the Court's other preemption cases. First, the Court dismissed the State's argument that the lack of an express preemption clause implied congressional approval. Justice Souter found this argument "unconvincing," and wrote that "[a] failure to provide for preemption expressly may reflect nothing more than the settled character of implied preemption doctrine that courts will dependably apply, and in any event, the existence of a conflict cognizable under the Supremacy Clause does not depend on express congressional recognition" of that conflict.[170.11] Moreover, unlike in *Florida Lime*, there was no mention of the traditional presumption against preemption when a state exercises its police powers. In a terse footnote, Justice Souter left "for another day a consideration in this context of a presumption against preemption."[170.12] Even assuming, he wrote, that *some* presumption was proper, "the state Act presents a sufficient obstacle to the full accomplishments of Congress's objectives under the federal Act to find it preempted."[170.13]

In *Geier v. American Honda Motor Company, Inc.* (2000), the Supreme Court held that ordinary conflict preemption principles precluded a state tort action against an automobile manufacturer for failing to equip its automobiles with driver's side airbags, where the manufacturer had complied with a federal vehicle safety standard issued by the Department of Transportation pursuant to a federal statute.[170.14] The statute had a saving clause, but the Court concluded that the clause did no more than to "remove[] tort actions from the scope of the express pre-emption clause."[170.15] "Nothing in the language of the saving clause," the Court wrote, "suggests an intent to save state-law tort actions that conflict with federal regulations."[170.16] The motor vehicle safety standard issued by the federal government, the Court found, "deliberately sought variety — a mix of several different passive restraint systems."[170.17] By contrast, the tort claim filed by Geier "depends upon its claim that manufacturers had a duty to install an airbag when they manufactured" the car in question. "Such a state law — *i.e*, a rule of state tort law imposing such a duty — by its terms would have required manufacturers of all similar cars to install airbags rather than other passive restraint systems. . . . It thereby would have presented an obstacle to the variety and mix of devices that the federal regulation sought."[170.18] Thus, the state tort action had to give way to the federal safety standard.

Justice Stevens, for the dissenters, argued that Honda had "not demonstrated that allowing a common-law no-airbag claim to go forward would impose an obligation on manufacturers that directly and irreconcilably contradicts any primary objective that the Secretary set forth with clarity in" the safety standard at issue.[170.19] Stevens further argued that the majority's decision flew in the face of the Court's oft-cited "presumption against preemption" of traditional state police powers.[170.20]

[170.1] *See* Crosby v. Nat'l Foreign Trade Council, 530 U.S. 363, 120 S. Ct. 2288 (2000). *See generally* Denning & McCall, Recent Decisions—Crosby v. Nat'l Foreign Trade Council, 120 S. Ct. 2288 (2000), 94 Am. J. Int'l L. 750 (2000); Symposium, Sanctions Reform?: Evaluating the Economic Weapon in Asia and the World, 32 Law & Pol'y Int'l Bus. 37 (2000) (articles by Price, Hannah & Carlson; Baker, Hahn, and Stumberg); Goldsmith, Statutory Foreign Affairs Preemption, 2000 Sup. Ct. Rev. 175; Hellwig, Note, The Retreat of the State?: The Massachusetts Burma Law and Local Empowerment in the Context of Globalization(s), 18 Wis. Int'l L.J. 477 (2000). *See also* Symposium, New Voices on the New Federalism, 46 Vill. L. Rev. 907 (2001) (articles by Cleveland, Halberstam, Vazquez and others); Barnico, The Road From Burma: State Boycotts After *Crosby v. National Foreign Trade Council*, 19 B.U. Int'l L.J. 89 (2001); Delahunty, Federalism Beyond the Water's Edge: State Procurement Sanctions and Foreign Affairs, 37 Stan. J. Int'l L. 1 (2001); Klein & Stern, Back to First Principles: The Constitutional Rationale for Invalidating Local Sanctions Against Foreign Trade, 33 Law & Pol'y Int'l Bus. 77 (2001); Cao, Comment, Limiting States' Roles in Foreign Commerce: Teaching Old-World Dogs New-World Tricks, 23 Houston J. Int'l L. 349 (2001); Miyaki-Murphy, Comment, In the Wake of *Crosby v. National Foreign Trade Council*, 34 J. Marshall L. Rev. 827 (2001); Moritsugu, Note, The Winding Course of the Massachusetts Burma Law: Subfederal Sanctions in a Historical Context, 34 Geo. Wash. Int'l L. Rev. 435 (2002); Pascoe, Note, Time for a New Approach?: Federalism and Foreign Affairs After *Crosby v. National Foreign Trade Council*, 35 Vand. J. Transnat'l L. 291 (2002); Sendleski, Note, Taking Our Money and Going Home: State Divestment Policy and the Foreign Affairs, Foreign Commerce, and Supremacy Clauses, 24 Suffolk Transnat'l L. Rev. 317 (2001); *see also* Swaine, The Undersea Word of Foreign Relations Federalism, 2 Chi. J. Int'l L. 337 (2001).

[170.2] National Foreign Trade Council v. Natsios, 181 F.3d 38 (1st Cir. 1999); National Foreign Trade Council v. Baker, 26 F. Supp. 2d 287 (D. Mass. 1998). *See generally* Denning & McCall, The Constitutionality of State "Sanctions" Against Foreign Countries: Affairs of State, States' Affairs, or a Sorry State of Affairs?, 26 Hastings Const. L.Q. 307 (1999); Denning & McCall, States' Rights and Foreign Policy, 79 For. Affairs 9 (Jan./Feb. 2000).

[170.3] *Crosby*, 530 U.S. at 366, 120 S. Ct. at 2291. *See also* 530 U.S. at 374 n.8, 120 S. Ct. at 2294 n.8 ("Because our conclusion that the state Act conflicts with federal law is sufficient to affirm the judgment below, we decline to speak to field preemption as a separate issue . . . or to pass on the First Circuit's rulings addressing the foreign affairs power or the dormant Foreign Commerce Clause.")

[170.4] *Crosby*, 530 U.S. at 373-374, 120 S. Ct. at 2294 (footnotes omitted). The state law had reached all persons or corporations wishing to do business with the State, and its definition of "doing business with Burma" swept quite broadly, and included only three narrow exceptions for medicine, newsgathering, and the like. The federal sanctions regime, by contrast, covered only "United States persons" and authorized the President to forbid "new investment" in Burma if certain conditions were obtained. However, the statute specifically exempted from the definition of "new investment" contracting for or financing a contract for the purchase of goods and services. *See Crosby*, 530 U.S. at 374-377, 120 S. Ct. at 2295-2296. For a similar approach, which treats "obstacle" or "frustration" preemption as a species of "conflict" preemption, *see* Clean Air Markets Group v. Pataki, 194 F. Supp. 2d 147, 158 (S.D.N.Y. 2002) (invalidating state law that imposed a penalty on emissions allowances of in-state producers choosing to trade with certain "upwind" states alleged to contribute to pollution in New York; penalty created an "obstacle" to federal Clean Air Act encouraging nationwide emissions trading and thus "actually conflict[ed] with" federal law).

[170.5] 530 U.S. at 376, 120 S. Ct. at 2296.

[170.6] *Id.* (footnote omitted).

[170.7] *Id.* Justice Souter also noted that Massachusetts's sanctions are "immediate . . . and perpetual," as opposed to the flexibility inherent in the federal act's delegation of authority to the President. *Id.* As a consequence, "if thc Massachusetts law is enforceable the President has less to offer and less economic and diplomatic leverage as a consequence." *Id.*

[170.8] *Crosby*, 530 U.S. at 378, 120 S. Ct. at 2297.

[170.9] *Crosby*, 530 U.S. at 383, 120 S. Ct. at 2300.

[170.10] *Id.* The United States was also hailed before the WTO by Japan and the European Union, both of which filed complaints with that body concerning the Massachusetts law. *Crosby*, 530 U.S. at 383, 120 S. Ct. at 2299-2300.

[170.11] *Crosby*, 530 U.S. at 387-388, 120 S. Ct. at 2302. Justice Souter also pointedly noted that the Court never passed on the validity of state and local sanctions against South Africa. *See Crosby*, 530 U.S. at 388, 120 S. Ct. at 2302.

[170.12] 530 U.S. at 374, 120 S. Ct. at 2294. A few months before *Crosby* was decided, the Court explicitly rejected the presumption against preemption when the State regulated an area in which the federal presence has historically been significant. *See* United States v. Locke, 529 U.S. 89, 120 S. Ct. 1135 (2000), discussed *infra* § 5.06[E]; *see also* Geier v. American Honda Motor Co., Inc., 529 U.S. 861, 120 S. Ct. 1913 (2000) (divided court) (holding that state tort action seeking to impose liability for failure to install airbags conflicted with safety standard issued by Department of Transportation pursuant to federal statute). The *Geier* majority did not even discuss the traditional presumption against preemption, for which it was criticized by Justice Stevens in his dissenting opinion. *See Geier*, 529 U.S. at 906-913, 120 S. Ct. at 1938-1942 (Stevens, J., dissenting).

[170.13] *Crosby*, 530 U.S. at 374 n.8, 120 S. Ct. at 2294 n.8. *See also* American Insurance Ass'n v. Garamendi, 539 U.S. 396, 124 S. Ct. 35 (2003) (divided court) (holding that, even in the absence of congressional legislation, executive agreements regarding litigation of Holocaust-era claims victims implicitly preempted California statute requiring disclosure of such information about insurance policies sold in Europe between 1920 and 1945 on pain of loss of licensure to do business in state).

[170.14] Geier v. American Honda Motor Co., Inc., 529 U.S. 861, 867, 120 S. Ct. 1913, 1917-1918 (2000) (divided court) *See generally* Ausness, Preemption of State Tort Law by Federal Safety Statutes: Supreme Court Preemption Jurisprudence Since *Cipollone*, 92 Ky. L.J. 913 (2003-2004); Haas, Note, Chipping Away at State Tort Remedies Through Pre-Emption Jurisprudence: *Geier v. American Honda Motor Co.*, 89 Cal. L. Rev. 1927

(2001); *see also* Scordato, Federal Preemption of State Tort Claims, 25 U. C. Davis L. Rev. 1 (2001); Carroll, Note, Federal Preemption of State Products Liability Claims: Adding Clarity and Respect for State Sovereignty to the Analysis of Federal Preemption Defenses, 36 Ga. L. Rev. 797 (2002).

[170.15] *Geier*, 529 U.S. at 869, 120 S. Ct. at 1919.

[170.16] *Id.*

[170.17] 529 U.S. at 878, 120 S. Ct. at 1924.

[170.18] 529 U.S. at 882, 120 S. Ct. at 1925.

[170.19] 529 U.S. at 906, 120 S. Ct. at 1938 (Stevens, J., dissenting).

[170.20] 529 U.S. at 906, 120 S. Ct. at 1939 (Stevens, J., dissenting). For an argument that "the presumption against preemption has no relevance to the express preemption analysis," and that "there is not much logic to a general presumption against preemption," *see* Dinh, *supra* note 151.

[E] Field and Frustration Preemption

Page 5-51, insert new footnote in third line after "to comply with both":

See, e.g., Clean Air Markets Group v. Pataki, 194 F. Supp. 2d 147, 158 (S.D.N.Y. 2002) (invalidating state law that imposed a penalty on emissions allowances of in-state producers choosing to trade with certain "upwind" states alleged to contribute to pollution in New York; penalty created an "obstacle" to federal Clean Air Act encouraging nationwide emissions trading and thus "actually conflict[ed] with" federal law).

Page 5-52, add to the end of note 171:

; *see also* Nelson, Preemption, 86 Va. L. Rev. 225 (2000) (arguing that field preemption risks preempting too much state law and should be abandoned by the Supreme Court).

Page 5-53, add to the end of note 177:

; *see also* Berger, Comment, Phoenix Grounded: The Impact of the Supreme Court's Changing Preemption Doctrine on State and Local Impediments to Airport Expansion, 97 Nw. U. L. Rev. 941 (2002).

Page 5-54, add to the end of the end of the carryover paragraph:

United States v. Locke (2000) saw a unanimous Court vigorously apply field preemption to invalidate a number of Washington State regulations relating to oil tankers.[181.1] Reversing both the district court and the Court of Appeals, the Court held that by including provisions of the Ports and Waterways Safety Act regulating design, construction, alteration, repair, maintenance, operation, equipping, personnel qualification, and manning of oil tankers, "Congress has left no room for state regulation of these matters."[181.2] In doing so, the Court repeatedly stressed both the "manifest" federal interest in the regulation of navigation "without embarrassment from intervention of the separate States" and the lessons drawn from *Cooley* that "there [are] instances in which state regulation of maritime commerce is inappropriate even absent the exercise of federal authority. . . ."[181.3]

The Court, moreover, limited the operation of one of the statute's savings clauses, relied upon by the lower courts in upholding the state regulations; in addition, it stated that assumptions of non-preemption do not attach when state laws "bear upon national and international maritime commerce. . . ."[181.4] The Court did allow that there might be some permissible state regulations. Where "local needs and conditions" necessitated, state regulations would be allowed, as they were in *Cooley.*[181.5] The Court listed the following factors as ones to be considered when addressing whether a "rule is justified by conditions unique to a particular port or waterway": (i) whether the rule has a "limited extraterritorial effect"; (ii) whether it poses a "minimal risk of innocent noncompliance"; (iii) whether or not it requires "adjustment of systemic aspects of the vessel"; and (iv) whether it "impose[s] a substantial burden on the vessel's operations within the local jurisdiction itself."[181.6]

[181.1] United States v. Locke, 529 U.S. 89, 111-112, 120 S. Ct. 1135, 1149 (2000); *see generally* Gudridge, Recent International Decisions, *United States v. Locke*, 120 S. Ct. 1135, 94 Am. J. Int'l L. 745 (2000); *see also* Allen, Federalism in the Era of International Standards: Federal and State Government Regulation of Merchant Vessels in the United States (pt. 4), 31 J. Mar. L. & Comm. 15 (2000); Avery, Comment, State Oil Spill Prevention Laws and Intertanko: When Is State Law Preempted?, 6 Ocean & Coastal L.J. 119 (2001); Carney, Note, The International Association of Independent Tanker Owners (Intertanko) v. Locke: Do Oil and State Tanker Regulation Mix?, 5 Ocean & Coastal L.J. 117 (2000); Vitt, Note, *United States v. Locke:* After a Rough Passage, Intertanko Crosses the Bar of State Regulation to Reach the Safe Harbor of Preemption, 25 Tul. Mar. L.J. 573 (2001).

[181.2] *Locke*, 529 U.S. at 111, 120 S. Ct. at 1149.

[181.3] 529 U.S. at 99, 120 S. Ct. at 1143; *see also* 529 U.S. at 115, 120 S. Ct. at 1151 (noting that even concurrent state regulations that seek only to augment federal regulation may fall if they interfere with a federal intent "to establish a workable, uniform system"). Following the Court's decision in *Locke*, one court has written that in railroad regulation, as in navigation, "an assumption of nonpreemption is not triggered when the state regulates in an area where there has been a history of significant federal presence." CSX Transportation, Inc. v. Plymouth, 92 F. Supp. 2d 643, 648 (E.D. Mich. 2000).

[181.4] 529 U.S. at 108, 120 S. Ct. at 1148. Citing *Rice v. Santa Fe Elevator Corp.*, 331 U.S. 218, 230, 67 S. Ct. 1146, 1147 (1947), the State argued, and the Court of Appeals had agreed, that a "clear and manifest purpose" of Congress needed to be demonstrated when the question arose whether Congress attempted to supersede "the historic police powers of the States." 529 U.S. at 107, 120 S. Ct. at 1147. The Court noted, however, that such an assumption "is not triggered when the State regulates in an area where there has been a history of significant federal presence." 529 U.S. at 108, 120 S. Ct. at 1147. Where the States do so, the Court continued, "we must ask whether the local laws in question are consistent with the federal statutory structure, which has as one of its objectives a uniformity for maritime commerce." 529 U.S. at 108, 120 S. Ct. at 1148. The Court, moreover, rejected as "an incorrect statement of law" State arguments that its regulations were valid where they are "similar to federal requirements." 529 U.S. at 115, 120 S. Ct. at 1151. "It is not always a sufficient answer to a claim of pre-emption to say that state rules supplement, or even mirror, federal requirements." *Id.* The "appropriate inquiry" was whether the rules were consistent with federal aims, such as securing uniformity. *Id.* For more on savings clauses, *see infra* § 5.06[G].

[181.5] 529 U.S. at 99, 120 S. Ct. at 1143.

[181.6] 529 U.S. at 111-112, 120 S. Ct. at 1149-1150. Under the Court's criteria, Washington's requirements of a state-approved training course, including frequent procedural drills; an English proficiency requirement; the navigation watch requirement; and a requirement that vessels report certain "marine casualties" were preempted. 529 U.S. at 112-116, 120 S. Ct. at 1150-1151. The Court left other parts of the state regulatory scheme to be addressed on remand, using the principles of conflict and field preemption it had articulated. 529 U.S. at 116-117, 120 S. Ct. at 1152. By contrast, in a previous case involving Washington's oil tanker requirements, the Court upheld—on grounds that it had both a "limited extraterritorial effect" and was based on "local peculiarities"—a requirement that certain vessels entering Washington's waters obtain a tug escort. *See* Ray v. Atlantic Richfield Co., 435 U.S. 151, 171, 98 S. Ct. 988, 1001 (1978) (divided court).

[F] Preemption and the Dormant Commerce Clause

Page 5-54, add to second line of note 182, after "(1953).":

For a recent article that classifies the Court's dormant Commerce Clause decisions as a species of preemption, *see* Dinh, *supra* note 151, at 2098, 2109-2112; Goldsmith, Statutory Foreign Affairs Preemption, 2000 Sup. Ct. Rev. 175; Spence & Murray, The Law, Economics, and Politics of Federal Preemption Jurisprudence: A Quantitative Analysis, 87 Cal. L. Rev. 1125, 1138-1145 (1999); *see also* Chen, Note, Organ Allocation and the States: Can the States Restrict Broader Organ Sharing?, 49 Duke L.J. 261, 275-289 (1999) (discussing both preemption and dormant Commerce

Clause doctrine problems with state schemes to keep organs harvested from donors from being used outside the state). For a recent case that seems to combine elements of traditional preemption jurisprudence the vocabulary of dormant Commerce Clause cases, *see* United States v. Locke, 529 U.S. at 99, 107, 112-116, 120 S. Ct. at 1143, 1147, 1150-1152 (mentioning, variously, the incompatibility of state regulations of oil tankers with federal interest in securing uniformity in areas of federal interest, with the need for the federal government "to speak with one voice" when setting international standards for tankers, and the problems of such regulations' extraterritorial effects); *see also* Crosby v. Nat'l Foreign Trade Council, 530 U.S. 363, 374 n.8, 120 S. Ct. 2288, 2294 n.8 (2000) (declining to pass on dormant Foreign Commerce Clause questions regarding state sanctions against companies doing business with foreign countries; relying on conflict preemption analysis to strike down state law); CSX Transportation, Inc. v. Plymouth, 92 F. Supp. 2d 643, 659 (E.D. Mich. 2000) (in concluding that federal statute preempted local regulation of length of time trains could block grade crossings, court added that "the fact that the regulation of length has been held to violate the Commerce Clause is relevant to the preemption analysis").

[G] Savings Clauses

Page 5-56, add to the end of note 188:

See also United States v. Locke, 529 U.S. 89, 106, 120 S. Ct. 1135, 1147 (2000) (holding that savings clause that applied to portion of statute dealing with liability for oil pollution did not save state oil tanker regulations from the preemptive effect of a separate statutory scheme; "[l]imiting the savings clauses . . . respects the established federal-state balance in matters of maritime commerce between the subjects as to which the States retain concurrent powers and those over which the federal authority displaces state control"); Geier v. American Honda Motor Co., Inc., 529 U.S. 861, 869, 120 S. Ct. 1913, 1919 (2000) (divided court) (concluding that the presence of saving clause in federal statute served only to remove state "tort actions from the scope of the express preemption clause" and that "[n]othing in the language of the saving clause suggests an intent to save state-law tort actions that conflict with federal regulations"; thus, implied preemption doctrine applies).

CHAPTER 6

THE "DORMANT" COMMERCE CLAUSE: RESTRICTIONS ON STATE REGULATORY POWERS

§6.01 INTRODUCTION

[A] Origin of the "Dormant" Concept

Page 6-4, add to note 7, after "see also":

Johnson, Homage to Clio: The Historical Continuity from the Articles of Confederation into the Constitution, 20 Const. Comment. 463 (2003-2004) (arguing that many features of the modern dormant Commerce Clause doctrine—especially its prohibitions of parochial discrimination in commercial regulation—were well established norms by 1787);

Page 6-5, add to the end of note 10:

In recent years, however, Justices Scalia and Thomas have indicated a willingness to entertain arguments that the doctrine should be radically reconceptualized. *See, e.g.*, Camps Newfound/Owatonna v. Harrison, 520 U.S. 564, 603, 117 S. Ct. 1590, 1611 (1997) (Scalia, J., dissenting); 520 U.S. at 609, 117 S. Ct. at 1614 (Thomas, J., dissenting) (arguing that Court should replace dormant Commerce Clause doctrine with strict application of Import-Export Clause, which, Justice Thomas argued, was intended to apply both to interstate and foreign commerce). For an analysis of Justice Thomas's opinion, *see* Denning, Justice Thomas, The Import-Export Clause, and *Camps Newfound/Owatonna v. Harrison*, 70 Colo. L. Rev. 155 (1999).

In 1999, responding to the apparent entreaties of these two Justices, the State of Alabama, in its defense of a corporate tax clearly unconstitutional under the Court's existing precedents, invited the Court to overturn its entire dormant Commerce Clause jurisprudence. *See* South Central Bell Tel. Co. v. Alabama, 526 U.S. 160, 119 S. Ct. 1180 (1999). The Court declined Alabama's invitation because the State failed to give adequate notice of its intent to argue that issue, which was not in the State's petition for certiorari. *South Central Bell*, 526 U.S. at 171, 119 S. Ct. at 1186. Justice O'Connor, concurring, added that she was not otherwise impressed by the State's argument on the merits. 526 U.S. at 171, 119 S. Ct. at 1187 (O'Connor, J., concurring). Justice Thomas agreed that the issue was not properly before the Court, but did not comment on the merits of Alabama's position. 526 U.S. at 171, 119 S. Ct. at 1187 (Thomas, J., concurring).

In 2003, the other shoe dropped for Justice Thomas. He announced in two cases that he would no longer enforce the dormant Commerce Clause doctrine against states. *See* Pharmaceutical Research and Manufacturers of America v. Walsh, 538 U.S. 644, 683, 123 S. Ct. 1855, 1878 (2003) (Thomas, J. concurring) (stating that the doctrine has "no basis in the text of the Constitution, mak[es] little sense, and [is] virtually unworkable in application") (quoting Camps Newfound/Owatonna v. Harrison, 520 U.S. 564, 610, 117 S. Ct. 1590, 1615 (1997) (Thomas, J., dissenting)); *see also* Hillside Dairy, Inc. v. Lyons, 539 U.S. 59, 68, 123 S. Ct. 2142, 2148 (2003) (Thomas, J., concurring in part and dissenting in part) (same). Justice Scalia's attitude, too, seems to have hardened a bit. His concurring opinion in *Walsh* implies that only in cases of facial discrimination or in cases involving nondiscriminatory action "of the precise sort hitherto invalidated" will he apply the dormant Commerce Clause doctrine. *Walsh*, 123 S. Ct. at 1874 (Scalia, J., concurring).

Page 6-5, add to fifth line of note 11, after "chronological order:":

Coenen, The Commerce Clause 209-342 (2004); 1 Tribe, American Constitutional Law § 6-2 (3d ed., Foundation Press, 2000); Carrubba & Rogers, National Judicial Power and the Dormant Commerce Clause, 19J.L. Econ. & Org. 543 (2003); Regan, Judicial Review of Member-State Regulation of Trade within a Federal or Quasi-Federal System: Protectionism and Balancing, Da Capo, 99 Mich. L. Rev. 1853 (2001); Spence & Murray, The Law, Economics of Federal Preemption Jurisprudence: A Quantitative Analysis, 87 Cal. L. Rev. 1125, 1138-1146 (1999) (characterizing dormant Commerce Clause cases as merely a species of federal preemption law); Stearns, A Beautiful Mend: A Game Theoretical Analysis of the Dormant Commerce Clause Doctrine, 45 Wm. & Mary L. Rev. 1 (2003) (an ambitious effort to explain the doctrine using law and economics and game theory);

Page 6-6, omit last sentence of carryover paragraph of note 11 beginning with "See also infra," and replace with:

See also Broll, Comment, The Economic Liberty Rationale of the Dormant Commerce Clause, 49 S.D. L. Rev. 824 (2003-2004); Jehangiri, The Dowling Thesis Revisited: Professor Dowling and Justice Scalia, 49 S.D. L. Rev. 867 (2003-2004); Larsen, Discrimination in the Dormant Commerce Clause, 49 S.D. L. Rev. 844 (2003-2004).

[C] "Commerce" and "Activities Affecting Commerce"

Page 6-8, insert at the end of note 19:

For an in-depth doctrinal analysis of the influence the Court's dormant Commerce Clause jurisprudence had on its treatment of congressional commerce power, *see* Cushman, Formalism and Realism in Commerce Clause Jurisprudence, 67 U. Chi. L. Rev. 1089 (2000).

§6.02 THE DORMANT COMMERCE CLAUSE AS A GRANT OF EXCLUSIVE AUTHORITY TO CONGRESS

Page 6-9, insert at the end of note 21:

See generally Williams, *Gibbons*, 79 N.Y.U. L. Rev. 1398 (2004).

[C] The Dormant Commerce Clause, "Judicial Activism," and the "Counter-Majoritarian Difficulty"

Page 6-18, add to the end of note 48:

But *see* Drahozal, Preserving the American Common Market: State and Local Governments in the United States Supreme Court, 7 Sup. Ct. Econ. Rev. 233 (1999) (arguing that Court is supplied with information from other cities and states, in the form of *amici* briefs, that allows it effectively to police the national common market).

§6.03 "NATIONAL" VS. "LOCAL" SUBJECTS: THE HERITAGE OF *COOLEY V. BOARD OF WARDENS*

Page 6-19, add to the end of note 51:

In a recent encounter with the same Washington regulations, the Court again cited *Cooley* in its invalidation of certain Washington State regulations regarding the operation of oil tankers in state waters. *See* United States v. Locke, 529 U.S. 89, 99, 120 S. Ct. 1135, 1143 (2000) (citing federal interest in uniformity for maritime regulations); *see also* CSX Transportation, Inc. v. Plymouth, 92 F. Supp. 2d 643, 648 (E.D. Mich.

2000) (in striking down a local ordinance regulating the length of time a train could block a grade crossing, the court stressed that "[b]oth Congress and the courts have traditionally recognized a need to regulate railroad operations at a national level").

Page 6-23, add to the end of note 63:

In striking down a state statute attempting to regulate sexually explicit content on the Internet, the Second Circuit invoked *Cooley*'s national-local distinction, opining that "it [is] likely that the internet will soon be seen as falling within that class of subjects that are protected from State regulation because they 'imperatively demand[] a single uniform rule.'" American Bookseller's Foundation v. Dean, 342 F.3d 96, 102-104 (2d Cir. 2003) (quoting Cooley v. Board of Wardens, 53 U.S. (12 How.) 299, 319 (1851)). While acknowledging the "abandon[ment]" of "the attempt to test state regulation by classifying its subject matter as local or national," Professor Tribe has described the legacy of *Cooley* as follows:

> The validity of state action affecting interstate commerce must be judged in light of the desirability, in terms of the Constitutional structure and goals, of permitting diverse responses to local needs and the undesirability, again evaluated by a constitutional metric, of permitting local interference with such uniformity as the unimpeded flow of interstate commerce may require.

1 Tribe, *supra* note 11, at 1048.

§ 6.04 "DIRECT" VS. "INDIRECT" EFFECTS ON INTERSTATE COMMERCE

Page 6-28, add to the end of note 78:

; CSX Transportation, Inc. v. Plymouth, 92 F. Supp. 2d 643, 659 (E.D. Mich. 2000) (finding that in addition to being preempted by federal law, local ordinance regulating length of time train could block grade crossing violated the Commerce Clause; *Pike* balancing test inapplicable because "in no event can a state law directly regulate interstate commerce"); A.G.G. Enterprises, Inc. v. Washington Co., 2000 WL 361892 (D. Or.

2000), at *9 (slip opinion) (concluding that local waste control ordinances "burden interstate commerce only indirectly and [that] the *Pike* test should be used to analyze their constitutionality"); American Meat Institute v. Barnett, 64 F. Supp. 2d 906 (D.S.D., 1999); *but see* CSX Transportation, Inc. v. Plymouth, 283 F.3d 812 (6th Cir. 2002) (rejecting direct/indirect test for dormant Commerce Clause doctrine violation; district court should have used *Pike* balancing; *held*, local time limit on grade crossing delays by passing trains preempted under federal law, dormant Commerce Clause analysis unnecessary).

§6.05 "BALANCING" STATE AND NATIONAL INTERESTS

Page 6-33, add to the end of note 95:

See generally Day, Revisiting *Pike*: The Origins of the Nondiscrimination Tier of the Dormant Commerce Clause Doctrine, 27 Hamline L. Rev. 45 (2004). For a recent, though short-lived, application of *Pike* balancing to enjoin enforcement of a state law, *see* National Electrical Manufacturing Ass'n v. Sorrell, 72 F. Supp. 2d 449, 450 (D. Vt. 1999) (enjoining enforcement of Vermont statute forbidding the sale of items containing mercury without state-mandated label notifying purchasers of presence of mercury and of buyer's responsibility to remove or recycle mercury before disposing of item; burden on commerce likely to be substantial); *see also* Phillip Morris Incorporated v. Reilly, 113 F. Supp. 2d 129, 149-151 (D. Mass. 2000) (striking down Massachusetts statute requiring tobacco companies to file disclosure statements detailing ingredients and nicotine yield of tobacco, which would then become public record; court concluded act impermissible, *inter alia*, because burden on interstate commerce—*i.e.*, publicity of trade secrets—clearly exceeded putative benefits; noting that "much, if not all, of the hoped for benefit could be achieved by disclosure requirements tailored to avoid loss of trade secrets"). Both decisions, however, were recently reversed. In *National Electrical Manufacturers Association v. Sorrell*, 272 F.3d 104 (2d Cir. 2001), the court of appeals found that a state law requiring labeling for mercury-containing light bulbs did not violate the dormant Commerce Clause doctrine. In *Philip Morris v. Reilly*, 267 F.3d 45 (1st Cir. 2001) (withdrawn from bound volume at request of the court), the court found that the Massachusetts statute requiring disclosure of ingredients by cigarette manufacturers was evenhanded, effectuated a legitimate interest (protecting the health and safety of state citizens) and that its benefits were not clearly exceeded by the burdens on interstate commerce. *Reilly*, 267 F.3d at 54. The court pointedly refused to consider increased costs to cigarette manufacturers as constituting a burden on interstate commerce "because the Clause protects the interstate market, not particular interstate firms, from prohibitive or burdensome regulations." *Id.* For commentary on these cases, *see* Nix, Comment, Statutory Disclosure of Tobacco Ingredients: Secrets Up in Smoke? 54 Ala. L. Rev. 1413 (2003); Ryan, Casenote, *Nema v. Sorrell*: It's "Lights Out" for the National Electrical Manufacturers Association—A Look at NEMA's Failed Commerce Clause Challenge, 14 Vill. Envt'l L.J. 349 (2003). For other instances of state laws failing *Pike* balancing, *see* Yamaha Motor Corp., U.S.A. v. Jim's Motorcycle, Inc., 401 F.3d 560, 570-574 (4th Cir. 2005) (striking down provision of Virginia law permitting motorcycle franchise holder to protest intent to establish competing franchise anywhere else in the state, triggering requirement that manufacturer prove inadequate representation in market); Alliant Energy Co. v. Bie, 303 F.3d 904, 914-915 (7th Cir. 2003) (striking down Wisconsin statute requiring that utilities holding companies be incorporated in the state of Wisconsin; concluding that burden on interstate commerce outweighs any local benefits, but upholding provision prohibiting transfer of utility license to foreign corporation and provisions regarding take-over of utilities); PSINET, Inc. v. Chapman, 362 F.3d 227, ____-____(4th Cir. 2004) (divided court) (striking down Virginia statute prohibiting use of Internet to display or provide access to offensive materials by juveniles; burdens on interstate commerce clearly excessive compared to local benefits); Union Pac. R. Co. v. California Pub. Utilities Comm'n, 2003 WL 21391674 (9th Cir. 2003), at *15 (California train safety rules held to have indubitable extraterritorial effect, thus rendering burden on interstate commerce "clearly excessive" when compared to local benefits); R & M Oil & Supply, Inc. v. Saunders, 307 F.3d 731, 735-776 (8th Cir. 2002) (striking down Missouri law requiring bulk propane sellers to maintain—but not necessarily to fill or use—an 18,000 gallon storage capacity tank in the state; burden on interstate commerce excessive as compared to *de minimis* local benefits); Southeast Booksellers Ass'n v. McMaster, 2005 WL 1322849 (D.S.C. 2005), at *11 (South Carolina statute prohibiting dissemination of material "harmful to minors" over the Internet invalid "because the burdens that it imposes on interstate commerce are excessive in relation to the local benefit conferred"); Center for Democracy & Technology v. Pappert, 2004 WL 2005938 (E.D. Pa. 2004), at ____(striking down state law requiring Internet service providers to remove or disable access to child pornography either stored on or available through its service; little evidence law is effective while "there is evidence that this Act places a substantial burden on interstate commerce"); Kraft Foods North America, Inc. v. Rockland Co. Dept. Weights & Measures, 2003 WL 554796 (S.D.N.Y.) (Feb. 26, 2003) (striking down county's method of enforcing state food labeling requirements that required weights on packages to meet or exceed weight on box under *Pike* balancing); Dakota, Minnesota & Eastern R. Corp. v. South Dakota, 236 F. Supp. 2d 989, 1020-1025 (D.S.D. 2002) (striking down part of state statute requiring railroad have financial resources necessary to complete expansion project to exercise power of eminent domain); Bioganic Safety Brands, Inc. v. Ament, 174 F. Supp. 2d 1168, 1184 (D. Colo. 2001) (holding that state prohibition of insecticide label reading "safe for kids" violated that dormant Commerce Clause doctrine, in part because of expense of removing it from all products sold in that single state).

Page 6-33, add to the end of note 96:

A recent court decision interpreted the language in *Pike* regarding "incidental" effects on interstate commerce to mean that "in no event can a state directly regulate interstate commerce." If it did, *Pike* was inapplicable. *See* CSX Transportation, Inc. v. Plymouth, 92 F. Supp. 2d 643, 659 (E.D. Mich. 2000); *but see* CSX Transportation, Inc. v. Plymouth, 283 F.3d 812 (6th Cir. 2002) (rejecting direct/indirect test for dormant Commerce Clause doctrine violation; district court should have used *Pike* balancing). *Compare* A.G.G. Enterprises, Inc. v. Washington Co., 2000 WL 361892 (D. Or. 2000), at *9 (concluding that local waste control ordinances "burden interstate commerce only indirectly and [that] the *Pike* test should be used to analyze their constitutionality"); *accord* A.G.G. Enterprises, Inc. v. Washington Co., 145 F. Supp. 2d 1215, 1225 (D. Or. 2001) (holding that because waste disposal ordinances "burden interstate commerce only indirectly . . . the *Pike* test should be used to analyze their constitutionality"). The judge in the A.G.G. Enterprises cases conflates the "direct-indirect" test with the general rule that statutes and ordinances that discriminate, facially or in effect, against interstate commerce are analyzed under a "virtually *per se*" rule of invalidity. For more on the dormant Commerce Clause doctrine and economic protectionism, *see infra* § 6.06[A].

For more conventional applications of *Pike* balancing, *see* Yamaha Motor Corp., U.S.A. v. Jim's Motorcycle, Inc., 401 F.3d 560, 570-574 (4th

Cir. 2005) (striking down provision of Virginia law permitting motorcycle franchise holder to protest intent to establish competing franchise anywhere else in the state, triggering requirement that manufacturer prove inadequate representation in market); Lenscrafters, Inc. v. Robinson, 2005 WL 850439 (6th Cir. 2005), at *6 (upholding statute prohibiting optometrists from practicing in or in conjunction with a retail store; "Lenscrafters has failed to show a genuine issue of material fact as to whether the burdens placed on interstate commerce are 'clearly excessive' in relation to the putative local benefits of the statute"); National Solid Waste Mgmt. Ass'n v. Pine Belt Regional Solid Waste Mgmt. Auth., 389 F.3d 491, 502-503 (5th Cir. 2004) (upholding regional flow control ordinance requiring disposal of waste at site owned by regional waste authority; burden on interstate commerce no greater than that on intrastate commerce); Alliant Energy Co. v. Bie, 330 F.3d 904, 914-915 (7th Cir. 2003) (striking down Wisconsin statute requiring that utilities holding companies be incorporated in the state of Wisconsin; concluding that burden on interstate commerce outweighs any local benefits, but upholding provision prohibiting transfer of utility license to foreign corporation and provisions regarding take-over of utilities); PSINET, Inc. v. Chapman, 362 F.3d 227, 239-240 (4th Cir. 2004) (divided court) (striking down Virginia statute prohibiting use of Internet to display or provide access to offensive materials by juveniles; burdens on interstate commerce clearly excessive compared to local benefits); Union Pac. R. Co. v. California Pub. Utilities Comm'n, 2003 WL 21391674 (9th Cir. 2003), at *15 (California train safety rules held to have indubitable extraterritorial effect, thus rendering burden on interstate commerce "clearly excessive" when compared to local benefits); National Audubon Society, Inc. v. Davis, 307 F.3d 835, 857-858 (9th Cir. 2002) (rejecting Commerce Clause challenge to state ban on use of certain traps; statute neither discriminated against out-of-state commerce, nor imposed an unreasonable burden on interstate commerce); Eby-Brown Co., LLC v. Wisconsin Dept. Agric., 295 F.3d 749 (7th Cir. 2002) (upholding state Unfair Sales Act against challenge by tobacco wholesaler; fact that statute made it more difficult to operate stores in state did not mean statute excessively burdened interstate commerce); Omya, Inc. v. Vermont, 2002 WL 730841 (2d Cir.) (April 25, 2002) (unpublished) (upholding state environmental board order limiting truck trips on federal highway to and from quarry and processing center; benefit ("enhance[ment of] aesthetic and historic preservation goals" and traffic congestion reduction) not "clearly exceeded" by incidental burdens on interstate commerce); Star Scientific, Inc. v. Beales, 278 F.3d 339, 357

(4th Cir. 2002) (upholding state legislation implementing nationwide tobacco settlement requiring tobacco companies not party to the settlement to escrow certain monies based on number of in-state sales; state benefit — "ensuring that Virginia has a source of recovery for future smoking-related healthcare costs" attributable to nonparty tobacco companies — was not clearly exceeded by burden on interstate commerce); Taxi Cab-vertising, Inc. v. Myrtle Beach, 2002 WL 23165 (4th Cir.) (Jan. 9, 2002) (unpublished) (per curiam) (city ban on roof-mounted taxicab advertising not clearly excessive in relation to putative benefits); Pharmaceutical Research and Manufacturers of America v. Concannon, 249 F.3d 66, 83-84 (1st Cir. 2001) (upholding Maine law requiring companies selling drugs in state to Medicaid beneficiaries to negotiate with the state for rebates with which state funds plan to offer drug discounts; act satisfies *Pike* balancing: "Arguably, the only burden imposed on interstate commerce by the Maine Act is its possible effects on the profits of individual manufacturers," while the "local benefits of the Act [are] substantial"), *aff'd on other grounds* 538 U.S. 644, 123 S. Ct. 1855 (2003); Hampton Feedlot, Inc. v. Nixon, 249 F.3d 814, 820 (8th Cir. 2001) (upholding Missouri law prohibiting certain forms of price discrimination in the buying of livestock in-state; any burdens falling on interstate commerce not clearly excessive in relation to local benefits); Grant's Dairy — Maine, L.L.C. v. Comm'r, 232 F.3d 8, 24 (1st Cir. 2000) (upholding Maine dairy price support legislation imposing minimum prices on dealers; "slim showing of an imagined burden does not suffice to trigger *Pike* balancing"; "modest burdens . . . are outweighed by the benefits Maine seeks to secure by imposing minimum price benefits that include ensuring an adequate instate supply of milk at reasonable prices and maintaining market stability"); American Target Advertising, Inc. v. Giani, 199 F.3d 1241, 1254 (10th Cir. 2000) (upholding a Utah law requiring professional fundraisers to apply and pay a fee before raising money within the state; "[t]he Utah Act plainly does not distinguish between in-state and out-of-state businesses" and its effects are "incidental," "not clearly excessive in relation to the putative local benefits" and Utah has a legitimate public interest in "curtailing fraudulent solicitations"); Southeast Booksellers Ass'n v. McMaster, 2005 WL 1322849 (D.S.C. 2005), at *11 (South Carolina statute prohibiting dissemination of material "harmful to minors" over the Internet invalid "because the burdens that it imposes on interstate commerce are excessive in relation to the local benefit conferred"); Pharmaceutical Care Mgmt. Ass'n v. Rowe, 2005 WL 757608 (D. Me. 2005), at *20 (rejecting Commerce Clause challenge to law regulating pharmaceutical benefits management companies by imposing fiduciary duties and required practices in their dealings with benefits providers); Nichols Media Group, LLC v. Babylon, 2005 WL 885501 (E.D.N.Y. 2005) (upholding town ban on billboards, subject to an on-premises advertising exception, against dormant Commerce Clause challenge); Center for Democracy & Technology v. Pappert, 2004 WL 2005938 (E.D. Pa. 2004), at ____ (striking down state law requiring Internet service providers to remove or disable access to child pornography either stored on or available through its service; little evidence law is effective while "there is evidence that the this Act places a substantial burden on interstate commerce"); Public Citizen, Inc. v. Pinellas Co., 2004 WL 1336308 (M.D. Fla. 2004) (rejecting argument that county ordinance regulating solicitation of charitable donations impermissibly burdens interstate commerce); Fidelity National Information Solutions, Inc. v. Sinclair, 2004 WL 764834 (E.D. Pa.) (March 31, 2004), at *16-*17 (rejecting claim that licensing requirements for real estate appraisers violated the dormant Commerce Clause under *Pike* balancing); BFI Waste Systems of North America v. Dekalb Co., 2004 WL 116540 (N.D. Ga. 2004), at *12-*15 (refusal to rezone land to permit landfill expansion did not fail *Pike* balancing); Cambridge Credit Counseling Corp. v. Foulston, 2003 WL 23279978 (D. Kan. 2003), at *4 (state ban on business of debt adjusting except where performed as an incident to the practice of law did not violate the dormant Commerce Clause under *Pike* balancing); Walgreen Co. v. Rullan, 292 F. Supp. 2d 298, 316-317 (D.P.R. 2003) (law requiring certificate of convenience and necessity to open new pharmacies did not constitute "clearly excessive" burden on interstate commerce as compared to local benefits); Power & Tel. Supply Co., Inc. v. Harmonic, Inc., 2003 WL 21448329 (W.D. Tenn. 2003), at *7 (upholding Tennessee statute requiring suppliers to repurchase unsold inventory from retailers under *Pike* balancing test); Lenscrafters, Inc. v. Wadley, 248 F. Supp. 2d 705, 738 (M.D. Tenn. 2003) (rejecting arguments that state restriction on optometrists practicing in retail establishments impermissibly burdened interstate commerce; "state's interest in restricting commercial interference with conduct of a medical professional is an indisputably legitimate exercise of its police power"); South Dakota Farm Bureau v. Hazeltine, 202 F. Supp. 2d 1020 (D.S.D. 2002) (employing *Pike* balancing to strike down amendments to state constitution prohibiting utilities from acquiring easements for transmission lines, pipelines, etc. within the state); Young v. Coloma-Agaran, 2001 WL 1677259 (D. Hawaii) (Dec. 27, 2001), at *15 (striking down ban on operation of tour boats in certain bay; state presented no evidence of local benefit, asserted benefits clearly exceeded by demonstrated burden on interstate commerce); Connecticut *ex rel* Blumenthal v. Crotty, 180 F. Supp. 2d 392 (N.D.N.Y. 2001) (striking down state emergency restrictions on lobstering; regulations impose impermissible burden on interstate commerce); Kafka v. Hagener, 176 F. Supp. 2d 1037, 1043 (D. Mont. 2001) (upholding moratorium on game farm licenses, ban of licenses transfers, and killing of exotic wildlife on game farms; "[a]t its core [dormant Commerce Clause claim] is an argument about state policy and a disagreement with the consequences of voting on a hotly-contested public issue"); Southern Union Co. v. Missouri Pub. Svc. Comm'n, 138 F. Supp. 2d 1201, 1208 (W.D. Mo. 2001) (upholding statute requiring utility companies operating in the state to receive prior approval of Public Service Commission before purchasing stock in another utility company; concluding that "Missouri has a valid interest in assuring the supply of natural gas for its citizens at reasonable rates, and that interest is protected by" the statute in question), *aff'd* 289 F.3d 503 (8th Cir. 2002); Cloverland — Green Spring Dairies, Inc. v. Penn. Milk Marketing Bd., 138 F. Supp. 2d 593, 607-613 (M.D. Pa. 2001) (upholding Pennsylvania Milk Marketing Law under *Pike* balancing); Camden v. Beretta, 123 F. Supp. 2d 245, 255 (D.N.J. 2000) (dismissing county complaint against gun manufacturers for negligent marketing and distribution of handguns; expressing skepticism that such suits might implicate the dormant Commerce Clause doctrine: "The Court finds that plaintiff's claims in this case would almost certainly have a negative effect upon interstate commerce, but also that there would undoubtedly be strong local benefits involved if the county succeeded in stemming the tide of gun violence within its borders."); *cf.* Crowley v. Cybersource Corp., 166 F. Supp. 2d 1263, 1272 (N.D. Cal. 2001) (noting doubts that state common law claims can violate the dormant Commerce Clause doctrine); New England Dragway, Inc. v. M-O-H Enterprises, 817 A.2d 288, 291-292 (N.H. 2003) (upholding state takeover disclosure act; burdens on interstate commerce not "clearly excessive" in comparison with state interest in guaranteeing *resident shareholders have* adequate information regarding tender offers); District of Columbia v. Beretta, U.S.A. Corp., 872 A.2d 633, 656-658 (D.C. Ct. App. 2005) (upholding D.C. ordinance imposing strict liability in tort for manufacturers of "machine guns" or "assault weapons" for injuries arising out of discharge of weapon within the District; burdens no "greater than [those] of other state laws imposing liability in tort on manufacturers of defective or abnormally dangerous products"); Bronco Wine Co. v. Jolly, 2005 WL 1244920 (Cal. Ct. App. 2005), at *22 (upholding state statute prohibiting the use of brand name using "Napa" to refer to wines unless substantial portion of grapes used to make the wine originated in Napa County; insufficient evidence to determine that impact on interstate commerce "clearly exceeds" benefits to state); Bean v. Bredesen, 2005 WL 1025767 (Tenn. Ct. App. 2005), at *7 (upholding state ban on private possession of white-tailed deer); State v. Kolla, 672 N.W.2d 1, 10-11 (Ct. App. Minn. 2003) (upholding provision of Minnesota requiring purchase of permit for hauling minnows through state and minnow hauler's vehicle license; laws requiring both did not differentiate between residents and nonresidents; valid under *Pike* balancing) Diehl, Inc. v. Ohio Dept. Agric., 2002 WL 31155100 (Ct. App. Ohio) (Sept. 30, 2002) (upholding milk inspection fee schedule against dormant Commerce Clause challenge; burdens not "clearly excessive" in relation to local benefits); Northern Springs, Inc. v. Wells, 2004 WL 844178 (Super. Ct. Me. 2004), at *4-*5 (closing of road to trucks of certain weight class did not violate the Commerce Clause). For some commentary on the cases described above, *see* Nave, Charitable State Registration and the Dormant Commerce Clause, 31 Wm. Mitchell L. Rev. 227 (2004); McEowen & Harl, South Dakota Amendment E Ruled Unconstitutional — Is There a Future for Legislative Involvement in Shaping the Structure of Agriculture, 37 Creighton L. Rev. 285 (2004); Pancoast, Comment, A Test Case for Re-Evaluation of the Dormant Commerce Clause: The Maine Rx Program, 4 U. Pa. J. Const. L. 184 (2001) (commenting on *Concannon*); Pietila, Note, "[W]e're Doing This to Ourselves": South Dakota's Anticorporate Farming Amendment, J. Corp. L. 149 (2001); Rhead, Note, *Hampton Feedlot, Inc. v. Nixon*: Slaughtering Price Discrimination Statutes with the Dormant Commerce Clause, 6 Great Plains Nat. Res. J. 77 (2001).

Page 6-33, add to the end of note 97:

For a critique of the use of balancing in trade regulation cases, *see* Regan, Judicial Review of Member-State Regulation of Trade within a Federal or Quasi-Federal System: Protectionism and Balancing, Da Capo, 99 Mich. L. Rev. 1853 (2001).

Page 6-34, add a new footnote to the end of the first full paragraph ending "the *aggregate* benefit).":

See generally Day, Revisiting *Pike*: The Origins of the Nondiscrimination Tier of the Dormant Commerce Clause Doctrine, 27 Hamline L. Rev. 45

(2004); Fox, State Benefits Under the *Pike* Balancing Test of the Dormant Commerce Clause: Putative or Actual?, 1 Ave Maria L. Rev. 175 (2003).

§ 6.06 ECONOMIC PROTECTIONISM: INTRODUCTION

Page 6-35, add to the end of note 99:

For an argument that the anti-discrimination norm was fully internalized during the Articles of Confederation, which obviated the need for an explicit textual prohibition, *see* Johnson, Homage to Clio: The Historical Continuity from the Articles of Confederation into the Constitution, 20 Const. Comment. 463 (2003-2004).

[A] Economic Protectionism as a Per Se Mark of Constitutional Invalidity

Page 6-35, add to the end of note 99:

For the role that railroads played in the development of the dormant Commerce Clause doctrine, see *Ely*, "The Railroad System Has Burst Through State Limits": Railroads and Interstate Commerce, 1830-1920, 55 Ark. L. Rev. 933, 937-965 (2003).

Page 6-36, add to the end of note 103:

Because of the concern with state regulation fettering *inter*state commerce, the dormant Commerce Clause doctrine has little to say about state laws that limit an *intra*state company's *intra*state operations. *See* Jamaica Ash & Rubbish Removal Co. v. Ferguson, 85 F. Supp. 2d 174, 189 (E.D.N.Y.) (Feb. 29, 2000) (noting that a challenge by "an intrastate plaintiff" to "an intrastate municipal law . . . affect[ing] the plaintiff's [intrastate] operations," which law lacks an interstate effect is missing a "crucial" element; denying injunctive relief).

Page 6-36, add to the end of note 105:

More recent milk pricing statutes, which do not require that out-of-state milk imported into a state has been purchased at no less than the minimum price required for in-state milk purchases, have fared much better. *See, e.g.*, Grant's Dairy — Maine, L.L.C., v. Comm'r, 232 F.3d 8, 24 (1st Cir. 2000) (upholding Maine dairy price support legislation imposing minimum prices on dealers; "slim showing of an imagined burden does not suffice to trigger *Pike* balancing"; "modest burdens . . . are outweighed by the benefits Maine seeks to secure by imposing minimum price benefits that include ensuring an adequate instate supply of milk at reasonable prices and maintaining market stability"); Cloverland — Green Spring Dairies, Inc. v. Penn. Milk Marketing Bd., 138 F. Supp. 2d 593 (M.D. Pa. 2001) (upholding Pennsylvania Milk Marketing Law). *But see* Cloverland-Green Springs Dairies, Inc. v. Pennsylvania Milk Marketing Board, 298 F.3d 201 (3d Cir. 2002) (concluding that state minimum price floors for wholesale sellers of milk could be found to have impermissible discriminatory effects if they eliminate competitive advantage of out-of-state milk dealers).

Page 6-39, add to the end of note 112:

For an argument that the application of the dormant Commerce Clause doctrine can frustrate other forms of state environmental regulation, *see* Engel, The Dormant Commerce Clause Threat to Market-Based Environmental Regulation: The Case of Electricity Deregulation, 26 Ecology L.Q. 243 (1999). *See also infra* § 6.06[B].

Page 6-40, add to first line of note 114, between "(emphasis added) *and* "For an earlier . . .":

Despite the Court's treatment of purpose in *Philadelphia v. New Jersey* — the Court concluded that the facial discrimination made New Jersey's purpose largely irrelevant — it is hornbook law that facially neutral statutes with a proven discriminatory purpose will suffice to invalidate a law under the dormant Commerce Clause. *See, e.g.*, Bacchus Imports, Ltd. v. Dias, 468 U.S. 268, 270, 104 S. Ct. 3049, 3054-3055 (1984) (divided court) ("A finding that state legislation constitutes 'economic protectionism' may be made on the basis of either discriminatory purpose . . . or discriminatory effect. . . ."); Minnesota v. Clover Leaf Creamery Co., 449 U.S. 456, 471 n.15, 101 S. Ct. 715, 727 n.15 (1981) (divided court); Hunt v. Washington State Apple Advertising Comm'n, 432 U.S. 333, 352-353, 97 S. Ct. 2434, 2446 (1977). For recent lower court cases involving discriminatory purpose, *see* Smithfield Foods, Inc. v. Miller, 367 F.3d 1061, 1065 (8th Cir. 2004) (listing the following factors as bearing on existence of discriminatory purpose: (1) statements by lawmakers; (2) use of irregular procedures in sequence of events leading up to statute's adoption; (3) whether a consistent pattern exists of disparate impact of a particular class of persons; (4) statute's historical background, including history of discrimination by the state; (5) use of highly ineffective means to promote state's asserted interest; absence of such information in record requires remand for further discovery); Walgreen Co. v. Rullan, 292 F. Supp. 2d 298, 314-315 (D.P.R. 2003) (local pharmacies grandfathered in after passage of act requiring certificate of convenience and necessity to open new pharmacies insufficient to establish discriminatory purpose).

Page 6-41, add to first line of note 117, after "2537":

; *see also* Used Tire Int'l, Inc. v. Diaz-Saldana, 155 F.3d 1, 3-4 (1st Cir. 1998) (rejecting similar environmental argument in striking down Puerto Rico act imposing unique requirements on imported used tires while exempting locally generated used tires);

Page 6-41, add to the end of note 117:

For a recent application of the "per se" rule of invalidity to a facially discriminatory measure, *see* McNeilus Truck and Manufacturing, Inc. v. Ohio, 226 F.3d 429 (6th Cir. 2000) (state statute licensing car dealers that placed burdens on out-of-state vehicle remanufacturers *vis-à-vis* in-state dealers protectionist and subject to "virtually *per se* rule of invalidity"; *held,* statute violates the dormant Commerce Clause doctrine); Jemal's Fairfield Farms, LLC v. Prince George's Co., 2004 WL 1219242 (D. Md. 2004), at *9 (invalidating county ordinances prohibiting use of land for marshalling trucks used to service out-of-county uses or buildings; "[a]bsent some compelling public interest which can be served by no less discriminatory alternatives, the County may not define a use permitted in certain zones to exclude activities that serve uses outside the County"); Hillside Dairy, Inc. v. Kawamura, 2004 WL 1068888 (E.D. Cal. 2004) (enjoining California statute requiring purchasers of out-of-state milk to contribute to fund from which payments were made to California milk producers; "[s]ince the 1997 amendment . . . requires out-of-state raw milk producers to pay for benefits received exclusively by California dairy businesses, it is similar to the milk pricing order invalidated in *West Lynn*"); National Solid Waste Management Assoc. v.

Pine Belt Solid Waste Mgmt. Auth., 2003 WL 21006321 (S.D. Miss. 2003) (striking down flow control ordinance requiring the disposal of solid waste at designated stations under contract with waste management authority and prohibiting disposal elsewhere); Smithfield Foods, Inc. v. Miller, 241 F. Supp. 2d 978 (S.D. Iowa 2003) (striking down state law prohibiting pork producers from owning or controlling pork production in the state unless affiliated with in-state farm cooperative; statute was facially discriminatory and enacted with impermissible protectionist purpose), *rev'd* 367 F.3d 1061, 1065 (8th Cir. 2004) (vacating trial court judgment, remanding for further discovery on issue of discriminatory effect); Homer Distributing Co., Inc. v. New Bedford, 188 F. Supp. 2d 33 (D. Mass. 2002) (ordinance charging "non-domestic transient vendors" $2,000 for license, which exempts domestic corporations, and where permanent local merchants charged $25.00 every four years for business license protectionist and *per se* invalid); Goya de Puerto Rico, Inc. v. Santiago, 59 F. Supp. 2d 274, 276-278 (D.P.R. 1999) (striking down Puerto Rico regulation requiring imported, but not locally produced, pigeon peas to undergo inspection and exacting an inspection fee on such imports); State v. Kolla, 672 N.W.2d 1, 10-11 (Ct. App. Minn. 2003) (striking down provision of Minnesota charging nonresidents more than residents for permits to haul minnows); Delaware v. Preferred Florist Network, Inc., 791 A.2d 8, 19-20 (Del. Ch. 2001) (striking down part of Delaware statute prohibiting out-of-state florists from listing local telephone numbers in local directories if calls to local number referred out-of-state; statute discriminated against out-of-state florists in favor of local businesses, subject to strict scrutiny); Children's Hospital and Medical Center v. Bonta, 118 Cal. Rptr.2d 629, 649 (Ct. App. Cal. 2002) (holding that California's method of reimbursing out-of-state hospitals for treatment of state Medicare patients at rates lower than that of in-state hospitals was subject to "*per se* rule of invalidity").

Page 6-42, add to the end of note 120:

The *Washington Apple* case is generally considered the leading "discriminatory effects" case. For recent lower court cases involving facially-neutral statutes alleged to have discriminatory effects, *see, for example*, Walgreen Co. v. Rullan, 405 F.3d 50, 55-56 (1st Cir. 2005) (striking down Puerto Rico requirement that new pharmacies must obtain a certificate of necessity and convenience where existing pharmacies may object and a certificate denied if grant of certificate will increase competition among existing pharmacies); Lenscrafters, Inc. v. Robinson, 2005 WL 850439 (6th Cir. 2005), at *5 (upholding statute prohibiting optometrists from practicing in or in conjunction with a retail store; statute did not "discriminate among in-state and out-of-state optical stores, as both are prohibited from leasing space to optometrists"); International Truck and Engine Corp. v. Bray, 372 F.3d 717, 726 (5th Cir. 2004) (upholding Texas law prohibiting truck manufacturers from acting as new or used vehicle dealers or as used truck dealers; in-state dealers and out-of-state manufacturers not similarly situated); Smithfield Foods, Inc. v. Miller, 367 F.3d 1061, 1065 (8th Cir. 2004) (vacating trial court judgment, remanding for further discovery on issue of discriminatory effect); Freedom Holdings, Inc. v. Spitzer, 2004 WL 26498 (2d Cir. 2004), at *9 (rejecting cigarette importers arguments that New York contraband statute discriminated in its effects against interstate commerce); Doran v. Massachusetts Turnpike Auth., 348 F.3d 315, 321-322 (1st Cir. 2003) (program permitting automobile drivers with special transponders to pay discounted tolls held not to discriminate against non-residents of Massachusetts; noting that "[a]ny traveler can qualify for a discount, but the decision whether to do so turns principally on anticipated frequency of travel."); CSX Transportation, Inc. v. Williams, 2005 WL 902130, at *21 (D.D.C. 2005) (upholding District prohibition of transportation of certain hazardous materials within 2.2 miles of the U.S. Capitol; suggests that "mere movement" risks harm, unlike in *Philadelphia v. New Jersey*); Kentucky Power Co. v. Huelsmann, 352 F. Supp. 2d 777, 784-787 (E.D. Ky. 2005) (striking down Kentucky law requiring utilities to curtail service to out-of-state customers instead of in-state customers in the event of a disruption of energy supply; *held*, statute has a discriminatory effect on interstate commerce); National Solid Waste Management Ass'n v. Granholm, 344 F. Supp. 2d 559, 566-567 (E.D. Mich. 2004) (upholding law requiring assurance prior to deposit of out-of-state waste in Michigan landfills that waste does not contain materials prohibited by Michigan law to be deposited in its landfills; no discriminatory effects on present record); Saunders v. Port Auth., 2004 WL 1077964 (S.D.N.Y. 2004) (rejecting similar challenge to New York Port Authority's E-ZPass system, which discounts tolls for participants); National Solid Wastes Management Association v. Wayne Co., 2004 WL 288615 (E.D. Mich. 2004) (striking down amendments to county waste disposal ordinance prohibiting disposal of out-of-county solid waste from waste generators not subject to beverage container deposit rate and whose bottle return rates are comparable to those in-state rates; effect is to automatically admit in-state waste and exclude most out-of-state waste); American Trucking

Ass'n, Inc. v. Whitman, 2004 WL 601659 (D.N.J. 2004) (striking down New Jersey statute restricting commercial carriers not originating or terminating trips in state to routes designed for interstate travel finding that exemption for intrastate travel impermissibly discriminated in its effects against interstate commerce); Alliance of Automobile Mfrs. v. Gwadosky, 2004 WL 288533 (D. Me. 2004), at *7-*8 (rejecting claim that state statute prohibiting automobile manufacturers from recovering costs paid to reimburse dealers for repairs performed under manufacturers' warranties discriminated against interstate commerce in its effects; statute "does not discriminate against out-of-state manufacturers, because as a matter of fact, there are no in-state manufacturers to be favored"); Walgreen Co. v. Rullan, 292 F. Supp. 2d 298, 315-316 (D.P.R. 2003) (fact that local pharmacies granted certificate of convenience and necessity to open new pharmacies granted certificates at higher rate than "mainland" pharmacies insufficient to establish discriminatory effects).

Where it is asserted that a facially neutral statute nevertheless discriminates against interstate commerce, either by design or by effect, plaintiffs will often need to assemble a factual record for the court. *See, e.g.*, Smithfield Foods, Inc. v. Miller, 367 F.3d 1061, 1065 (8th Cir. 2004) (vacating trial court judgment, remanding for further discovery on issue of discriminatory effect); National Solid Waste Management Ass'n v. Granholm, 344 F. Supp. 2d 559, 566-567 (E.D. Mich. 2004) (upholding law requiring assurance prior to deposit of out-of-state waste in Michigan landfills that waste does not contain materials prohibited by Michigan law to be deposited in its landfills; no discriminatory effects on present record); American Trucking Ass'n, Inc. v. Whitman, 136 F. Supp. 2d 343, 351-352 (D.N.J. 2001) (action challenging New Jersey regulations limiting certain trucks traveling through the state, with neither origin nor destination in the state, to the use of "National Network Roads" in order to reduce volume of traffic on other New Jersey highways; denying motion for partial summary judgment; characterizing as "premature" a determination whether "the Regulations discriminate in their effect against out-of-state interests"); New Rochelle v. Mamaroneck, 111 F. Supp. 2d 353, 362-363 (S.D.N.Y. 2000) (declining to dismiss, prior to discovery, claim that town ordinance requiring approval of construction projects in areas adjacent to town after review for impact on town; while not *per se* violation of dormant Commerce Clause doctrine, "discovery might reveal that the law was . . . aimed solely at preventing national or international retail 'superstores' from being built in the area" or that town "was looking to keep out streams of shoppers from across the Connecticut border").

Page 6-44, add to the end of note 128:

Though one might wonder whether the *Exxon* case, were it decided today, would come out the same way, courts have nevertheless found it a handy precedent for giving the benefit of the doubt to questionable statutes in close cases. For recent examples *see* Lenscrafters, Inc. v. Robinson, 2005 WL 850439 (6th Cir. 2005), at *5 (upholding statute prohibiting optometrists from practicing in or in conjunction with a retail store; statute did not "discriminate among in-state and out-of-state optical stores, as both are prohibited from leasing space to optometrists"); International Truck and Engine Corp. v. Bray, 372 F.3d 717, 726 (5th Cir. 2004) (upholding Texas law prohibiting truck manufacturers from acting as new or used vehicle dealers or as used truck dealers; in-state dealers and out-of-state manufacturers not similarly situated); Philip Morris v. Reilly, 267 F.3d 45 (1st Cir. 2001) (withdrawn from bound volume at request of the court) (upholding state law requiring tobacco companies to file list of ingredients with state; "Commerce Clause . . . protects the interstate market, not particular interstate firms, from prohibitive or burdensome regulations," citing *Exxon*); Maharg, Inc. v. Van Wert Solid Waste Mgmt. Dist., 249 F.3d 544, 552-555 (6th Cir. 2001) (upholding county waste management plan that prohibited export of waste to site in adjoining state, which site declined to meet conditions for designation as county-approved site, including collection of surcharge and remittance to county); Southern Union Co. v. Missouri Pub. Svc. Comm'n, 138 F. Supp. 2d 1201, 1207-1208 (W.D. Mo. 2001) (upholding Missouri statute requiring Commission approval for stock purchases of other utilities; "[t]he fact that Southern Union does not have the unfettered right to participate in the interstate market of utility stocks does not mean that the market has been impermissibly burdened."), *aff'd* 289 F.3d 503 (8th Cir. 2002); Alliance of Automobile Manufacturers v. Hull, 137 F. Supp. 2d 1165, 1174 (D. Ariz. 2001) (relying on *Exxon* in rejecting motion for injunction against Arizona law that, *inter alia*, prohibits automobile manufacturers from selling services in competition with in-state dealers); *see also* Pharmaceutical Research and Manufacturers of America v. Concannon, 249 F.3d 66, 84 (1st Cir. 2001) (citing *Exxon* for the proposition that the dormant Commerce Clause doctrine does not protect particular interstate firms from "prohibitive or burdensome regulations"); Grant's Dairy — Maine, L.L.C., v. Comm'r, 232 F.3d 8, 21-22 (1st Cir. 2000) ("Grant's argument is nothing more than a lament that the Maine minimum [price for milk] burdens it relative to fully federally regulated handlers located in southern

Maine. This lament should be addressed to the Maine legislature, not to the federal courts. The dormant Commerce Clause does not protect intrastate competition, but, rather, safeguards interstate markets from discriminatory regulation."; citing *Exxon*).

Page 6-47, add to the end of carryover paragraph before "In Wyoming v. Oklahoma":

As *Exxon* and *Clover Leaf Creamery* suggest, those challenging statutes lacking overt, facial discrimination, bear a heavier burden convincing courts of either discriminatory effects or impermissible purposes.[139.1]

[139.1] *See, e.g.*, International Truck and Engine Corp. v. Bray, 372 F.3d 717, 726 (5th Cir. 2004) (upholding Texas law prohibiting truck manufacturers from acting as new or used vehicle dealers or as used truck dealers; in-state dealers and out-of-state manufacturers not similarly situated); Brown & Williamson Tobacco Corp. v. Pataki, 320 F.3d 200 (2d Cir. 2003) (upholding New York law prohibiting sales of cigarettes through the mail or over the Internet; statute did not facially discriminate against in-state and out-of-state sellers); CSX Transportation, Inc. v. Williams, 2005 WL 902130, at *21 (D.D.C. 2005) (upholding District prohibition of transportation of certain hazardous materials within 2.2 miles of the U.S. Capitol; suggests that "mere movement" risks harm, unlike in *Philadelphia v. New Jersey*); National Solid Waste Management Ass'n v. Granholm, 344 F. Supp. 2d 559, 566-567 (E.D. Mich. 2004) (upholding law requiring assurance prior to deposit of out-of-state waste in Michigan landfills that waste does not contain materials prohibited by Michigan law to be deposited in its landfills; no discriminatory effects on present record); Doran v. Massachusetts Turnpike Auth., 2003 WL 1877870 (D. Mass. 2003) (state program offering discounts on tolls to subscribers purchasing electronic toll collection system does not discriminate against out-of-state drivers in its effects; collection system available to in-state and out-of-state residents alike); Lenscrafters, Inc. v. Wadley, 248 F. Supp. 2d (M.D. Tenn. 2003) (rejecting argument that state law prohibiting optometrists from practicing in any retail store or other establishment where merchandise was displayed for sale; no discriminatory effects present), *aff'd sub. nom.* Lenscrafters, Inc. v. Robinson, 2005 WL 850439 (6th Cir. 2005); Hatch v. Employers Insurance of Wausau, 644 N.W.2d 820, 837 (Ct. App. Minn. 2002) (upholding state law requiring state approval of negotiated releases between insurers and policyholders concerning certain in-state landfills).

[B] State Regulation of Solid Waste Disposal

Page 6-49, add to second line of note 155, after "(divided court)":

; *see also* U & I Sanitation v. Columbus, 205 F.3d 1063 (8th Cir. 2000) (striking down city ordinance requiring all waste collected in the city and not destined for out-of-state disposal be processed at city-owned transfer station. National Solid Waste Management Assoc. v. Pine Belt Solid Waste Mgmt. Auth., 261 F. Supp. 2d 644 (S.D. Miss. 2003) (striking down flow control ordinance requiring the disposal of solid waste at designated stations under contract with waste management authority and prohibiting disposal elsewhere), *rev'd* 389 F.3d 491, 502-503 (5th Cir. 2004); National Solid Waste Management Association v. Wayne Co., 2004 WL 288615 (E.D. Mich. 2004) (striking down amendments to county waste disposal ordinance prohibiting disposal of out-of-county solid waste from waste generators not subject to beverage container deposit rate and whose bottle return rates are comparable to those in-state rates; effect is to automatically admit in-state waste and exclude most out-of-state waste); Waste Management Holdings, Inc. v. Gilmore, 64 F. Supp. 2d 537 (E.D. Va. 1999) (refusing to dismiss dormant Commerce Clause claim that state statutes aimed at preventing the importation of garbage for in-state disposal), *aff'd* 252 F.3d 316, 336 (4th Cir. 2001) (concluding that no reasonable juror could have concluded that state waste management plan was *not* intended to discriminate against out-of-state waste), *cert. denied sub nom.* Murphy v. Waste Management Holding, Inc., 122 S. Ct. 1203 (2002); Coastal Carting Ltd. v. Broward County, 75 F. Supp. 2d 1350 (S.D. Fla. 1999) (striking down flow control ordinance prohibiting the transportation of garbage outside the county); Ecological Systems, Inc. v. Dayton, 2002 WL 125702 (Ct. App. Ohio) (Feb. 1, 2002) (unpublished) (striking down city ordinance prohibiting any discharge of wastewater originating outside city into city's sewers or wastewater facilities); *but see* Blue Ribbon Properties, Inc. v. Hardin Co. Fiscal Court, 2002 WL 1893515 (6th Cir.) (Aug. 15, 2002) (concluding that denial of application to operate landfill, where one member of voting body may have been motivated by desire to discriminate against out-of-state waste, insufficient to demonstrate impermissible discriminatory purpose, nor did denial fail *Pike* balancing); CSX Transportation, Inc. v. Williams, 2005 WL 902130, at *21 (D.D.C. 2005) (upholding District prohibition of transportation of certain hazardous materials within 2.2 miles of the U.S. Capitol; suggests that "mere movement" risks harm, unlike in *Philadelphia v. New Jersey*); National Solid Waste Management Ass'n v. Granholm, 344 F. Supp. 2d 559, 566-567 (E.D. Mich. 2004) (upholding law requiring assurance prior to deposit of out-of-state waste in Michigan landfills that waste does not contain materials prohibited by Michigan law to be deposited in its landfills; no discriminatory effects on present record); East Coast Recycling, Inc. v. Port of St. Lucie, 234 F. Supp. 2d 1259 (S.D. Fla. 2002) (upholding ordinance that restricted garbage collection to firm chosen through competitive bidding process, but did not otherwise direct the flow of garbage, and separate city-county agreement that city send garbage to county landfill); A.G.G. Enterprises, Inc. v. Washington Co., 2000 WL 361892 (D. Or. 2000), at *9 (upholding, under *Pike* balancing, a county ordinance that proscribed the storage, transportation, or disposal of solid waste without a certificate, license, or permit, where no additional waste disposal franchises had been awarded in over thirty years and where no process existed for the award of new franchises under a competitive bidding process).

Page 6-49, add to seventh line of note 155 after "see generally":

Carlson, Federalism, Preemption, and Greenhouse Gas Emissions, 37 U.C. Davis L. Rev. 281 (2003); Connolly, Small Town Trash: A Model Comprehensive Solid Waste Ordinance for Rural Areas of the United States, 53 Cath. U. L. Rev. 1 (2003); Cox, Garbage In, Garbage Out: Court Confusion About the Dormant Commerce Clause, 50 Okla. L. Rev. 155 (1997); Diederich, Municipalities Regain Control Over Trash—"Flow Control" Revisited, 35 Urb. Law. 687 (2003); Epstein, Waste & the Dormant Commerce Clause, 3 Green Bag 2d 29 (1999); Adler, Waste and the Dormant Commerce Clause—A Reply, 3 Green Bag 2d 353 (2000); Epstein, Waste and the Dormant Commerce Clause—A Reprise, 3 Green Bag 2d 363 (2000); Green, Public Participation, Federalism and Environmental Law, 6 Buff. Envtl. L.J. 169 (1999); Henning, Misguided Federalism, 68 Mo. L. Rev. 389 (2003); Hodas, State Reponses to Global Warming: Is It Constitutional to Think Globally and Act Locally? 21 Pace Envt'l L. Rev. 53 (2003); Klein, The Environmental Commerce Clause, 27 Harv. Envtl. L. Rev. 1 (2003); Lazarus, Restoring What's Environmental About Environmental Law in the Supreme Court, 47 U.C.L.A. L. Rev. 703, 755-756 (2000); Murray & Spence, Fair Weather Federalism and America's Waste Disposal Crisis, 27 Harv. Envtl. L. Rev. 71 (2003); Nolon, In Praise of Parochialism: The Advent of Local Environmental Law, 26 Harv. Envt'l L. Rev. 365 (2002); Percival, "Greening" the Constitution—Harmonizing Environmental and Constitutional Values, 32 Envtl. L. 809 (2002); Turner, Solid Waste Flow Control: The Commerce Clause and Beyond, 19 Miss. College L. Rev. 53 (1998); Chuang, Note, Who Should Win the Garbage Wars? Lessons from the Low-Level Radioactive Waste Act, 72 Fordham L. Rev. 2403 (2004); Davies, Comment, If You Give the Court a Commerce Clause: An Environmental Justice Critique of Supreme Court

Interstate Waste Jurisprudence, 11 Fordham Envtl. L.J. 207 (1999); Korot, Note, *Waste Management Holdings v. Gilmore*: The Anything but Dormant Problem of Interstate Waste, 13 Vill. Envt'l L.J. 315 (2002); McCracken, Comment, Constitutional Law—Combating Canadian Trash Under the Guise of the Dormant Commerce Clause, 82 U. Det. Mercy L. Rev. 59 (2004); Peake, Note, South Carolina Loses a Battle in the Hazardous Waste Wars: Using the Dormant Commerce Clause to Invalidate South Carolina's Hazardous Waste Laws in *Environmental Technology Council v. Sierra Club*, 76 N.C. L. Rev. 650 (1998); Thompson, Note, Public Health, Environmental Protection, and the Dormant Commerce Clause: Maintaining State Sovereignty in the Federalist Structure, 55 Case W. Res. L. Rev. 213 (2004);

Page 6-51, add to note 159 after "(1992);" *and before* "*see also*":

CSX Transportation, Inc. v. Williams, 2005 WL 902130, at *21 (D.D.C. 2005) (upholding District prohibition of transportation of certain hazardous materials within 2.2 miles of the U.S. Capitol; suggests that "mere movement" risks harm, unlike in *Philadelphia v. New Jersey*);

Page 6-55, add to second line of note 176, before "Stickney,":

For commentary on *Carbone*, *see* Cox, *supra* note 155; Turner, *supra* note 155;

Page 6-56, add to the end of note 179:

For a new twist on local-processing requirement, see the Arizona law challenged in *Alliance for Automobile Manufacturers v. Hull*, 137 F. Supp. 2d 1165 (D. Ariz. 2001). Designed to protect independent, in-state automotive dealerships from abuses by automobile manufacturers, the law "forbids manufacturers from owning or operating a dealership in [Arizona], or from directly selling vehicles, parts, services, financing, or accessories directly to customers in [Arizona]. It also precludes manufacturers from dictating prices or otherwise discriminating against the dealerships." *Alliance for Automotive Manufacturers*, 137 F. Supp. 2d at 1169. Specifically, manufacturers were required to offer cars to dealers in Arizona at a price no greater than that paid by any other dealer in the United States, subject to a few exceptions. *See id.* at 1172. In addition, the law required that "when a lead of a prospective retail customer is discovered, the manufacturer must forward that lead to a dealer within the same geographic area as the prospective customer." *Id.* at 1175. The effect of the latter would mean that manufacturers could not be able, for instance, to sell cars to Arizona residents over the Internet. The discriminatory pricing section of the law survived a motion for injunctive relief because the judge found the factual record too incomplete to ascertain plaintiffs' likelihood of success on the merits of their claims. *Id.* at 1172-1173. The ban on provision of aftermarket services survived based on *Exxon. Id.* at 1174. Finally, the "leads forwarding" provision likewise survived because the judge concluded that the plaintiffs had not met their burden of proof that the law was, in fact, protectionist or discriminatory. *Id.* at 1176. After discovery, however, it would be surprising if the plaintiffs were not able to establish that the law was drafted to protect in-state car dealerships at the expense of out-of-state manufacturers, and to ensure the dealerships' survival in the event that car makers attempt large-scale attempts (over the Internet or otherwise) to sell directly to their customers. If such a foundation is laid, *Exxon* notwithstanding, the case would seem indistinguishable from others cited in this section in which strict scrutiny would apply.

For recent post-*Carbone* decisions concerning flow-control ordinances, *see* Maharg, Inc. v. Van Wert Solid Waste Mgmt. Dist., 249 F.3d 544 (6th Cir. 2001) (upholding county waste management plan that prohibited export of waste to site in adjoining state, which site declined to meet conditions for designation as county-approved site, including collection of surcharge and remittance to county); Huish Detergents, Inc. v. Warren Co., 214 F.3d 707 (6th Cir. 2000) (striking down county ordinance incorporating by reference franchise contract for exclusive collection and disposal of municipal solid waste, operation of city-owned transfer station, and requiring in-state disposal of waste); U & I Sanitation v. Columbus, 205 F.3d 1063 (8th Cir. 2000) (striking down city ordinance requiring all waste collected in the city and not destined for out-of-state disposal be processed at city-owned transfer station); United Waste Systems of Iowa, Inc. v. Wilson, 189 F.3d 762 (8th Cir., 1999) (upholding Iowa flow control statute that required in-county waste to be disposed of at county-designated processing plant, unless shipped out of state); Sal Tinnerello & Sons, Inc. v. Stonington, 141 F.3d 46, 55-56 (2d Cir. 1998); National Solid Waste Management Assoc. v. Pine Belt Solid Waste Mgmt. Auth., 2003 WL 21006321 (S.D. Miss. 2003) (striking down flow control ordinance requiring the disposal of solid waste at designated stations under contract with waste management authority and prohibiting disposal elsewhere), *rev'd*, 389 F.3d 491, 502-503 (5th Cir. 2004); Randy's Sanitation, Inc. v. Wright Co., 65 F. Supp. 2d 1017, (D. Minn.1999) (striking down county ordinance requiring all waste to be disposed of in the county to be disposed of in designated processing plant); Waste Management Holdings, Inc. v. Gilmore, 64 F. Supp. 2d 537 (E.D. Va. 1999) (refusing to dismiss dormant Commerce Clause claim against state statutes aimed at preventing the importation of garbage for in-state disposal), *aff'd* 252 F.3d 316, 336 (4th Cir. 2001) (concluding that no reasonable juror could have concluded that state waste management plan was *not* intended to discriminate against out-of-state waste), *cert. denied sub nom.* Murphy v. Waste Management Holding, Inc., 122 S. Ct. 1203 (2002); Coastal Carting Ltd. v. Broward County, 75 F. Supp. 2d 1350 (S.D. Fla. 1999) (striking down flow control ordinance prohibiting the transportation of garbage outside the county).

The contradictory outcomes in the Eighth Circuit were explained by the *U & I Sanitation* panel as turning on the fact that the plaintiff landfill in the *United Waste Systems* case argued that the state law "caused it to lose business, and that it was precluded from purchasing additional fuel, equipment and supplies from out-of-state businesses because it had not been chosen by a sufficient number of counties as a disposal site." *U & I Sanitation*, 205 F.3d at 1069 n.3. According to the *U & I Sanitation* court, the court in *United Waste Systems* "concluded . . . that the alleged business loss resulted from poor marketing techniques and not from the state regulation." *Id.* In contrast, the *U & I Sanitation* court did not limit its analysis "to the burdens suffered by the particular parties before us," but rather, it felt obliged "to adopt an aggregate analysis whereby we consider the interstate effect on the . . . market if several jurisdictions were to adopt similar ordinances." *Id.* at 1069. When it did so, it found that the impact on the interstate market for recyclables would be marked, since the city-owned processing plant had "virtually no recycling capabilities." *Id.* at 1072.

For a recent decision upholding a local flow control ordinance, *see* A.G.G. Enterprises, Inc. v. Washington Co., 2000 WL 361892 (D. Or. 2000), at *9 (upholding, under *Pike* balancing, a county ordinance that proscribed the storage, transportation, or disposal of solid waste without a certificate, license, or permit, where no additional waste disposal franchises had been awarded in over thirty years and where no process existed for the award of new franchises under a competitive bidding process). The facts in *A.G.G. Enterprises* were strikingly similar to those in *Carbone*, yet the judge reached a different result. The district court opinion is notable for (i) its focus on whether the county ordinance at issue "directly" or "indirectly" regulated commerce and (ii) the judge's failure to analyze the facts of the case at bar in light of *Carbone*, even though the judge cited the case. *See id.* at *8-*9. The judge did, however, strike down part of the ordinance on preemption grounds, *see id.* at *8, but was reversed by the Ninth Circuit. A.G.G. Enterprises, Inc. v. Washington Co., 281 F.3d 1324 (9th Cir. 2001).

Page 6-57, add to the end of note 181:

For recent critiques of the Supreme Court's application of the dormant Commerce Clause doctrine in the area of waste regulation, *see* Epstein, Waste & the Dormant Commerce Clause, 3 Green Bag 2d 29 (1999); Green, Public Participation, Federalism and Environmental Law, 6 Buff. Envtl. L.J. 169 (1999); Henning, Misguided Federalism, 68 Mo. L. Rev. 389 (2003); Houck, Environmental Law and the General Welfare, 16 Pace Envt'l L. Rev. 1, 8, 9 (1998); Klein, The Environmental Commerce Clause, 27 Harv. Envtl. L. Rev. 1 (2003); Lazarus, Restoring What's Environmental About Environmental Law in the Supreme Court, 47 U.C.L.A. L. Rev. 703, 755-756 (2000); Murray & Spence, Fair Weather Federalism and America's Waste Disposal Crisis, 27 Harv. Envtl. L. Rev. 71 (2003); Nolon, In Praise of Parochialism: The Advent of Local Environmental Law, 26 Harv. Envt'l L. Rev. 365 (2002); Percival, "Greening" the Constitution—Harmonizing Environmental and Constitutional Values, 32 Envtl. L. 809 (2002); *see also* Adler, Waste and the Dormant Commerce Clause—A Reply, 3 Green Bag 2d 353 (2000); Epstein, Waste and the Dormant Commerce Clause—A Reprise, 3 Green Bag 2d 363 (2000); Chuang, Note, Who Should Win the Garbage Wars? Lessons from the Low-Level Radioactive Waste Act, 72 Fordham L. Rev. 2403 (2004); Davies, Comment, If You Give the Court a Commerce Clause: An Environmental Justice Critique of Supreme Court Interstate Waste Jurisprudence, 11 Fordham Envtl. L.J. 207 (1999); McCracken, Comment, Constitutional Law—Combating Canadian Trash Under the Guise of the Dormant Commerce Clause, 82 U. Det. Mercy L. Rev. 59 (2004); Thompson, Note, Public Health, Environmental Protection, and the Dormant Commerce Clause: Maintaining State Sovereignty in the Federalist Structure, 55 Case W. Res. L. Rev. 213 (2004);

[C] Regulations Relating to Natural Resources

[1] Fish and Game

Page 6-58, add to note 184, line 8, after "or less"):

; Connecticut *ex rel.* Blumenthal v. Crotty, 180 F. Supp. 2d 392 (N.D.N.Y. 2001) (striking down New York regulation conditioning the grant of license to take lobsters in New York waters on agreement to refuse to take lobsters in areas outside state jurisdiction), *aff'd*, 346 F.3d 84, 100 (2d Cir. 2003); *see also* Young v. Coloma-Agaran, 2001 WL 1677259 (D. Hawaii) (Dec. 27, 2001), at *15 (striking down ban on operation of tour boats in certain bay; state presented no evidence of local benefit, asserted benefits clearly exceeded by demonstrated burden on interstate commerce);

Page 6-58, add to note 184, second from last, before "See generally":

Kafka v. Hagener, 176 F. Supp. 2d 1037, 1043 (D. Mont. 2001) (upholding, against dormant Commerce Clause challenge, moratorium on game farm licenses, ban of licenses transfers, and killing of exotic wildlife on game farms); Bean v. Bredesen, 2005 WL 1025767 (Tenn. Ct. App. 2005), at *7 (upholding state ban on private possession of white-tailed deer);

Page 6-58, add to note 184, second line from last, after "See generally":

Irrang, Note, Poof, Up in Smoke! The Coal Industry Gets Burned: The Seventh Circuit Incinerates State Autonomy with Its Strict Interpretation of the Dormant Commerce Clause in *Alliance for Clean Coal v. Miller*, 8 Villanova Envt'l L.J. 259 (1997) (criticizing Seventh Circuit opinion striking down state law that attempted to require coal-burning electrical plants to use some high-sulfur coal); Nicolaysen, Comment, Reserving Wildlife for Resident Consumption: Is the Dormant Commerce Clause the Outfitters' White Knight?, 32 Land & Water L. Rev. 125 (1997);

Page 6-60, add to the end of note 193:

Cf. Hagener v. Wallace, 47 P.3d 847, 855-857 (Mont. 2003) (holding that prohibition on transfer of elk from game farm to person outside state in violation of state statute did not violate the dormant Commerce Clause; state had legitimate interest in preventing harm to wild elk populations); Bean v. Bredesen, 2005 WL 1025767 (Tenn. Ct. App. 2005), at *7 (upholding state ban on private possession of white-tailed deer). The First Circuit recently resisted attempts to characterize a state's minimum price scheme for milk as the sort of "resource-hoarding" that warrants application of strict scrutiny under the dormant Commerce Clause doctrine. *See* Grant's Dairy—Maine, L.L.C. v. Comm'r, 232 F.3d 8, 22-23 (1st Cir. 2000) (finding the comparison inapposite because (i) "the suggestion of resource hoarding contradicts Grant's admission . . . that, with the Maine minimum in place, Grant finds it more profitable to sell milk out of state than in most in-state markets" and (ii) "Grant's argument about producers' incentives to sell to handlers with the smallest percentage of interstate distribution is woven out of the gossamer strands of speculation and surmise, unsupported by even the slimmest evidentiary thread").

[D] Restrictions on Out-of-State Corporations

Page 6-65, add to the end of note 203:

For an argument that cities and states should be allowed to protect their citizens from large chain stores like Wal-Mart and Home Depot, *see* Shoemake, Note, The Smalling of America?: Growth Management Statutes and the Dormant Commerce Clause, 48 Duke L.J. 891 (1999). This desire to defend against the feared onslaught of "urban sprawl" may have motivated the Town of Mamaroneck to pass an ordinance that "requires that its Town Board review the impact of certain major development projects in an area outside of, but adjacent to, Mamaroneck." The law makes the granting of certain permits contingent upon "a showing that the impact of the development on the Town will be mitigated." New Rochelle v. Mamaroneck, 111 F. Supp. 2d 353, 357 (S.D.N.Y. 2000). The City of New Rochelle alleged that the ordinance was passed in response to its attempt to acquire land adjacent to Mamaroneck so that a national home furnishings store could be built there—a move that Mamaroneck vociferously opposed. New Rochelle argued that this ordinance discriminated against interstate commerce. While the court noted that the ordinance did not discriminate on its face, and thus was not *per se* illegal, it refused to grant Mamaroneck's motion to dismiss because "discovery might reveal that the law was, in fact, aimed solely at preventing national or international retail 'superstores' from being built in the area. Or it might be revealed that Mamaroneck was looking to keep out streams of shoppers from across the Connecticut border. . . ." *New Rochelle*, 111 F. Supp. 2d at 362-363. The controversial development plan was later abandoned in the face of the neighborhood resistance. *See* Hu, A Neighborhood Adjusts, Warily, to Life After Ikea, N.Y. Times, July 5, 2002.

Page 6-65, add to the end of note 206:

In Alabama, for example, a state statute forbids a corporation not qualified to do business in Alabama from enforcing in a state court a contract made in the state. While the state supreme court has recognized that the statute does not apply to businesses engaged in interstate commerce, the state court has not interpreted that concept expansively. *See, e.g.*, Hays Corp. v. Bunge Corp., 777 So. 2d 62 (Ala. 2000) (Georgia corporation, not qualified to do business in Alabama, that contracted with other out-of-state corporation to provide construction services in Alabama sued for breach of contract; *held*, contract to provide construction services is intrastate commerce, thus claim barred by state statute); *ex parte* Dial Kennels of Alabama, Inc., 771 So. 2d 419, 426 (Ala. 1999) ("We have stated that a nonqualified foreign corporation is conducting intrastate business in Alabama when it has engaged in some activity toward establishing a continuing presence in the state, over and above merely shipping commodities between the states."). Companies have also successfully challenged state laws that toll the statute of limitations for persons who leave the state without appointing an agent for service of process. *See, e.g.*, Bendix Autolight Corp. v. Midwesco Enterprises, Inc., 486 U.S. 888, 108 S. Ct. 2218 (1988) (divided court) (statute burdened interstate commerce); Rademeyer v. Farris, 284 F.3d 833, 838-839 (8th Cir. 2002) (striking down similar Missouri statute); *but see* Argonaut Insurance Co. v. Halvanon Ins. Co., 2001 WL 1579619 (9th Cir.) (July 10, 2001) (unpublished) (divided court) (upholding a tolling statute where defendant was a foreign corporation not otherwise subject to service of process; "[w]here the defendant is not subject to service of process, the state interest in preserving a litigation forum is more compelling" (footnote omitted)).

Page 6-66, add to the end of note 211:

Similarly, state statutes that seek to protect their citizens working on commission from sharp-dealing, out-of-state corporations by, *inter alia*, requiring those businesses not maintaining a fixed place of business within the state to negotiate written contracts with their in-state sales personnel, on pain of treble damages, have also faired poorly in court. *See, e.g.*, Lett v. Paymentech, Inc., 81 F. Supp. 2d 992, 995-1001 (N.D. Cal. 1999) and cases cited therein; *but see* Sandra F. Monroe & Co., Inc. v. Nat'l Equipment Services, Inc., 2000 WL 420746 (N.D. Ill. 2000) (upholding Illinois Business Brokerage Act as applied to a Delaware corporation with its principal place of business in Illinois and a Massachusetts business broker who allegedly arranged the sale of a Massachusetts business to the defendant corporation; *held*, statute voiding the contract of a business broker not registered to do business in the state was valid; no dormant Commerce Clause violation because statute was even-handed and applied only to corporations "domiciled" in state).

Page 6-67, add to the end of note 212:

But see Southern Union Co. v. Missouri Pub. Svc. Comm'n, 138 F. Supp. 2d 1201, 1209-1210 (W.D. Mo. 2001) (upholding Missouri law prohibiting utilities from acquiring stock in other utilities without approval by the Public Service Commission), *aff'd* 289 F.3d 503 (8th Cir. 2002).

[F] State Restrictions on Prices of Alcoholic Beverages

Page 6-75, add to the end of note 242:

For the use of *Brown-Forman* and *Healy*'s reasoning to strike down other state laws with extraterritorial effects, *see* American Bookseller's Foundation v. Dean, 342 F.3d 96, 102-104 (2d Cir. 2003) (striking down Vermont's statute governing sexually-explicit content on the Internet; concluding that statute is impermissible extraterritorial regulation); Southeast Booksellers Ass'n v. McMaster, 2005 WL 1322849 (D.S.C. 2005), at *10 (South Carolina statute prohibiting dissemination of material "harmful to minors" over the Internet invalid because act "regulat[es] commerce occurring wholly outside of South Carolina"); Center for Democracy & Technology v. Pappert, 2004 WL 2005938 (E.D. Pa. 2004), at ____ (striking down state law requiring Internet service providers to remove or disable access to child pornography either stored on or available through its service; the Act "has the practical effect of exporting Pennsylvania's domestic policies"); Pepsico, Inc. v. Marion Pepsi-Cola

Bottling Co., 2003 WL 22594235 (S.D. Ill. 2003), at *7 (striking down Illinois statute granting soft drink distributors rights against suppliers; "many provisions of the Act have the practical effect of controlling conduct which occurs outside of this State" and "requires Pepsi to tailor its commercial activity outside of Illinois to the Illinois regulatory scheme"); Philip Morris, Inc. v. Reilly, 113 F. Supp. 2d 129, 149-150 (D. Mass. 2000) (striking down Massachusetts law requiring disclosure of specific ingredients contained in tobacco products, and requirement that such disclosures be available to the public, even if protected as "trade secrets" under federal law and exempt from disclosure; "the 'practical effect' of the Disclosure Act would be to alter competitive relationships in the market for tobacco products in places wholly outside Massachusetts by withdrawing . . . the competitive advantage [plaintiffs'] otherwise have in those places by reason of their ingredient trade secrets. . . . The effect of requiring disclosure of the secret cannot be localized within a single State."), *rev'd* 267 F.3d 45 (1st Cir. 2001) (withdrawn from bound volume at request of the court) (distinguishing *Healy*; act "does not purport to regulate across state lines, nor is it an attempt at economic protectionism . . . ; its out-of-state effect is merely incidental to an in-state . . . regulatory scheme and any resulting loss of competitive advantage is unrelated to interstate commerce"); National Electrical Man. Assoc. v. Sorrell, 72 F. Supp. 2d 449, 450 (D. Vt. 1999) (enjoining enforcement against Vermont statute forbidding the sale of items containing mercury without state-mandated label "which essentially requires lamp manufacturers to label all lamps in conformity with Vermont law"; "Vermont is presuming to legislate outside its own boundaries"), *rev'd* 272 F.3d 104, 110 (2d Cir. 2001) (plaintiff's "extraterritoriality contention fails because the statute does not inescapably require manufacturers to label all lamps wherever distributed"); Knoll Pharmaceutical Co. v. Sherman, 57 F. Supp. 2d 615, 622-624 (E.D. Ill. 1999) (striking down Illinois law prohibiting the advertisement, within the state, of an FDA-approved weight-loss drug; *held*, compliance with advertising ban not possible without cessation of national advertising campaign); In re Lead Paint, 2002 WL 31474528 (N.J. Superior Ct.) (Nov. 4, 2002) (unpublished) (rejecting attempt to impose punitive damages on lead paint manufacturers; suit seeks to regulate conduct that takes place outside the borders of state); *but see* Freedom Holdings, Inc. v. Spitzer, 2004 WL 26498 (2d Cir. 2004), at *11 (rejecting cigarette importers arguments that New York contraband statute operated with impermissible extraterritorial effects); Gravquick A/S v. Trimble Navigation Int'l Ltd., 323 F.3d 1219,

1223-1225 (9th Cir. 2003) (state statute protecting equipment dealers did not operate with impermissible extraterritorial reach with respect to contract between parties that supported California choice of law; statute "only applies to this case because the parties chose to be governed by California law"); Southern Union Co. v. Missouri Pub. Svc. Comm'n, 289 F.3d 503, 507 (8th Cir. 2002) (rejecting claim that law requiring administrative approval for stock purchases of other utility companies); Pharmaceutical Research and Manufacturers of America v. Concannon, 249 F.3d 66, 80-83 (1st Cir. 2001) (refusing to enjoin Maine Act requiring pharmaceutical companies wishing to supply drugs to State Medicaid patients to negotiate with the State for discounts on drugs, which fund state subsidy program designed to reduce cost of prescription drugs; no extraterritorial effect: "Act does not interfere with regulatory schemes in other states" or seek to regulate activity outside Maine's borders), *aff'd sub nom.* Pharmaceutical Research and Manufacturers of America v. Walsh, 538 U.S. 644, 123 S. Ct. 1855 (2003) (divided court). The court went on to draw further distinctions between the Maine Act and other price-affirmation statutes struck down by the Supreme Court:

> Unlike . . . price affirmation and price control statues, the Maine Act does not regulate the price of any out-of-state transaction, either by its express terms or by its inevitable effect. Maine does not insist that manufacturers sell their drugs to a wholesaler for a certain price. Similarly, Maine is not tying the price of its in-state products to out-of-state prices. There is nothing within the Act that requires the rebate to be a certain amount dependent upon the price of prescription drugs in other states. The Act merely states that the Commissioner of the Maine Department of Human Services shall use "best efforts to obtain an initial rebate amount equal to or greater than the rebate calculated under the Medicaid program. . . ." Furthermore . . . the Maine Act does not impose direct controls on a transaction that occurs wholly out-of-state. *Id.* at 81-82.

The U.S. Supreme Court quoted the First Circuit's analysis with approval in Pharmaceutical Research and Manufacturers of America v. Walsh, 538 U.S. 644, 123 S. Ct. 1855, 1871 (2003) (divided court), implying, without stating explicitly, that the Court may be inclined to restrict extraterritoriality analysis to the facts of *Healy* and *Brown-Forman.* For other recent judicial rejections of extraterritoriality arguments, *see* District of

Columbia v. Beretta, U.S.A. Corp., 872 A.2d 633, 656-658 (D.C. Ct. App. 2005) (upholding D.C. ordinance imposing strict liability in tort for manufacturers of "machine guns" or "assault weapons" for injuries arising out of discharge of weapon within the District; no extraterritorial regulation where only "regulation" is possible imposition of tort damages); Alliance of Automobile Mfrs. v. Gwadosky, 2004 WL 288533 (D. Me. 2004), at *6-*7 (rejecting claim that state statute prohibiting automobile manufacturers from recovering costs paid to reimburse dealers for repairs performed under manufacturers' warranties operated with impermissible extraterritorial effects); Pharmaceutical Care Management Ass'n v. Rowe, 2004 WL 438320 (D. Me. 2004), at ____ (rejecting extraterritoriality challenge to state law establishing fiduciary duty between pharmaceutical benefits management companies and benefits plans supplied by them with prescription drugs); Cambridge Credit Counseling Corp. v. Foulston, 2003 WL 23279978 (D. Kan. 2003), at *5-*6 (state ban on business of debt adjusting except where performed as an incident to the practice of law was not impermissible extraterritorial regulation; "the transactions involved contracts formed between citizens of one state and a corporation located in another state. . . . [T]he transactions did not occur wholly outside of Kansas."); Pharmaceutical Research & Mfrs. of America v. Michigan Dept. Community Health, 2003 WL 1701416 (D.D.C.) (March 28, 2003) (state Medicaid initiative requiring drug manufacturers to discount drugs sold to state to avoid prior authorization requirements did not operate with impermissible extraterritorial effect; no attempt to tie prices charged in state to those charged elsewhere); Mariana v. Fisher, 226 F. Supp. 2d 575 (M.D. Pa. 2002) (rejecting argument that Master Settlement Agreement between tobacco companies and states to settle claims stemming from costs states bear to treat ill smokers constituted impermissible extraterritorial regulation); Bronco Wine Co. v. Jolly, 2005 WL 1244920 (Cal. Ct. App. 2005), at *16-*17 (upholding state statute prohibiting the use of brand name using "Napa" to refer to wines unless substantial portion of grapes used to make the wine originated in Napa County; because statute limited to wine produced in-state and offered for sale either in-state or out-of-state, no extraterritorial effect); Volkswagen of America, Inc. v. Quillian, 569 S.E.2d 744 (Ct. App. Va. 2002) (upholding state new vehicle allocation statute against allegation statute regulated extraterritorially). For articles on extraterritoriality generally, *see* Felmly, Comment, Beyond the Reach of States: The Dormant Commerce Clause, Extraterritorial State Regulation, and the Concerns of Federalism, 55 Me. L. Rev. 467 (2003); *see also* Hull,

Extraterritoriality and Punitive Damages: Is There a Workable System, 70 Def. Couns. J. 439 (2003).

Gun manufacturers who have been subjected to suits by municipalities for allegedly engaging in tortious marketing and distribution practices have objected, on extraterritoriality grounds, to those suits. In part, manufacturers claim that the remedies sought, including injunctive relief mandating changes in nationwide marketing and distribution of their products, operate with impermissible extraterritorial effects. One court accepted that argument, but it did not survive appeal. *See* Gary v. Smith & Wesson Corp., 2001 WL 333111 (Super. Ct. Ind. 2001), at *6 ("Defendants suggest that the City's lawsuit, in violate of the Commerce Clause, seeks to regulate the lawful conduct of defendants outside Gary's borders, in their production, distribution and sales practices. As such, the City's proposed claim and relief inevitably have an unconstitutional and extraterritorial effect."), *rev'd*, 801 N.E.2d 1222, 1236-1237 (Ind. 2003); *see also* District of Columbia v. Beretta U.S.A. Corp., 2002 WL 31811717 (D.C. Super. Ct.) (Dec. 16, 2002) (suggesting, without holding, that the District of Columbia's Strict Liability Act governing the liability of firearms manufacturers constitutes impermissible extraterritorial regulation); *but see* District of Columbia v. Beretta, U.S.A. Corp., 872 A.2d 633, 656-658 (D.C. Ct. App. 2005) (upholding D.C. ordinance imposing strict liability in tort for manufacturers of "machine guns" or "assault weapons" for injuries arising out of discharge of weapon within the District; no extraterritorial regulation where only "regulation" is possible imposition of tort damages); Ileto v. Glock, Inc., 349 F.3d 1191, 1216-1217 (9th Cir. 2003) (divided court); New York v. Beretta U.S.A. Corp., 2004 WL 764959 (E.D.N.Y. 2004), at *23-*24; City of Cincinnati v. Beretta U.S.A. Corp., 768 N.E.2d 1136 (Ohio 2002) (rejecting argument that municipal tort suit against gun manufacturer seeking injunctive relief forcing changes in marketing and distribution of firearms did not constitute impermissible extraterritorial regulation); Camden v. Beretta, 123 F. Supp. 2d 245, 254-255 (D.N.J. 2000) (dismissing county complaint against gun manufacturers for negligent marketing and distribution of handguns; expressing skepticism that such suits might implicate the dormant Commerce Clause doctrine: "The Court finds that plaintiff's claims in this case would almost certainly have a negative effect upon interstate commerce, but also that there would undoubtedly be strong local benefits involved if the county succeeded in stemming the tide of gun violence within its borders."). *See generally* Denning, Constitutional Limitations on Regulating the Gun Industry Through Tort Litigation: The Second Amendment and the Dormant Commerce Clause, *in* Suing the Gun Industry: A Battle at the Crossroads of Gun Control and Mass Torts (Lytton ed., 2005); Rostron, The Supreme Court, the Gun Industry, and the Misguided Revival of Strict Territorial Limits on the Reach of State Law, 2003 Mich. St. U.-D.C. L. Rev. 115, 151-56.

[G] Subsidies and Economic Protectionism

Page 6-76, add to the end of note 243:

For a recent case rejecting a dormant Commerce Clause challenge to a state medical school's admission policy that, all things being equal, favored long-term over short-term residents in admissions decisions, *see* Buchwald v. University of New Mexico School of Medicine, 159 F.3d 487, 496 n.9 (10th Cir. 1998). A recent student note, on the other hand, suggests that Georgia's HOPE scholarship program, which provides state money for Georgia residents to attend in-state public or private schools, may be unconstitutional under the dormant Commerce Clause doctrine. *See* Cross, Note, Dormant Danger?: A Potential Constitutional Challenge to Georgia's HOPE Scholarship, 34 Ga. L. Rev. 1381 (2000).

[1] Constitutional Status of Subsidies

Page 6-76, add to note 245, after "See generally":

Cross, Note, Dormant Danger?: A Potential Constitutional Challenge to Georgia's HOPE Scholarship, 34 Ga. L. Rev. 1381 (2000);

Page 6-77, add to end of note 246 after "see also":

Enrich, Business Tax Incentives: A Status Report, 34 Urb. Law. 415 (2002); Dale, Comment, Economic Development Incentives, Accountability Legislation, and the Double Negative Commerce Clause, 46 St. Louis U. L. J. 247 (2002); Little, Comment, Corporate Welfare Wars: The Insufficiency of Current Constraints on State Action and the Desirability of a Federal Legislative Response, 22 Hamline L. Rev. 849 (1999). For the application of game theory by a political scientist to the question of incentives' effectiveness in attracting businesses, *see* Rogers, The Effectiveness and Constitutionality of State Tax Incentive Policies for Locating Businesses: A Simple Game Theoretic Analysis, 53 Tax Law. 431 (2000).

The Sixth Circuit recently accepted a portion of Professor Enrich's theory by invalidating, on dormant Commerce Clause grounds, an Ohio business incentive statute granting tax credits for the placement of certain types of heavy equipment in the state. *See* Cuno v. DaimlerChrysler, 386 F.3d 738 (6th Cir. 2004). For more on the *Cuno* case, for which a petition for certiorari is pending at the time of this writing, *see infra* § 8.05.

Page 6-81, add new footnote to paragraph ending "with those in the West Lynn case.":

For a possible confirmation of this speculation, see *Pharmaceutical Research and Manufacturers of America v. Walsh*, 538 U.S. 644, 123 S. Ct. 1855 (2003) (divided court). The "Maine Rx Program" required drug manufacturers and retailers to rebate a certain percentage of Medicaid drug sales to the state in order to avoid a prior authorization requirement in the state's Medicaid program. The money from the rebate was then segregated into a "Maine Rx Fund" and was used to reimburse in-state pharmacies (which were required to pay the rebates) for filling discount prescriptions for non-Medicaid-eligible state citizens. Despite the availability of a brilliant argument that the parallels between *West Lynn Creamery* and the Maine Rx Program should result in the latter's invalidation, *see* Denning, The Maine Rx Prescription Drug Plan and the Dormant Commerce Clause Doctrine: The Case of the Missing Link[age], 29 Am. J. L. & Med. 7 (2003), the Supreme Court upheld the program. Justice Stevens, joined on this point by all of his colleagues, wrote:

> Unlike the situation in *West Lynn* . . . the Maine Rx Program will not impose a disparate burden on any competitors. A manufacturer could not avoid its rebate obligation by opening production facilities in Maine and would receive no benefit from the rebates even if it did so; the payments to the local pharmacists provide no special benefit to competitors of rebate-paying manufacturers.

Walsh, 538 U.S. at 670, 123 S. Ct. at 1871.

[H] Overlapping Constitutional Coverage: The Commerce Clause and the Privileges and Immunities Clauses

[1] The Privileges and Immunities Clause of Article IV

Page 6-83, add to the end of note 265:

For a recent historical examination of the meaning of "privileges and immunities," *see* Upham, Note, *Corfield v. Coryell* and the Privileges and Immunities of Federal Citizenship, 83 Tex. L. Rev. 1483 (2005).

[a] Economic Protectionism and the Privileges and Immunities Clause of Article IV

Page 6-84, add to the end of note 268:

Similarly, the Court recently reversed a Ninth Circuit decision holding that to trigger scrutiny under the Privileges and Immunities Clause of Article IV, a state statute needed to discriminate on its face on the basis of citizenship or residency. Hillside Dairy, Inc. v. Lyons, 539 U.S. 59, 123 S. Ct. 2142 (2003). Justice Stevens, noted that holding was "inconsistent" with an older case, *Chalker v. Birmingham & Northwestern R. Co.*, 249 U.S. 522, 39 S. Ct. 366 (1919), in which the Court applied the Privileges and Immunities Clause to a state tax that "did not on its face draw any distinction based on citizenship or residence." *Hillside Dairy*, 539 U.S. at 67, 123 S. Ct. at 2147. The tax in *Chalker*, while not facially discriminating on the basis of citizenship or residency, *did* facially discriminate based on the location of a taxpayer's chief office. Companies whose chief offices were located outside the state paid $100 per year while those in state paid only $25 per year. 249 U.S. at 525-26, 39 S. Ct. at 367. The *Chalker* Court reasoned that since it was likely that persons who had chief offices outside the state were citizens and residents of other states, the practical effect of the tax's structure was to discriminate against those out-of-state residents. 249 U.S. at 527, 39 S. Ct. at 367. It is not clear, however, that *any* facially neutral regulation not as transparent as the one in *Chalker* would be examined under the Privileges and Immunities Clause for discriminatory effects. *Hillside Dairy* explicitly declined to decide "[w]hether *Chalker* should be interpreted as merely applying the Clause to classifications that are but proxies for differential treatment against out-of-state residents, or as prohibiting any classification with the practical effect of discriminating against such residents . . ." 539 U.S. at 67, 123 S. Ct. at 2147. For an argument that the Privileges and Immunities Clause of Article IV does not extend to facially neutral laws with discriminatory effects, and that fact makes it a poor substitute for the dormant Commerce Clause doctrine, as some have suggested, *see* Denning, Why the Privileges and Immunities Clause of Article IV Cannot Replace the Dormant Commerce Clause Doctrine, 88 Minn. L. Rev. 384 (2003).

Page 6-85, add to third line of note 269, before "In a previous case,. . . . ":

; *see also* New York v. State, 709 N.Y.S. 2d 122 (N.Y. 2000) (striking down New York commuter tax on both Privileges and Immunities Clause and dormant Commerce Clause doctrine grounds); New York v. State, 696 N.Y.S. 2d 426, 427 (N.Y. App. Div. 1999) (striking down amended commuter tax on those who work in New York City, but do not reside in the State; no reliable evidence that intrastate commuters are burdened by taxes, which interstate commuters escape); Igoe v. Pataki, 696 N.Y.S. 2d 355 (Sup. Ct. 1999) (striking down state commuter tax that exempted commuters to New York City that commuted from points within the state, *inter alia*, as a violation of Article IV's Privileges and Immunities Clause).

Page 6-85, add to note 269, after "See generally":

Firestone, Does a Commuter's Choice of Where to Reside Implicate the Dormant Commerce Clause?, 49 N.Y.L.S. L. Rev. 943 (2004-2005); Schultz, State Taxation of Interstate Commuters: Constitutional Doctrine in Search of Empirical Analysis, 16 Touro L. Rev. 435 (2000);

Page 6-85, add to first line of note 273 after "See also":

Connecticut ex rel. Blumenthal v. Crotty, 346 F.3d 84, 100 (2d Cir. 2003) (striking down New York law barring nonresident holders of state commercial lobstering permits from taking lobsters from certain areas of New York waters); Council of Insurance Agents + Brokers v. Gallagher, 287 F. Supp. 2d 1302, 1312 (N.D. Fla. 2003) (striking down state rules prohibiting licensed, nonresident insurance agents from engaging in certain activities unless accompanied by a resident agent);

Page 6-86, add to first line of note 276 after "See also":

Lee v. Minner, 2005 WL 1138913 (D. Del. 2005), at * ____ (striking down Delaware's "citizens only" requirement from state Freedom of Information Act under the Privileges and Immunities Clause); Council of Insurance Agents & Brokers v. Juarbe-Jimenez, 363 F. Supp. 2d 47, 55 (D.P.R. 2005) (striking down Puerto Rico regulation prohibiting direct sales of insurance by nonresident insurance agents unless provided through a resident insurance agent required to countersign policies or contracts of insurance); Bach v. Pataki, 289 F. Supp. 2d 217, 226-228 (N.D.N.Y.) (holding that New York's concealed carry scheme did not violate nonresident's right to travel guaranteed by Article IV, § 2), *aff'd* 2005 WL 1052565 (2d Cir 2005);

[b] Hiring Preferences

Page 6-87, add to the fifteenth line of note 278 before "See generally":

; C.S. McCrossan Construction, Inc. v. Rahn, 96 F. Supp. 2d 1238, 1249 (D.N.M. 2000) (striking down a New Mexico statute granting bidding preference to certain in-state corporations whose majority shareholders were state citizens domiciled in New Mexico as not being "closely or substantially related to its purpose").

Page 6-87, add to end of note 278:

For an unusual hiring preference case involving positions in the Wyoming National Guard, *see* Nelson v. Geringer, 295 F.3d 1082, 1095-1096 (10th Cir. 2002) (concluding that residency requirement for positions in Wyoming National Guard violated the Privileges and Immunities Clause of Article IV).

Page 6-87, add to seventh line of note 280 after "See also":

C.S. McCrossan Construction, Inc., 96 F. Supp. 2d at 1247-1248 (striking down a New Mexico statute granting bidding preference to corporations whose majority shareholders were state citizens domiciled in New Mexico; statute abridged majority stockholder plaintiff's "right to own shares, in a meaningful manner" sufficient to grant standing to bring Article IV Privileges and Immunities Clause claim).

[c] The Right to Practice Professions and Vocations

Page 6-88, add to note 282, after "But see":

Paciulan v. George, 229 F.3d 1226, 1228-1229 (9th Cir. 2000) (rejecting a Privileges and Immunities Clause challenge to California rule allowing nonresident lawyers to be admitted *pro hac vice*, but excluding California residents from rule; "Appellants argue not that California is favoring its residents in violation of the Privilege and Immunities Clause, but rather that it is discriminating against its own residents in violation of the Clause. Such a broad interpretation of the Privileges and Immunities Clause would prohibit a state from basing admission to its bar on standards any more stringent than those of the least restrictive state. . . . The Constitution does not compel such a result.");

Page 6-88, add to last line of note 282, after "See generally":

Barton, An Institutional Analysis of Lawyer Regulation: Who Should Control Lawyer Regulation—Courts, Legislatures, or the Market? 37 Ga. L. Rev. 1167 (2003); Perlman, A Bar Against Competition: The Unconstitutionality of Admission Rules for Out-of-State Attorneys, 18 Geo. J. Legal Ethics ____ (forthcoming 2004);

Page 6-89, add to the end of note 282:

; Balderson, Note, *Birbrower, Montalbano, Condon & Frank, P.C. v. Superior Court*: A Defensible Outcome, but a Striking Example of the Need to Reform Unauthorized Practice of Law Provisions, 36 San Diego L. Rev. 871, 893 n.118 (1999) (suggesting potential Privileges and Immunities problems with certain California laws regarding the unauthorized practice of law). A recent article suggests that the United States emulate our European counterparts and relax restraints on interstate legal practice using the Privileges and Immunities Clause and the dormant Commerce Clause doctrine. *See* Goebel, The Liberalization of Interstate Legal Practice in the European Union: Lessons for the United States?, 34 Int'l Law.307 (2000).

Page 6-89, add to the end of note 283:

For a recent application of the *Piper* "substantiality" test to strike down a discriminatory commuter tax, see New York v. State, 709 N.Y.S.2d 122 (N.Y. 2000).

Page 6-89, add to the end of note 284:

See also C.S. McCrossan Construction, Inc. v. Rahn, 96 F. Supp. 2d 1238, 1249 (D.N.M. 2000) (striking down a New Mexico statute granting bidding preference to certain in-state corporations whose majority shareholders were state citizens domiciled in New Mexico as not being "closely or substantially related to its purpose").

[2] Differences between Commerce Clause and the Privileges and Immunities Clause of Article IV

Page 6-89, add new footnote to the end of first paragraph of subpart [2], ending "differences between the two":

See generally Denning, Why the Privileges and Immunities Clause of Article IV Cannot Replace the Dormant Commerce Clause Doctrine, 88 Minn. L. Rev. 384 (2003).

Page 6-90, add to the end of note 285:

But see C.S. McCrossan Construction, Inc. v. Rahn, 96 F. Supp. 2d 1238, 1247-1248 (D.N.M. 2000) (striking down a New Mexico statute granting bidding preference to in-state corporations whose majority shareholder was a state citizen domiciled within the state; *held*, the statute violated majority stockholder plaintiff's "right to own shares, in a meaningful manner" and provided him with sufficient standing to claim a violation of the Privileges and Immunities Clause of Article IV).

Page 6-90, add to the end of the first full paragraph, ending "on this protective shield":

Similarly, the Court has refused to create a "market-participant" exception, like that created for the dormant Commerce Clause doctrine, to the Privileges and Immunities Clause of Article IV.[286.1] This means that a state or local measure insulated from dormant Commerce Clause scrutiny is still vulnerable to invalidation under the Privileges and Immunities Clause, if the plaintiff is not a corporation.

[286.1] *See* United Building and Construction Trades Council v. Camden, 465 U.S. 208, 104 S. Ct. 1020 (1984). For more on the market-participant exception to the dormant Commerce Clause doctrine, *see infra* §§ 7.01-7.07.

Page 6-90, add to the end of note 287:

But see Hillside Dairy, Inc. v. Lyons, 539 U.S. 59, 123 S. Ct. 2142 (2003). In *Hillside Dairy* the Court reversed a Ninth Circuit holding that the Privileges and Immunities Clause of Article IV required facial discrimination on the basis of citizenship or residency before its protections could be invoked. The Court, per Justice Stevens, held that this holding was "inconsistent" with an older case, *Chalker v. Birmingham & Northwestern R. Co.*, 249 U.S. 522, 39 S. Ct. 366 (1919), in which the Court applied the Privileges and Immunities Clause to a state tax that "did not on its face draw any distinction based on citizenship or residence." *Hillside Dairy*, 539 U.S. at 67, 123 S. Ct. at 2147. The tax in *Chalker*, while not facially discriminating on the basis of citizenship or residency, *did* facially discriminate based on the location of a taxpayer's chief office. Companies whose chief offices were located outside the state paid $100 per year while those in state paid only $25 per year. 249 U.S. at 525-26, 39 S. Ct. at 367. The *Chalker* Court reasoned that since it was likely that persons who had chief offices outside the state were citizens and residents of other states, the practical effect of the tax's structure was to discriminate against those out-of-state residents. 249 U.S. at 527, 39 S. Ct. at 367. It is not clear, however, that *any* facially neutral regulation not as transparent as the one in *Chalker* would be examined under the Privileges and Immunities Clause for discriminatory effects. *Hillside Dairy* explicitly declined to decide "[w]hether *Chalker* should be interpreted as merely applying the Clause to classifications that are but proxies for differential treatment against out-of-state residents, or as prohibiting any classification with the practical effect of discriminating against such residents. . . ." 539 U.S. at 67, 123 S. Ct. at 2147. For an argument that the Privileges and Immunities Clause of Article IV does not extend to facially neutral laws with discriminatory effects, and that fact makes it a poor substitute for the dormant Commerce Clause doctrine, as some have suggested, *see* Denning, Why the Privileges and Immunities Clause of Article IV Cannot Replace the Dormant Commerce Clause Doctrine, 88 Minn. L. Rev. 384 (2003).

[3] Fourteenth Amendment's Privileges and Immunities Clause

Page 6-91, add to the beginning of note 291:

The Supreme Court's decision in *Saenz v. Roe*, 526 U.S. 489, 119 S. Ct. 1518 (1999), which reaffirmed the right to travel, and struck down a state durational residency requirement that limited the welfare benefits of new state residents, has spawned discussion among commentators about whether the Court is poised to reconsider the *Slaughter House Cases* and perhaps begin filling the Fourteenth Amendment's Privileges or Immunities Clause with substantive content. *See, e.g.*, Bunch, The Original Understanding of the Privileges and Immunities Clause: Michael Perry's Justification for Judicial Activism or Robert Bork's Constitutional Inkblot?, 10 Seton Hall Const. L.J. 321 (2000); Tribe, *Saenz* Sans Prophecy: Does the Privileges or Immunities Revival Portend the Future or Reveal the Structure of the Present?, 113 Harv. L. Rev. 110 (1999); Winick, Comment, A New Chapter in Constitutional Law: *Saenz v. Roe* and the Revival of the Fourteenth Amendment's Privileges or Immunities Clause, 28 Hofstra L. Rev. 573 (1999).

[I] Economic Protectionism and the Equal Protection Clause

Page 6-93, add to the end of note 299:

See also C.S. McCrossan Construction, Inc. v. Rahn, 96 F. Supp. 2d 1238, 1244 (D.N.M. 2000) (upholding a New Mexico statute granting bidding preference to certain in-state corporations whose majority shareholders were state citizens domiciled in New Mexico under the Equal Protection Clause; "[t]he New Mexico legislature could have believed rationally at the time it passed the law, as does at least one expert economist, that the resident contractor preference would help this state"). The New Mexico statute was, however, struck down on Article IV Privileges and Immunities grounds. The statute, the district court found, impermissibly burdened the rights of the majority shareholder "to own shares, in a meaningful manner." 96 F. Supp. 2d at 1247-1248. For more on the Privileges and Immunities Clause of Article IV, *see supra* § 6.06[H][1].

Page 6-94, add to the end of note 301:

But see New York v. State, 709 N.Y.S.2d 122 (N.Y. 2000); New York v. State, 696 N.Y.S.2d 426, 427 (N.Y. App. Div. 1999) (striking down a commuter tax on those who work in New York City, but do not reside in the State; State "fail[ed] to offer a substantial reason for subjecting [interstate] commuters . . . to a New York City income tax while exempting from such tax [intrastate] commuters . . ."); Igoe v. Pataki, 696 N.Y.S.2d 355, 364 (Sup. Ct. 1999) (holding that basing tax burdens on residency alone "is a wholly arbitrary and irrational basis on which to create distinctions among taxpayers"). For the more familiar deferential judicial posture towards state tax legislation, *see* Rylander v. 3 Beall Bros. 3, Inc., 2 S.W.3d 562 (Ct. App. Tex. 1999) (upholding state franchise tax imposed on corporation no longer subject to state's taxing jurisdiction; greater tax imposed on corporations maintaining fiscal year accounting records as opposed to those electing calendar year basis not "irrational or unreasonable").

§ 6.07 EXPOSURE OF INTERSTATE COMMERCE TO MULTIPLE STATE REGULATORY BURDENS: BACKGROUND

Page 6-98, add to the end of note 317:

See generally Palmore, The Not-So-Strange Career of Interstate Jim Crow: Race Transportation, and the Dormant Commerce Clause, 1878-1946, 83 Va. L. Rev. 1173 (1997).

[A] Current Law

Page 6-98, add to note 318 before "; but see":

; Bioganic Safety Brands, Inc. v. Ament, 174 F. Supp. 2d 1168, 1184 (D. Colo. 2001) (relying in part on *Bibb* to strike down state law regulating labeling of certain pesticides; "[a] state can violate the Dormant Commerce Clause [if] the state's law [conflicts] with other states' laws").

Page 6-98, add to the end of note 318:

; American Trucking Associations, Inc. v. Whitman, 136 F. Supp. 2d 343, 350-351 (D.N.J. 2001) (denial of summary judgment motion involving

New Jersey regulations prohibiting trucks passing through State of New Jersey that have neither originated nor terminated their trips there from using other than "National Network" Roads: "[t]he principal commerce clause cases involving highway safety regulations were all decided only after the development of extensive evidentiary records").

Page 6-100, add to the end of note 322:

In many cases, courts will take care to interpret state statutes to minimize any "extraterritorial" effects that would render them vulnerable to a ormant Commerce Clause doctrine challenge. *See, e.g.*, Star Scientific, Inc. v. Beales, 278 F.3d 339, 356 (4th Cir. 2002) (upholding state legislation implementing nationwide tobacco settlement requiring tobacco companies not party to the settlement to escrow certain monies based on number of in-state sales; rejecting extraterritoriality claim because "Virginia's qualifying statute . . . rather than aiming at or reacting to commerce outside of Virginia, specifically limits its applicability to the sale of cigarettes 'within the Commonwealth.'"); Morley-Murphy Co. v. Zenith Electronics Corp., 142 F.3d 373, 378-381 (7th Cir. 1998) (applying such a saving construction to the Wisconsin Fair Dealership Law); Hampton Feedlot, Inc. v. Nixon, 249 F.3d 814, 819 (8th Cir. 2001) (construing Missouri statute prohibiting price discrimination in the buying of livestock to sales of livestock in Missouri only); Union Underwear Co., Inc. v. Barnhart, 50 S.W.3d 188, 193 (Ky. 2001) (divided court) (holding that Kentucky's Civil Rights Act did not apply to employer whose headquarters were in Kentucky, when the acts giving rise to the lawsuit occurred in another state: "[i]mposing the policy choices by the Commonwealth on the employment practices of our sister states should be done with great prudence and caution out of respect for the sovereignty of other states, and to avoid running afoul of the Commerce Clause of the United States Constitution.").

Page 6-100, add to the end of note 324:

; Pharmaceutical Research and Manufacturers of America v. Concannon, 249 F.3d 66, 82 (1st Cir. 2001) (dismissing claim that Maine statute requiring negotiated rebates to state to fund program to subsidize drug purchase by citizens not eligible for state Medicaid program as a precondition to supplying drugs to Medicaid beneficiaries would burden pharmaceutical companies if scheme replicated in other states: "[t]he most apparent effect of similar statues being passed in other states would be a loss in profits for manufacturers"), *aff'd sub nom.* Pharmaceutical Research and Manufacturers of America v. Walsh, 538 U.S. 644, 123 S. Ct. 1855 (2003) (divided court).

[C] Jurisdiction to Regulate as Prerequisite

Page 6-101, add to the end of note 326:

For examples of a court interpreting a state statute narrowly to avoid impermissible extraterritorial effects, *see* Star Scientific, Inc. v. Beales, 278 F.3d 339, 357 (4th Cir. 2002) (upholding state legislation implementing nationwide tobacco settlement requiring tobacco companies not party to the settlement to escrow certain monies based on number of in-state sales; state benefit — "ensuring that Virginia has a source of recovery for future smoking-related healthcare costs" attributable to nonparty tobacco companies — was not clearly exceeded by burden on interstate commerce); Dean Foods Co. v. Brancel, 187 F.3d 609, 614-616 (7th Cir. 1999); Hampton Feedlot, Inc. v. Nixon, 249 F.3d 814, 819 (8th Cir. 2001) (construing Missouri statute prohibiting price discrimination in the buying of livestock to sales of livestock in Missouri only); Northland Ins. Co. v. New Hampshire Ins. Co., 63 F. Supp. 2d 128, 137 (D.N.H 1999); Union Underwear Co., Inc. v. Barnhart, 50 S.W.3d 188, 193 (Ky. 2001) (divided court) (holding that Kentucky's Civil Rights Act did not apply to conduct occurring outside the state: "[i]mposing the policy choices by the Commonwealth on the employment practices of our sister states should be done with great prudence and caution out of respect for the sovereignty of other states, and to avoid running afoul of the Commerce Clause of the United States Constitution.").

§ 6.08 SUING STATES FOR VIOLATIONS OF THE DORMANT COMMERCE CLAUSE

Page 6-103, add to the end of note 331:

Note, however, that a plaintiff bringing suit under § 1983 must otherwise satisfy procedural requirements, like standing. *See* To-Ro Trade Shows v. Collins, 997 P.2d 960 (Ct. App. Wash. 2000) (holding that trade show promoter did not have standing to file § 1983 action against state for ordering out-of-state corporation not qualified to do business in state to close display at trade show, resulting in financial loss to promoter). In addition, a California court of appeals refused to enjoin the application of a city business tax ordinance to writers who worked from their homes. The plaintiffs had sought relief under § 1983; the court held that it had no power to enjoin the tax. *See* Writers Guild of America, West, Inc. v. Los Angeles, 77 Cal. App. 4th 475 (Ct. App. Cal. 2000). The court held that the plaintiffs should first pay the tax under protest, then seek a refund.

CHAPTER 7

MARKET PARTICIPATION: AN EXCEPTION TO THE DORMANT COMMERCE CLAUSE DOCTRINE

§7.02 SCOPE OF MARKET PARTICIPATION EXCEPTION

[A] Sales by State-Owned Plants

Page 7-8, add to the end of note 16:

Assisting citizens in the purchase of prescription drugs is one such area of state "expansion" now seen by many as "indispensable." In defending its novel plan to require drug companies to negotiate with the state for rebates on prescription drugs as a condition for supplying drugs to state Medicaid beneficiaries — with the "rebates" funding a state subsidy program for those citizens *not* eligible for Medicaid — the State of Maine claimed that it was merely acting as a market-participant. The First Circuit turned aside this proffer of a defense, but upheld the plan against a dormant Commerce Clause challenge anyway. *See* Pharmaceutical Research and Manufacturers of America v. Concannon, 249 F.3d 66, 80 (1st Cir. 2001) ("Maine is not a market buyer of prescription drugs, except as required by the Medicaid statute. Its citizens will continue to directly purchase prescription drugs as needed. Nothing in the Act makes Maine a market participant."), *aff'd sub nom.* Pharmaceutical Research and Manufacturers of America v. Walsh, 538 U.S. 644, 123 S. Ct. 1855 (2003). The market-participant ruling was not appealed to the Supreme Court.

However, the Seventh Circuit turned aside a dormant Commerce Clause challenge to the City of Chicago's use of tolls collected from users of the Chicago Skyway on non-Skyway related transportation projects, contrary to past practices. *See* Endsley v. Chicago, 230 F.3d 276, 284-285 (7th Cir. 2000). The plaintiff had claimed that the tolls unreasonably burdened interstate commerce, insofar as they were not related to the use and operation of the Skyway; the City claimed that it operated the Skyway as a market participant, and not as a market regulator. *Endsley*, 230 F.3d at 284. The Seventh Circuit agreed with the City, and dismissed the dormant Commerce Clause challenge, in part because the plaintiff's own complaint stated that the City operated the Skyway as a "proprietary enterprise," and not in its "governmental capacity." *Id.* The plaintiff's inartful pleading notwithstanding, the court also concluded that the facts — the City had sold revenue bonds to pay for the Skyway's construction and funded its operation and maintenance by the imposition of tolls on its users — "suggest that the City was acting as a property owner, using its property to raise money, not as a regulator." *Id.* at 285.

Page 7-9, add to the end of note 19:

; *cf.* Red River Service Corp. v. Minot, 146 F.3d 583, 586-590 (8th Cir. 1998) (permitting limitations imposed on waste disposal in municipal-owned and operated landfill undertaken "to prolong the useful life of its landfill").

Page 7-10, add to the end of note 22:

See generally Baranski, Comment, Is Local Government the Equivalent of State Government for Purposes of the Market Participant Exception to the Dormant Commerce Clause?, 104 Dick. L. Rev. 687 (2000).

[C] Sales of State-Owned Natural Resources

Page 7-14, add to the end of note 38:

For a similar argument that state and local proposals to purchase firearms for official use only from manufacturers agreeing to make design changes to firearms and change marketing strategies is "regulation" not "market participation," and thus not eligible for the exception, *see* Grast, Gun Control's "Third Way": State and Local Purchase Preference Plans and the Dormant Commerce Clause, 88 Va. L. Rev. 167 (2002).

Page 7-14, add to the end of note 40:

A court recently refused to dismiss a § 1983 claim against a county airport alleging that it required that all pilots storing aircraft at the facility buy fuel only from the private company selected by the county to manage the airport. The judge turned aside the county's argument that the dormant Commerce Clause complaint must be rejected because the county was acting as a market-participant. The court wrote that the county "does not merely collect fees from renters or licensees in exchange for space; it imposes a restriction that benefits a third-party in a market in which it does not directly participate — the market for aircraft fuel." The case, the court continued, closely resembled *South-Central Timber.* Cedarhurst Air Charter, Inc. v. Waukesha Co., 110 F. Supp. 2d 891, 899 (E.D. Wis. 2000).

[D] Foreign Commerce

Page 7-17, add to first line of note 52 before "See generally":

But *see* Antilles Cement Corp. v. Calderon, 288 F. Supp. 2d 187, 197 (D.P.R. 2003) (declining to apply the market-participant doctrine to situation involving foreign dormant Commerce Clause doctrine).

Page 7-17, replace citation at the end of note 53:

see Denning & McCall, The Constitutionality of State and Local "Sanctions" Against Foreign Countries: Affairs of State, States' Affairs, or a Sorry State of Affairs?, 26 Hastings Const. L.Q. 307 (1999); *see also* National Foreign Trade Council v. Natsios, 181 F.3d 38, 62 (1st Cir. 1999) (rejecting the argument that state sanctions on foreign countries, enforced by forbidding companies doing business with such countries from bidding for state contracts, was protected by the market participant exception; doubting whether market participant exception even applied in foreign commerce context); *but see* Sommers, Comment, Massachusetts, Myanmar, Market Participation, and the Federal Shutdown of Selective Purchasing Laws: Is the Power to Purchase Really the Power to Regulate?, 21 Nw. J. Int'l L. & Bus. 317 (2000); Jenkins, National Foreign Trade Council v. The Common- wealth of Massachusetts: A State Acting As a "Market Participant" Should Trump the Federal Government's Right to Regulate Foreign Affairs Unless Congress Expressly Declares Otherwise, 14 Conn. J. Int'l L. 593 (1999). Though the U.S. Supreme Court sustained the First Circuit's decision striking the law, it did so on preemption grounds, and declined to address the dormant Foreign Commerce Clause doctrine, including the state's claim that the market-participant doctrine provided a defense. *See* Crosby v. Nat'l Foreign Trade Council, 530 U.S. 363, 374 n.8, 120 S. Ct. 2288, 2294 n.8 (2000). For post-*Crosby* commentary on state and local sanctions, *see* Symposium, New Voices on the New Federalism, 46 Vill. L. Rev. 907 (2001) (articles by Cleveland, Halberstam, Vazquez and others); Barnico, The Road From Burma: State Boycotts After *Crosby v. National Foreign Trade Council*, 19 B.U. Int'l L.J. 89 (2001); Delahunty, Federalism Beyond the Water's Edge: State Procurement Sanctions and Foreign Affairs, 37 Stan. J. Int'l L. 1 (2001); Klein & Stern, Back to First Principles: The Constituitonal Rationale for Invalidating Local Sanctions Against Foreign

Trade, 33 Law & Pol'y Int'l Bus. 77 (2001); Cao, Comment, Limiting States' Roles in Foreign Commerce: Teaching Old-World Dogs New-World Tricks, 23 Houston J. Int'l L. 349 (2001); Miyaki-Murphy, Comment, In the Wake of *Crosby v. National Foreign Trade Council*, 34 J. Marshall L. Rev. 827 (2001); Moritsugu, Note, The Winding Course of the Massachusetts Burma Law: Subfederal Sanctions in a Historical Context, 34 Geo. Wash. Int'l L. Rev. 435 (2002); Pascoe, Note, Time for a New Approach?: Federalism and Foreign Affairs After *Crosby v. National Foreign Trade Council*, 35 Vand. J. Transnat'l L. 291 (2002); Sendleski, Note, Taking Our Money and Going Home: State Divestment Policy and the Foreign Affairs, Foreign Commerce, and Supremacy Clauses, 24 Suffolk Transnat'l L. Rev. 317 (2001); *see also* Swaine, The Undersea Word of Foreign Relations Federalism, 2 Chi. J. Int'l L. 337 (2001).

§7.03 THE RELEVANT "MARKET"

Page 7-20, add to the end of note 65:

For a suggestion that a state is a market-participant when participating in the market for educational services, *viz.*, by operating a state university, *see* Buchwald v. University of New Mexico School of Medicine, 159 F.3d 487, 496 n.9 (10th Cir. 1998) (rejecting a dormant Commerce Clause challenge to applicant's rejection for spot in state medical school based, *inter alia*, on admissions policy favoring long-term over short- term residents; stating that "[t]he University of New Mexico's educational activities constitute participation in the market for educational services, not regulation of that market"). A recent student note argues that a state scholarships program limited to in-state students is permissible as applied to state universities, under the market-participant doctrine, but that its application to state private schools as well constitutes an impermissible downstream restriction that takes the state's action outside the exception and may run afoul of the dormant Commerce Clause doctrine. *See* Cross, Note, Dormant Danger?: A Potential Constitutional Challenge to Georgia's HOPE Scholarship, 34 Ga. L. Rev. 1381 (2000). For more on the limits of the exception, *see* §7.02[C] *supra.*

Page 7-21, add to the end of note 66:

; *see also* Evac, LLC v. Pataki, 89 F. Supp. 2d 250, 263 (N.D.N.Y. 2000) (rejecting a §1983 challenge by a private air ambulance company to

New York State's free air ambulance service; "[t]he actions Evac complains of fall squarely within [the market-partcipant] doctrine and, thus, Evac cannot maintain a Commerce Clause claim").

Page 7-22, add to the end of note 74:

See generally Foreman, Comment, Nondiscrimination Ordinance 101, San Francisco's Nondiscrimination in City Contracts and Benefits Ordinance: A New Approach to Winning Domestic Partnership Benefits, 2 U. Penn. J. Lab. & Employment L. 319 (1999).

Page 7-22, insert new paragraph before **"7.04 Municipal Waste Removal: The Markets":**

Recent cases have seen states defend against alleged dormant Commerce Clause violations in the provision of health care services by invoking the market participant exception. In *Pharmaceutical Research and Manufacturers of America v. Concannon* (2001), the First Circuit rejected Maine's claim that its plan to require drug companies wishing to supply drugs to its Medicaid patients to negotiate rebates with the state to fund a drug subsidy for its citizens was insulated from dormant Commerce Clause scrutiny because it was acting as a market participant.[70] Though the court upheld the plan against a dormant Commerce Clause challenge, the First Circuit found the market participant doctrine to be inapplicable. "Maine is not a market buyer of prescription drugs," the court wrote. "Its citizens will continue to directly purchase prescription drugs as needed."[71] In June 2002 the U.S. Supreme Court granted certiorari in this case and will hear it next term.[72]

Similarly, a California appeals court rejected that state's claim that reimbursement schedules favoring in-state health care providers over those located out-of-state constituted market participation.[73] The court wrote:

> [T]he state is not itself a consumer of the service in question, nor does it pick and choose service providers. Discharging conventional regulatory responsibilities imposed on it by state and federal law, the state . . . merely reimburses those service providers selected by Medi-Cal recipients in need of medical care. The level of reimbursement . . . is clearly not responsive to market forces . . . [T]here is no genuine private market regarding the

> delivery of care to Medi-Cal patients in which the state could participate. . . . In sum, when it determines the level of compensation hospitals are entitled to receive for the treatment of MediCal patients, [the state] is not participating in an open market, but simply carrying out a traditional state regulatory responsibility. The market participation exception therefore does not apply.[74]

[70] Pharmaceutical Research and Manufacturers of America v. Concannon, 249 F.3d 66 (1st Cir. 2001), *aff'd sub nom.* Pharmaceutical Research and Manufacturers of America v. Walsh, 538 U.S. 644, 123 S. Ct. 1855 (2003). The market-participant holding was not appealed to the Supreme Court.

[71] *Concannon*, 249 F.3d at 80.

[72] 2002 WL 1393606 (June 28, 2002).

[73] Children's Hospital and Medical Center v. Bonta, 118 Cal. Rptr. 2d 629 (Ct. App. Cal. 2002).

[74] *Children's Hospital and Medical Center*, 118 Cal. Rptr. 2d at 650.

§ 7.04 MUNICIPAL WASTE REMOVAL: THE MARKETS

Page 7-23, add to the first line of note 78, after "See, e.g.,":

Rockville Centre v. Hempstead, 196 F.3d 395 (2d Cir. 1999) (upholding contractual arrangement between Town of Hempstead and nearby villages requiring disposal of waste at Town's disposal center under the market-participant exception); Sal Tinnerello & Sons, Inc. v. Stonington, 141 F.3d 46, 55-56 (2d Cir. 1998) (upholding local flow control statute where local government was both market regulator and market participant; as market participant, contracts for waste-hauling insulated from dormant Commerce Clause challenge);

Page 7-23, add to the end of note 78:

; *cf.* Waste Connections of Kansas, Inc. v. Bel Aire, 191 F. Supp. 2d 1238 (D. Kan. 2002) (refusing to enjoin city recycling plan whereby city charged residents monthly fee for recycling services and entered into contract with provider to provide such services, but where scheme neither required participation, prevented citizens from paying for alternative recycling collection, nor required local processing of recyclables; *held*, city was participant in the market for recycling services and thus exempt from dormant Commerce Clause doctrine); *but see* Houlton Citizens' Coalition v. Houlton, 175 F.3d 178, 187-188 (1st Cir. 1999) (declining to follow the rationale of *Smithtown* and *Babylon* because of uncertainty "whether or not the Supreme Court eventually will adopt their ratio decidendi"; upholding local flow control ordinance, *held*, that open bidding process did not discriminate against interstate commerce, and that incidental burdens not clearly excessive in light of legitimate public goal); *see also* Waste Connections of Kansas, Inc. v. Bel Aire, 191 F. Supp. 2d 1253 (D. Kan. 2002) (alleged violation of state sunshine law resulting in "unfair" consideration of bids for provision of recycling services did not remove city from market participant exemption; distinguishing *Houlton Citizens' Coalition*). For a recent decision following *Smithtown, see* BFI Waste Systems of North America, Inc. v. Broward Co., 2003 WL 21313748 (S.D. Fla. 2003), at *8-*12 (upholding county flow control ordinance requiring waste haulers to use specified facilities as part of contract between haulers and county; held, county was market participant).

Page 7-23, add to the end of note 79:

The facts of *Huish Detergents, Inc. v. Warren Co.*, 214 F.3d 707 (6th Cir. 2000), provide a nice illustration of the importance of correctly identifying the relevant markets in municipal waste disposal cases. The County had, after soliciting bids, awarded an exclusive franchise contract to Monarch for the collection and processing of all municipal solid waste in Bowling Green, Kentucky. Under the contract, Monarch was required to manage the city's waste transfer station and to dispose of all refuse at a state-approved landfill, which, as the court noted, "effectively prohibit[ed] the use of out-of-state disposal sites." 214 F.3d at 708-709. The franchise agreement, moreover, specified that "all residential, commercial, and industrial entities that generate municipal solid waste in Bowling Green must employ Monarch to remove that waste. . . ." *Id.* at 709. Monarch's "customers" were prohibited from disposing of their own waste and from using any company other than Monarch. *Id.* When the contract took effect, the County "passed an ordinance 'executing' franchise agreement and incorporating its provisions by reference. In essence," the court wrote, "the ordinance transform[ed] the franchise agreement provisions into law." *Id.*

The ordinance and the contract were challenged by the plaintiff as being, *inter alia*, a violation of the dormant Commerce Clause doctrine.

The district court rejected its challenge, finding that the County had acted to "take over" the waste collection, processing, and disposal markets and that the County had acted as a market participant in awarding the exclusive contract to Monarch. *Id.* The Sixth Circuit reversed. First, the court concluded that the district court had improperly characterized the plaintiff's challenge to the County's plan. "Specifically," it wrote, "by grouping several challenged activities together under the heading of a County 'takeover,' the court overlooked the unique aspects of two provisions of the [County] scheme: (1) the requirement that Monarch process all waste at one location within Bowling Green; and (2) the prohibition on out-of-state disposal." *Id.* at 715. Moreover, the district court erred when it characterized Monarch as the exclusive franchisee for waste disposal because these services had to be purchased by Monarch from third parties. *Id.* The Sixth Circuit recharacterized the plaintiff's challenge as encompassing three different aspects of the County plan: "(1) the designation of a single in-state processing station for municipal waste; (2) the prohibition on out-of-state waste disposal; and (3) the award of an 'exclusive franchise' to Monarch for waste collection and processing." *Id.*

The Sixth Circuit went on to conclude that in none of these three areas was the County acting as a market participant. As for the designation of the single in-state processing center, "the County was not acting in a proprietary capacity in forcing all municipal waste to flow through the city's transfer station. The County was not 'purchasing' the processing services with public funds, nor was it 'selling' its own processing services." *Id.* at 715. The exception was equally unavailable for the County's prohibition on out-of-state disposal: "[E]ven if the County's 'agreement' with Monarch constitutes market participation in either the waste collection or processing markets, the market participant exception would insulate the County's regulation of the separate waste disposal market, which is downstream from the collection and processing markets." *Id.* at 716. Finally, as far as the designation of Monarch as the exclusive franchisee for waste collection and processing, the court concluded that the County had "used its regulatory powers—not its proprietary purchasing power—to retain Monarch's services by requiring the County's residents to pay for those services. . . . [T]he County used its regulatory power to grant an exclusive right to collect and process Bowling Green waste, a result that no private party could accomplish on an open market." *Id.* at 717. Because it concluded that the market-participant exception did not operate to exempt the County's actions from dormant Commerce Clause scrutiny, the Sixth Circuit remanded the case to the district court. *Id.*

Page 7-24, add to the end of note 83:

At least one court has specifically held that landfill space is not a "natural resource," the hoarding of which might make the market-participant exception unavailable. *See* Whitehouse v. New England Ecological Development, Inc., 1999 WL 1001188 (R.I. Super. Ct.) (Oct. 28, 1999), at *3. Nevertheless, courts are generally unsympathetic to attempts to cloak prohibitions on the importation of garbage with the market-participant mantle. *See* Waste Management Holdings, Inc. v. Gilmore, 64 F. Supp. 2d 537, 544 (E.D. Va. 1999) (exception not available for Virginia statutes aimed at curtailing importation of garbage for in-state disposal), *aff'd*, 252 F.3d 316 (4th Cir. 2001), *cert. denied sub nom.* Murphy v. Waste Management Holding, Inc., 122 S. Ct. 1203 (2002).

§7.06 STATE-WIDE MANDATES TO SUBORDINATE POLITICAL LEGAL ENTITIES

Page 7-27, add to note 95, after "See generally":

Baranski, Comment, Is Local Government the Equivalent of State Government for Purposes of the Market Participant Exception to the Dormant Commerce Clause?, 104 Dick. L. Rev. 687 (2000);

CHAPTER 8

STATE AND LOCAL TAXATION

§8.01 INTRODUCTION

Page 8-3, add to the end of note 1:

According to the Eighth Circuit, another threshold issue is whether the matter taxed by the state is "contraband." If it is "property that it is unlawful to possess," then it is "not an object of interstate trade protected by the Commerce Clause." Predka v. Iowa, 186 F.3d 1082, 1084 (8th Cir. 1999).

Page 8-4, add to the second line of note 6, after "see also":

Schoettle, Big Bucks, Cloudy Thinking: Constitutional Challenges to State Taxes — Illumination from the GATT, 19 Va. Tax Rev. 277 (1999) (criticizing Supreme Court approaches to adjudicating state tax cases under the dormant Commerce Clause doctrine).

Page 8-4, add to the fourth line of note 6, between "still useful);" and "Sedler, The Negative":

Choper & Yin, State Taxation and the Dormant Commerce Clause: The Object-Measure Approach, 1998 Sup. Ct. Rev. 193; Joondeph, Rethinking the Role of the Dormant Commerce Clause in State Tax Jurisdiction, 24 Va. Tax Rev. 109 (2004); Schmudde, Constitutional Limitations on State Taxation of Nonresident Citizens, 1999 Mich. St. U.– Det. Col. L. Rev. 95, 111-113, 114-126;

Page 8-4, add to the end of note 6:

For literature on what is shaping up to be the next area in which the dormant Commerce Clause doctrine will be involved to strike down state and local taxes — state and local taxation of Internet commerce — *see generally* Symposium, Jurisdiction to Tax Income and Consumption in the New Economy: International, National, and Subnational Perspectives, 38 Ga. L. Rev. 1 (2003) (articles by Hellerstein, Cockfield, Freidman, Libin & Gillis, and Swain); Symposium, Debating the Prospect of E-Commerce Taxation, 13 Harv. J.L. & Tech. 549-657 (2000) (articles by Hellerstein, McClure, Bick, Groves, and Varian); Symposium on Taxation of Electronic Commerce, 2000 B.Y.U. L. Rev. 1-183 (articles by Fleming, Houghton and Hellerstein, McLure, and McKeown); Camilli, Run for the Border!: Evasion of Sales and Use Taxes by Mail-Order and Internet Sellers, 19 J.L. & Comm. 137 (1999) (recommending that Congress pass legislation permitting states and localities to collect sales and use taxes); Forgione, Weaving the Continental Web: Exploring Free Trade, Taxation, and the Internet, 9 L. & Bus. Rev. Am. 513 (2003); Gulick & Jones, The Internet's Impact on State Tax Systems: A Proposal to Impose a Use Tax Collection Duty on Remote Vendors, 33 Urb. Law. 479 (2001); Smith, Internet Taxes: Congressional Efforts to Control States' Ability to Tax the World Wide Web, 7 Rich. J.L. & Tech. 3 (2000); Houghton & Hellerstein, State Taxation of Electronic Commerce: Perspectives on Proposals For Change and Their Constitutionality, 2000 B.Y.U. L. Rev. 9; Hellerstein, State and Local Taxation of Electronic Commerce: Reflections on the Emerging Issues, 52 U. Miami L. Rev. 691 (1998); Hellerstein, State Taxation of Electronic Commerce, 52 Tax L. Rev. 425 (1997); Swain, Cybertaxation and the Commerce Clause: Entity Isolation or Affiliate Nexus, 75 S. Cal. L. Rev. 419 (2002); Williams, The Role of Caesar in the Next Millennium?: Taxation of E-Commerce: An Overview and Analysis, 27 Wm. Mitchell L. Rev. 1703 (2001); Bassinger, Note, Dormant Commerce Clause Limits on State Regulation of the Internet: The Transportation Analogy, 32 Ga. L. Rev. 889 (1999); Gray, Comment, The Constitutionality of Federal Preemption of State Taxation of Internet Transactions, 17 St. Louis U. Pub. L. Rev. 451 (1998) (arguing that the federal moratorium on state taxation of Internet commerce was unconstitutional); Lundy, Comment, The Taxation of E-Commerce: The Inapplicability of Physical Presence Necessitates an Economic Presence Standard, 8 Rich. J. L. & Tech. 12 (2001); Masterson, Note, Collecting Sales and Use Tax Electronic Commerce: E-Confusion or E-Collection, 79 N.C. L. Rev. 203 (2000); Morris, Commentary, Interstate Commerce and the Future of State Sales and Use Taxes, 54 Ala. L. Rev. 1393 (2003); Trahan, Note, The Future of Sales and Use Tax on Electronic Commerce: Promoting Uniformity After *Quill,* 21 Va. Tax Rev. 101 (2001); Way, Note, State and Local Sales Tax on Internet Commerce: Developing a Neutral and Efficient Framework, 19 Va. Tax Rev. 115 (1999); Wilde, Comment, *Western Wireless Corp. v. Department of Revenue*: State Taxation on Interstate Transactions and How to Comply with the Dormant Commerce Clause, 49 S.D. L. Rev. 341 (2003-2004).

§8.05 DISCRIMINATION AGAINST INTERSTATE COMMERCE

Page 8-11, add to the beginning of note 25:

See, e.g., South Central Bell Tel. Co. v. Alabama, 119 S. Ct. 1180, 1185-1186 (1999) (striking down "facially discriminat[ory]" Alabama law taxing stock of in-state corporations at par value while taxing out-of-state corporations based on actual capital employed in the state); Birth Hope Adoption Agency, Inc. v. Arizona Health Care Cost Containment System, 218 F.3d 1040, 1044-1045 (9th Cir. 2000) (striking down Arizona statute requiring out-of-state adopting parents — but not those from in-state — to pay for prenatal and delivery of adopted child); Simon Aviation, Inc. v. Dept. St. Rev., 805 N.E.2d 920, 929 (Ind. 2004) (striking down Indiana use tax that did not credit taxpayer for taxes paid out-of-state on vehicles, aircraft, or watercraft; "Indiana's use tax results in a greater tax burden on aircraft purchased out-of-state than aircraft purchased in-state [thus] it impermissibly discriminates against interstate commerce"); D.D.I., Inc. v. North Dakota, 657 N.W.2d 228, 233, 235 (N.D. 2003) (striking down a "dividends received deduction to a dividend recipient to the extent the dividend payor's income was subject to North Dakota corporate income tax" but which did not "grant a dividends received deduction to a dividend recipient if the dividend payor's income was not subject to North Dakota corporate income tax"); Chapman v. Comm'r Rev., 651 N.W.2d 825, 834-835 (Minn. 2002) (invalidating facially discriminatory provision permitting deductions for contributions for in-state charities under state Alternative Minimum Tax); Rhoade v. Indiana Dept. Rev., 774 N.E.2d 1044, 1049-1050 (Ind. Tax Ct. 2002) (invalidating state use tax provision requiring purchasers of out-of-state vehicles to pay state use tax where statute permits exemption for purchasers who have paid in-state sales tax); PPG Industries, Inc. v. Pennsylvania, 790 A.2d 261, 269 (Penn. 2001) (divided court) (striking down tax exemption that "afford[ed] preferential treatment to corporations engaged in manufacturing in the Commonwealth"); Yonkers Racing Corp. v. New York, 705 N.Y.S.2d 193, 197 (Sup. Ct. N.Y. 2000) (striking down a discriminatory state tax on harness racing fees received for simulcasting races to off-track betting establishments in Connecticut). A threshold issue would be whether interstate commerce is implicated at all. *See* Stelzner v. Comm'r Rev., 621 N.W.2d 736, 741 (Minn. 2001) (concluding that nonresident domiciliaries' income derived in part from activities occurring in Arizona and taxed by Minnesota insufficient to establish "either discrimination against or an undue burden on interstate commerce to implicate the Commerce Clause"); *cf.* In the Matter of the Appeal of Barton-Dobenin, 9 P.3d 9, 18 (Kan. 2000) (concluding that taxpayers with substantial income-generating operations in the Czech Republic, which the state taxed without allowing credit for taxes paid to Czech Republic even when credit offered for taxes paid to other domestic states, did not "substantially affect" foreign commerce and thus not subject to analysis under the Foreign Commerce Clause); *see also* Jefferson Smurfit Corp. v. Court of Claims, 639 N.W.2d 269, 280 (Ct. App. Mich. 2001) (upholding state tax deduction against claim of discrimination; "[s]tates may compete with one another for a share of interstate commerce, they just may not discriminatorily tax the products manufactured or the business operations performed in other states"); Kraft General Foods, Inc. v. Comptroller, 2001 WL 699558 (Md. Tax Ct.) (June 8, 2001), at *5 (striking down state tax scheme that treated dividends from foreign corporations differently than those from domestic corporations in computation of state tax liability).

Page 8-12, add to the end of note 25:

; Tennessee Gas Pipeline Co. v. Urbach, 708 N.Y.S. 2d 193, 196 (Sup. Ct. N.Y. 2000) (upholding a New York tax on "gas importers," where gas importer was defined in an even-handed manner). As in nontax dormant Commerce Clause cases, the corollary to the anti-discrimination principle is that nondiscriminatory taxes will generally be upheld, unless the tax suffers from one of the other defects described *infra* §§ 8.07–8.11, 8.14. *See, e.g.,* American Trucking Ass'ns, Inc. v. Mich. Pub. Svc. Comm'n, __ U.S. __, 125 S. Ct. 2419, 2425 (2005) (flat fee imposed upon trucks engaged in intrastate commercial hauling did not violate the dormant Commerce Clause doctrine; "petitioners . . . failed to show that . . . fee, which does not seek to tax a share of interstate transactions, which focuses upon local activity, and which is assessed evenhandedly, either burdens or discriminates against interstate commerce . . ."); Waste Connections of Nebraska, Inc. v. Lincoln, 2005 WL 1335480 (Neb. 2005), at *7 (upholding $7/ton tax imposed on garbage either collected within the city to be disposed therein or collected outside the city and disposed of at municipal landfill; tax was held not to discriminate); McClane Western, Inc. v. Dept. Rev., 2005 WL 1038994, at *5 (Colo. Ct. App. 2005) (upholding tobacco excise tax against claim tax discriminated against interstate commerce by coercing distributors to locate activities in-state; "[o]ut-of-state manufacturers or distributors may engage in commerce within Colorado without suffering any burden from which local distributors or manufacturers are exempted"). For an interesting heterodox argument that the Court should eliminate its scrutiny of discriminatory taxes, *see* Zelinsky, Restoring Politics to the Commerce Clause: The Case for Abandoning the Dormant Commerce Clause Prohibition on Discriminatory Taxation, 29 Ohio N.U. L. Rev. 29 (2002).

Page 8-13, add to the end of note 29:

; Buck, Note, *General Motors Corp. v. Tracy,* 20 Energy L.J. 345 (1999). For an application of *Tracy* to a California law that cars registered in California that were last registered in another state, and thus had not been certified under California emissions laws, *see* Jordan v. Dept. Motor Vehicles, 75 Cal. App.4th 449 (Ct. App. 1999) (holding *Tracy* inapplicable; lower court did not err in finding the California tax violated the dormant Commerce Clause doctrine).

Page 8-13, insert at the end of note 30:

; Smith v. New Hampshire Dept. Rev. Admin., 813 A.2d 372 (N.H. 2002) (relying on *General Motors Corp.* to reject challenge to state interest and dividend tax previously invalidated on ground provisions exempting return on investment in state banks was facially discriminatory; court held that tax was not discriminatory as to all out-of-state investment income; out-of-state nonbank investment sources and in-state bank investments not similarly situated).

Page 8-14, add to the end of note 35:

See also New York v. State, 709 N.Y.S. 2d 122 (N.Y. 2000) (striking down discriminatory New York commuter tax on both Privileges and Immunities Clause and dormant Commerce Clause doctrine grounds).

Page 8-14, add to the end of note 36:

; *see also* Chapman v. Comm'r of Revenue, 651 N.W.2d 825, 833 (Minn. 2002) (no *de minimis* defense to challenge that tax is facially discriminatory); Westlake Transportation, Inc. v. Michigan Pub. Svc. Comm'n, 2003 WL 1038837 (Ct. App. Mich.) (March 11, 2003), at *14 (same).

Page 8-16, add new paragraph following text at note 50:

In *Cuno v. DaimlerChrysler, Inc.* (2004), the Sixth Circuit, relying heavily on the Supreme Court's decisions in *Boston Exchange* and *Westinghouse,* surprised many by striking down a fairly common investment tax credit granted by the State of Ohio to DaimlerChrysler under the dormant Commerce Clause doctrine.[50.1] The court held that the statute, which "grant[ed] a taxpayer a non-refundable credit against the state's corporate franchise tax" if the taxpayer purchased new machinery and installed that machinery in Ohio,[50.2] "coerce[ed]" businesses subject to Ohio's franchise tax to expand in-state, rather than in some other state.[50.3] The court rejected the defendants' arguments "liken[ing] the investment tax credit to a direct subsidy, which would . . . have the same economic effects. . . ."[50.4] The court felt compelled by Supreme Court cases to treat "attempts to create location incentives through the state's power to tax . . . differently from direct subsidies despite their similarity in terms of end-result economic impact."[50.5] Consequently, the court invalidated the tax credit as discriminatory even though DaimlerChrysler's tax liability would not have *increased* had it not located the property in Ohio, and despite the fact that it was available to in-state and out-of-state corporations equally.[50.6] After the Sixth Circuit denied DaimlerChrysler's petition for rehearing and petition for rehearing en banc, the company petitioned the U.S. Supreme Court for a writ of *certiorari*, which is pending as of this writing.

[50.1] Cuno v. DaimlerChrysler, Inc., 386 F.3d 738 (6th Cir. 2004). For articles endorsing the court's approach, *see* Enrich, Saving States from Themselves: Commerce Clause Restraints on State Tax Incentives for Business, 110 Harv. L. Rev. 377 (1996); Hellerstein & Coenen, Commerce Clause Restraints on State Business Incentives, 81 Cornell L. Rev. 789 (1996). Professor Enrich was the lawyer for the plaintiffs in *Cuno*.

[50.2] *Cuno*, 386 F.3d at 741.

[50.3] *Id.* at 743, 746. The court's coercion analysis borrowed heavily from *Hellerstein & Coenen, supra* note 50.1.

[50.4] *Id.* at 746.

[50.5] *Id. See* Westinghouse Elec. Corp. v. Tully, 466 U.S. 388, 104 S. Ct. 1856 (1984); Maryland v. Louisiana, 451 U.S. 725, 101 S. Ct. 2114 (1981); Boston Stock Exchange v. State Tax Comm'n, 429 U.S. 318, 97 S. Ct. 599 (1977).

[50.6] The court refused to strike down a personal property tax exemption, however. "Unlike an investment tax credit that reduces pre-existing income tax liability, the personal property exemption does not reduce any existing property tax liability," the court explained. "The exemption merely allows a taxpayer to avoid tax liability for new personal property put into a first use in conjunction with a qualified new investment." *Id.* at 747. "Thus, a taxpayer's failure to locate new investments within Ohio simply means that the taxpayer is not subject to the state's property tax at all, and any discriminatory treatment between a company that invests in Ohio and one that invests out-of-state cannot be attributed to the Ohio tax regime. . . ." *Id.* The court also rejected a challenge under the Ohio constitution's equal protection clause. *Id.* at 748–749.

§8.06 "COMPENSATORY" TAXES

Page 8-17, add to the end of note 52:

See Haag & Boekhaus, Note, The Final Nail in the Compensatory Tax Coffin? The Impact of the Supreme Court's Decision in *Fulton Corp. v. Faulkner*, 516 U.S. 325 (1996), on the Doctrine of Compensatory Taxes, 21 Hamline L. Rev. 451 (1998).

Page 8-18, add to end of note 55:

; *see also* Revenue Cabinet v. Lazarus, Inc., 49 S.W.3d 172, 177 (Ky. 2001) (relying on *D.H. Holmes* to uphold use tax on catalogues).

Page 8-18, add to the end of note 56:

The Supreme Court recently refused to apply the doctrine to an Alabama franchise tax that discriminated against in-state and out-of-state corporations by allowing the former to pay tax only on the par value of its stock, with the result that "the average domestic corporation pa[id] only one-fifth the franchise tax it would pay" if it were a foreign corporation. South Central Bell Tel. Co. v. Alabama, 119 S. Ct. 1180, 1185-1186 (1999); *see also* Birth Hope Adoption Agency, Inc. v. Arizona Health Care Cost Containment System, 218 F.3d 1040, 1044-1045 (9th Cir. 2000) (Arizona statute requiring out-of-state residents, but not in-state residents, to pay full cost of prenatal care and delivery of adopted children not a valid compensatory tax; statute "imposes a personal liability on out-of-state adoptive parents which is not imposed . . . on in-state adoptive parents and, therefore, creates a tax burden not born by in-state parents. Thus, the state does not meet the first condition necessary for a valid compensatory tax", *viz.*, identification of an intrastate tax burden for which the interstate tax is attempting to compensate); D.D.I., Inc. v. North Dakota, 657 N.W.2d 228, 234 (N.D. 2003) (rejecting argument that discriminatory dividends received deduction constitutes a valid compensatory tax; "Commissioner has not identified any specific in-state activity or benefit received by the taxpayers to justify the compensatory levy on their dividends received from out-of-state corporations"; tax further does not roughly approximate tax on interstate commerce); New York v. State, 709 N.Y.S.2d 122 (N.Y. 2000) (striking down a commuter tax on those who work in New York City, event triggering taxation, interstate travel, not "substantially equivalent" to other taxes not paid by interstate commuters); Annenberg v. Commonwealth, 757 A.2d 338, 342-346 (Pa. 2000) (holding that discriminatory state personal property tax whose effect was to tax only the stock of corporations that do not do business in Pennsylvania was not a valid compensatory tax).

Page 8-18, add to the end of note 57:

Another type of permitted exaction allows states or their political subdivisions to seek reimbursement for services rendered or for the use of their facilities, as long as the user fees are (i) nondiscriminatory; (ii) a fair approximation of benefits received; and (iii) not excessive in light of the cost of the benefit supplied. *See* Massachusetts v. U.S., 435 U.S. 444, 462, 98 S. Ct. 1153, 1165 (1978); Doran v. Massachusetts Turnpike Auth., 348 F.3d 315, 318-321 (1st Cir. 2003) (rejecting argument that discounts offered to subscribers to state toll booth program constituted an unapportioned flat tax on interstate commerce; "the tolls are assessed uniformly in direct proportion to the use of the toll facilities and have not been shown to be excessive"); Park Shuttle N Fly, Inc. v. Norfolk Airport Auth., 352 F. Supp. 2d 688, ___ (E.D. Va. 2004) (upholding 8% gross receipts fee charged off-premises parking facility operators for access to airport to pick up and drop off passengers; fee was based on fair approximation of use of facilities; not excessive; and not discriminatory); President Riverboat Casino-Missouri, Inc. v. Missouri Gaming Comm'n, 13 S.W.3d 635, 639 (Mo. 2000) (rejecting challenge to $2 per customer "admission fee" levied on riverboat casino customers; fee does not discriminate, "pay[s] exact cost of . . . law enforcement, a fair approximation of the benefit to the boats," and is not excessive). *See generally* Coenen, State User Fees and the Dormant Commerce Clause, 50 Vand. L. Rev. 795 (1997).

Page 8-20, add to note 61 after "See generally":

Symposium, Jurisdiction to Tax Income and Consumption in the New Economy: International, National, and Subnational Perspectives, 38 Ga.

L. Rev. 1 (2003) (articles by Hellerstein, Cockfield, Freidman, Libin & Gillis, and Swain); Forgione, Weaving the Continental Web: Exploring Free Trade, Taxation, and the Internet, 9 L. & Bus. Rev. Am. 513 (2003); Gulick & Jones, The Internet's Impact on State Tax Systems: A Proposal to Impose a Use Tax Collection Duty on Remote Vendors, 33 Urb. Law. 479 (2001); Swain, Cybertaxation and the Commerce Clause: Entity Isolation or Affiliate Nexus, 75 S. Cal. L. Rev. 419 (2002); Williams, The Role of Caesar in the Next Millennium?: Taxation of E-Commerce: An Overview and Analysis, 27 Wm. Mitchell L. Rev. 1703 (2001);

Page 8-20, add to end of note 61:

; Morris, Commentary, Interstate Commerce and the Future of State Sales and Use Taxes, 54 Ala. L. Rev. 1393 (2003); Trahan, Note, The Future of Sales and Use Tax on Electronic Commerce: Promoting Uniformity After *Quill,* 21 Va. Tax Rev. 101 (2001).

Page 8-20, add to note 62 before "See generally":

; *see also* Baker & Taylor, Inc. v. Kawafuchi, 82 P.3d 804, 816 (Haw. 2004) (concluding that foreign corporation's activities in state in connection with sales of books to library constituted nexus with state's taxing jurisdiction when corporation's representatives made visits to service library by whom contract was awarded); Kevin Associates, L.L.C. v. Crawford, 2004 WL 178610 (La. 2004) (concluding that it did not violate the dormant Commerce Clause for state to impose taxes on Delaware holding company for corporate entities whose commercial domicile was in state, despite fact the holding company had no contacts with the state); Moran Towing Corp. v. Urbach, 2003 WL 1562207 (N.Y.) (Mar. 27, 2003) (rejecting facial challenge to tax imposed on fuel imported into state for consumption within the state; set of facts exist in which nexus is present sufficient to support constitutional application of the tax); In the Matter of the Appeal of Family of Eagles, Ltd., 2003 WL 1894609 (Kan.) (Apr. 18, 2003), at *8 (taxpayer selling materials in the state through independent sales representatives had sufficient presence in state to justify imposition of use tax without violating the Commerce Clause); In the Matter of the Appeal of Intercard, Inc., 14 P.3d 1111, 1122 (Kan. 2000) (installation of credit card readers in taxing state did not constitute a "substantial nexus" necessary to sustain imposition of sales and use taxes); Borders Online, LLC v. St. Bd. Equalization, 2005 WL 1274623 (Cal. Ct. App. 2005), at *9-*14 (concluding that relationship between on-line bookseller and seller's in-state retail stores rendered out-of-state Internet retailer physically present in the state and subject to state's use tax); Inova Diagnostics, Inc. v. Strayhorn, 2005 WL 1241116, at *7 (Tex. Ct. App. 2005) (subjecting to state franchise tax business employing in-state resident seven to ten days a month to solicit orders for product in the taxing state; *held*, single employee's activities constituted physical presence in the state); Dell Catalog Sales, L.P. v. Comm'r Rev., 834 A.2d 812, 822-823 (Super. Ct. Conn. 2003) (holding that relationship between seller of computers and in-state company contracted to perform on-site repair did not provide sufficient nexus between seller and state for purposes of imposing sales taxes on seller's sales to state residents); Hi-Tech Housing, Inc. v. Dept. Treasury, 2001 WL 1081598 (Ct. App. Mich.) (Sept. 14, 2001) (unpublished), at *7 (use of carriers in-state; solicitation of sales in-state by company personnel; use of field representatives in-state periodically during year; delivery of parts in-state; express warranty using in-state builders to make repairs; use of in-state contractors to make repairs on company's behalf; and use of personnel to make repairs on modular homes sold by company constituted "sufficient nexus" to sustain imposition of use tax on sales to in-state customers); Moran Towing Corp. v. Urbach, 726 N.Y.S.2d 748 (Sup. Ct. N.Y. 2001) (state lacked substantial nexus to tax fuel purchased outside state and brought into state in engines and consumed through movement in-state); Rylander v. Bandag Licencing Corp., 18 S.W.3d 296 (Ct. App. Tex. 2000) (mere possession of a certificate to do business in a state not sufficient nexus to sustain taxation by state, where corporation "did not own, possess, use, or maintain any real property in the state," employ any persons in the state, or send employees into the state, to conduct business); J.C. Penney National Bank v. Johnson, 19 S.W.3d 831 (Ct. App. Tenn. 1999) (applying *Quill* to strike down application of franchise and excise taxes to appellant national bank's credit card activities in the state; credit cards issued by appellant insufficient to supply "substantial nexus," as was maintenance of unaffiliated retail stores owned by appellant's parent company).

Page 8-20, add to end of note 62:

; Swain, State Income Tax Jurisdiction: A Jurisprudential and Policy Perspective, 45 Wm. & Mary L. Rev. 319 (2003); McGinnis, Comment, Marching to the Beat of the Itinerate Drummer: States Increasingly Refuse to Get Physical Before Finding Nexus, 32 Cap. U. L. Rev. 149 (2003); Wilde, Comment, *Western Wireless Corp. v. Department of*

Revenue: State Taxation on Interstate Transactions and How to Comply with the Dormant Commerce Clause, 49 S.D. L. Rev. 341 (2003-2004).

Page 8-21, add to the end of note 64:

The extent to which the subject of taxation must be "present" in a state is still the subject of controversy among commentators. *Compare* Fatale, State Tax Jurisdiction and the Mythical "Physical Presence" Constitutional Standard, 54 Tax Law 105 (2000) *and* Lundy, Comment, The Taxation of E-Commerce: The Inapplicability of Physical Presence Necessitates an Economic Presence Standard, 8 Rich. J. L. & Tech. 12 (2001) *with* Ervin, Comment, State Taxation of Financial Institutions: Will Physical Presence or Economic Presence Win the Day?, 19 Va. Tax Rev. 515 (2000) (arguing against the adoption of "economic presence" standard).

Another interesting question is whether states may tax out-of-state "intellectual property holding companies" to whom corporations pay hefty "royalties" for the use of intellectual property that the company has transferred to a wholly owned subsidiary without a physical presence in the taxing state. *See generally* Diehl, Is the IP Holding Company Dead? 37 Md. Bar J. 43 (Jan./Feb. 2004); Chiang, Comment, State Income Taxation of Out-of-State Trademark Holding Companies, 70 U. Chi. L. Rev. 1533 (2003).

§8.07 MULTIPLE STATE TAX BURDENS

Page 8-24, add to the beginning of note 71:

Pfizer, Inc. v. Lancaster Bd. Equalization, 616 N.W.2d 326, 338 (Neb. 2000) (concluding that personal property tax levied on assets acquired by taxpayer, including real property, did not violate Commerce Clause: "there is a substantial nexus between Nebraska and the subject of the tax, as the property at issue is located within the state").

§8.10 *COMPLETE AUTO TRANSIT, INC. V. BRADY*

Page 8-35, add to note 108 after "'taxed' is required).":

; Owner-Operator Independent Drivers Association v. Urbach, 699 N.Y.S.2d 268, 271 (Sup. Ct. N.Y. 1999) (upholding otherwise nondiscriminatory state tax on fuel use on commercial vehicles based on miles driven on New York State Thruway; "plaintiffs may never need the services of the fire or police departments, but these services are available if needed"); Shannon v. State, 2003 WL 576253 (Ct. App. Tex.) (Feb. 27, 2003), at *3 (permit and registration fee required by city for transportation of non-hazardous waste upheld against Commerce Clause challenge; rejecting claim that fees not "fairly related" to services provided: "[a]pellant, like all people traveling in Houston, will benefit by a clean, nonhazardous sewage and road system"; noting that "only those vehicles actually picking up waste products within the city limits need to be registered"); *see also* Northwood Construction Co. v. Township of Upper Moreland, 802 A.2d 1269, 1276 (Pa. Commonw. Ct. 2002) (holding that "enjoy[ment of] certain governmental services" sufficient to satisfy "fairly related" prong); Anderson v. Dept. Rev., 758 N.E.2d 597, 601-602 (Ind. Tax Ct. 2001) (upholding fuel tax; "[t]he fourth prong of *Complete Auto* requires that the [tax] only be fairly related to the multitude of services provided to the citizens by the State. . . . This requirement . . . does not call for a rigid quantification of services provided."); Owner-Operator Independent Drivers Association v. Bower, 757 N.E.2d 627, 634-637 (Ct. App. Ill. 2001) (upholding state fuel tax as being fairly related to services provided by state).

Page 8-36, add to the end of note 112:

In *Hunt-Wesson, Inc. v. Franchise Tax Bd.* (2000), the U.S. Supreme Court struck down California's rules that reduced a company's interest expense by the amount of interest and dividends received from "non-unitary" businesses that the state was not otherwise able to tax. Hunt-Wesson, Inc. v. Franchise Tax Bd., 528 U.S. 458, 120 S. Ct. 1022 (2000). Justice Breyer, writing for a unanimous court, held that since "the relevant income . . . is income that . . . by itself bears no 'rational relationship' or 'nexus' to California" then "this 'nonunitary income' may not constitutionally be taxed by a State other than the corporation's domicile, unless there is some other connection between the taxing state and the income." 528 U.S. at 464, 120 S. Ct. at 1026. The Court rejected California's argument that its rule was merely a "proper allocation of the deduction." The state assumed, wrote the Court, "that a corporation that borrows any money at all has really borrowed that money to 'purchase or carry' . . . its nonunitary investments . . . even if the corporation has put no money at all into nonunitary business that year." 528 U.S. at 466, 120

S. Ct. at 1027. In doing so, California pushed the idea of reasonable allocation "past reasonable bounds." *Id.*

For an application of the *Brady* test to uphold state and local airport "user fees" for off-site rental car companies, *see* Enterprise Leasing Co. v. Wayne, 191 F.3d 451 (6th Cir. 1999), and cases cited therein.

§8.11 INTERNAL AND EXTERNAL "CONSISTENCY"

Page 8-39, add to the end of note 122:

For evaluations of state taxes under the "internal" and "external" consistency tests, *see, for example*, Northwood Construction Co. v. Upper Moreland, 2004 WL 1949335, at *10-*12 (Pa. 2004) (striking down township tax on 100% of gross receipts of local business where business performed extensive work in other jurisdictions; business privilege tax neither internally nor externally consistent); Baker & Taylor, Inc. v. Kawafuchi, 82 P.3d 804, 816-17 (Haw. 2004) (imposition of excise tax on sales proceeds originating from purchasers in state internally consistent; "[i]f every state were to impose a general excise tax, the mainland states where Baker's goods originate would not be able to tax the transactions where goods are shipped to Hawai'i with the Hawai'i consumer having the power to accept or reject the goods. . . . Because the sales activities took place only in Hawai'i, Hawai'i appears to be the only jurisdiction that can tax the transaction"; tax externally consistent as well; "[s]ince the general excise tax system only places a tax on sales made to consumers located in Hawai'i and requires some business activity in the state to generate these sales, it properly taxes only the in-state component of transactions for external consistency"); Stryker Corp. v. Director, 773 A.2d 674, 682-684 (N.J. 2001) (state tax on receipts of sales shipped by in-state subsidiary to points out of state satisfies "internal consistency" test); Pfizer, Inc. v. Lancaster Bd. Equalization, 616 N.W.2d 326, 338-339 (Neb. 2000) (personal property tax levied on assets acquired by taxpayer, including real property, located in the taxing state satisfied both internal and external consistency tests); General Motors Corp. v. Denver, 990 P.2d 59 (Colo. 1999) (upholding city and county use tax on automobiles owned by GM); Westcott Communications, Inc. v. Strayhorn, 104 S.W.3d 141, 146-148 (Ct. App. Tex. 2003) (upholding franchise tax imposed on company producing training programs for transmission to subscribers via satellite; tax internally and externally consistent); Shannon v. Texas,

2004 WL 63925 (Ct. App. Tex. 2004), at *2-*3 (concluding that flat fee for transporting waste into City of Houston unconstitutional because they were not fairly apportioned); Shannon v. Texas, 2003 WL 576253 (Ct. App. Tex.) (Feb. 27, 2003), at *2 (permit and license fee imposed on transport of non-hazardous waste originating in Houston internally consistent; transport can originate in only one city); Northwood Construction Co. v. Township of Upper Moreland, 802 A.2d 1269, 1275-1276 (Pa. Commonw. Ct. 2002) (holding that gross receipts tax both internally and externally consistent); In the Matter of Zelinsky, 753 N.Y.S.2d 144, 148 (N.Y. App. Div. 2002) (rejecting argument that imposition of New York tax on total salary of law professor though part of work performed in Connecticut not "out of all appropriate proportion to the business that petitioner transacted in New York"); Hi-way Disptach, Inc. v. Dept. Rev., 756 N.E.2d 587, 603-604 (Ind. Tax Ct. 2001) (upholding state fuel tax under external consistency test); Texas Eastern Transmission Corp. v. Tax Appeals Tribunal, 699 N.Y.S. 2d 560 (Sup. Ct. N.Y. 1999).

§ 8.13 FEDERAL INTERVENTION

[A] Congressional Consent to Levy of Otherwise Unconstitutional State and Local Taxes

Page 8-41, add to the end of note 126:

See Jordan v. Dept. Motor Vehicles, 89 Cal. Rep. 2d 333, 342-343 (Ct. App. 1999) (congressional intent to exempt state or local tax from dormant Commerce Clause analysis must be "unmistakably clear") (citing Maine v. Taylor, 477 U.S. 121, 138-139, 106 S. Ct. 2440, 2447 (1986) (divided court)).

[B] The Interstate Commerce Tax Act

Page 8-43, add to the end of note 133:

In 1998, Congress passed, and the President signed, a three-year moratorium on state and local taxes on Internet commerce. *See* Pub. L. 105-277,

§ 1101 (1998). For more on the problem of taxing Internet commerce, *see supra* § 3.06[D].

§8.14 STATE TAXATION OF FOREIGN COMMERCE

Page 8-44, add to the end of note 136:

A threshold issue, of course, would be whether foreign commerce was involved at all. For the somewhat surprising conclusion that a taxpayer who ran substantial business operations located in the Czech Republic from his home in Kansas, and who challenged a state law permitting a credit for income taxes paid in other states, but not in foreign nations, was not involved in foreign commerce, *see* In the Matter of the Appeal of Barton-Dobenin, 9 P.3d 9, 18 (Kan. 2000).

[C] Impairment of Federal Uniformity

Page 8-50, add to the end of note 155:

For a recent application of the *Japan Line* test by a state court to a state tax on fuel sold by an American gas station located less than two miles away from the Canadian border, *see* Ammex, Inc. v. Dept. Treasury, 603 N.W.2d 308, 314-315 (Ct. App. Mich. 1999) (tax as applied did not constitute an impermissible state taxation of foreign commerce).

[D] Discrimination against or in Favor of Foreign Commerce

Page 8-50, add to the end of note 156:

For a recent application of the nondiscrimination principle in a foreign commerce case, *see* Emerson Electric Co. v. Tracy, 735 N.E.2d 445, 447-449 (Ohio 2000) (divided court) (concluding that state statute limiting the deductibility of dividends from "foreign source income" to 15% of the amount of dividends while allowing full deduction of dividends from domestic subsidiaries was discriminatory and violated the Foreign Commerce Clause); *see generally* Warren, Income Tax Discrimination Against International Commerce, 54 Tax L. Rev. 131 (2001).

Page 8-51, add to the end of note 159:

; *but see* Caterpillar, Inc. v. Dept. Rev. Admin., 741 A.2d 56 (N.H. 1999) (declining to apply *Kraft* to strike down state taxation of royalty and interest payments made to domestic company by foreign subsidiaries; *held,* state apportionment formula did not discriminate between foreign and domestic subsidiaries in a unitary business).

CHAPTER 9

CONGRESSIONAL CONSENT TO OTHERWISE UNCONSTITUTIONAL STATE REGULATIONS OF COMMERCE ("RECONVEYANCE")

§9.04 CURRENT LAW

Page 9-14, add to end of note 37:

The Act still serves to insulate state regulation of insurance companies from dormant Commerce Clause challenges. *See, e.g.*, Tancredi v. Metropolitan Life Ins. Co., 149 F. Supp. 2d 80, 90 (S.D.N.Y. 2001)(rejecting challenge to conversion of mutual insurance company to stock insurance company under state statute; "the McCarran-Ferguson Act, which designates the regulation and taxation of the insurance business to the states, insulates state insurance regulations from Commerce Clause challenge") (footnote omitted).

Page 9-16, add to the end of note 41:

One way Congress may express its consent for more than one state to do that which is otherwise forbidden by the dormant Commerce Clause doctrine is to approve an interstate compact. *See* U.S. Const. art. I, § 10, cl. 2 ("No State shall, without the Consent of Congress...enter into any agreement or Compact with another State. . . ."); New York State Dairy Foods, Inc. v. Northeast Dairy Compact Comm'n, 198 F.3d 1, 12 (1st Cir. 1999) (rejecting dormant Commerce Clause challenge to regulations promulgated by commission; "there is no question that Congress affirmatively contemplated otherwise invalid state legislation" by "explicitly consenting to the Compact").

§9.06 PROVING CONGRESSIONAL CONSENT

Page 9-17, add to note 44, after "(divided court)":

; *see also* Hillside Dairy, Inc. v. Lyons, 539 U.S. 59, 66, 123 S. Ct. 2142, 2147 (2003) ("Congress certainly has the power to authorize state regulations that burden or discriminate against interstate commerce . . . but we will not assume that it has done so unless such an intent is clearly expressed.") (citations omitted).

Page 9-17, add to end of note 44:

For lower court applications of the "expressly stated" formula, *see, for example,* Southwest Air Ambulance, Inc. v. Las Cruces, 268 F.3d 1162,

1177 (10th Cir. 2001) (holding that by enacting statute permitting municipalities to impose certain user fees on airport use Congress exhibited sufficient intent to permit regulation free of the prohibitions of the dormant Commerce Clause doctrine); Waste Management Holdings, Inc. v. Gilmore, 252 F.3d 316, 346-347 (4th Cir. 2001), *cert. denied sub nom.* Murphy v. Waste Management Holding, Inc., 122 S. Ct. 1203 (2002) (agreeing that "isolated bits of legislative history and . . . broadly worded statutory language . . . do not come close to expressing an 'unmistakably clear' intent on the part of Congress to exempt state laws relating to solid waste from the limitations of the dormant Commerce Clause") (internal quotation marks omitted); Oxygenated Fuels Association, Inc. v. Davis, 163 F. Supp. 2d 1182, 1188 (E.D. Cal. 2001) (dismissing dormant Commerce Clause claim against California ban on use of fuel additive; finding "Congress has specifically authorized California to enact prohibitions and controls respecting fuels and fuel additives" in the Clean Air Act).

Page 9-18, add to the end of note 45:

Of course, congressional consent is often in the eye of the beholding judge. *Compare* Shamrock Farms Co. v. Veneman, 146 F.3d 1177, 1180-1181 (9th Cir. 1998) (interpreting a savings clause in the Nutritional Labeling Act of 1990, which stated that neither the provisions of the Act, nor "any other provision of law" should "be construed to preempt, prohibit, or otherwise limit" California's regulation of its dairy industry, to remove dormant Commerce Clause disabilities from state dairy regulations; "other provision of law" interpreted to include the Constitution as well as case law, not merely statutes) *with* Jordan v. Dept. Motor Vehicles, 89 Cal. Rep. 2d 333, 343 (Ct. App. 1999) (refusing, under the "unmistakably clear" standard, to exempt from dormant Commerce Clause scrutiny California law imposing a $300 tax on automobiles titled in-state that were first titled in another state).

Page 9-18, add new paragraph of text at end of chapter:

Similarly, the Court is also reluctant to broadly construe redelegation provisions in statutes to encompass subjects not clearly within their text. In *Hillside Dairy, Inc. v. Lyons* (2003), for example, the Court reviewed a Ninth Circuit case in which the Court had applied language in a congressional statute authorizing states to legislate milk composition and labeling requirements free from the strictures of the Commerce Clause to state milk pricing and pooling laws as well.[47] The Supreme Court unanimously reversed. While acknowledging that "[t]he text of the federal statute plainly covers California laws regulating the composition and labeling of fluid milk products" it "does not mention laws regulating pricing."[48] The Court acknowledged that Congress could, if it wished, also exempt such laws from Commerce Clause scrutiny, but held that the "mere fact that the composition and labeling laws relate to the sale of fluid milk is by no means sufficient to bring them within the scope of" the statute and, thus, Congress had not clearly expressed its intent to exempt those subjects from dormant Commerce Clause review.[49]

[47] Hillside Dairy, Inc. v. Lyons, 539 U.S. 59, 64, 123 S. Ct. 2142, 2146 (2003).
[48] *Hillside Dairy, Inc.*, 539 U.S. at 66, 123 S. Ct. at 2147.
[49] 539 U.S. at 66, 123 S. Ct. at 2147.

CHAPTER 10

THE FOREIGN AND INDIAN COMMERCE POWERS

§ 10.01 INTRODUCTION: THE FOREIGN COMMERCE CLAUSE

Page 10-3, add to the end of note 1:

For an argument that the three portions of the Commerce Clause should be interpreted uniformly, and that cases departing from this "presumption of intrasentence uniformity" are mistaken, *see* Prakash, Our Three Commerce Clauses and the Presumption of Intrasentence Uniformity, 55 Ark. L. Rev. 1149 (2003). For a response, which concludes that such differentiation is not objectionable, *see* Vermeule, Three Commerce Clauses? No Problem, 55 Ark. L. Rev. 1175 (2003).

Page 10-3, add to the end of note 2:

For doubts about this conclusion, *see* Nelson & Pushaw, Rethinking the Commerce Clause: Applying First Principles to Uphold Federal Commercial Regulation but Preserve State Control over Social Issues, 85 Iowa L. Rev. 1, 46 n.85 (1999); Ramsey, The Power of the States in Foreign Affairs: The Original Understanding of Foreign Policy Federalism, 75 Notre Dame L. Rev. 341 (1999).

§ 10.02 THE "AFFIRMATIVE" CONGRESSIONAL POWER OVER FOREIGN COMMERCE

Page 10-4, add to the end of note 4:

For evidence supporting Professor Henkin's statement, *see* Made in the USA Foundation v. U.S., 56 F. Supp. 2d 1226, 1316-1323 (N.D. Ala. 1999) (suggesting that Congress's power over foreign commerce, the Necessary and Proper Clause, and the President's authority over foreign affairs, taken together, were sufficient to sustain the constitutionality of NAFTA, despite its not being ratified according to the Treaty Clause of the Constitution). *See generally* Recent Cases, 113 Harv. L. Rev. 1234 (2000). While praising the district court's "remarkably learned and thorough opinion," the Eleventh Circuit concluded that the issue whether NAFTA was a "treaty" requiring Senate ratification was a nonjusticiable political question. *See* Made in the USA Foundation v. United States, 242 F.3d 1300, 1302 (11th Cir. 2001). For a similar endorsement of a broad power to regulate foreign commerce, *see* Casebeer, The Power to

Regulate "Commerce with Foreign Nations" in a Global Economy and the Future of American Democracy: An Essay, 56 U. Miami L. Rev. 25 (2001). *But cf.* Equal Access Education v. Merten, 305 F. Supp. 2d 585, 608-611 (E.D. Va. 2004) (rejecting argument that state law prohibiting illegal aliens from enrolling in state-sponsored, post-secondary educational institutions violated dormant foreign Commerce Clause doctrine; state admission policy "are by no stretch of the imagination a regulation of foreign commerce").

Page 10-4, add to end of note 7:

But see United States v. Cummings, 281 F.3d 1046, 1049-1050 (9th Cir. 2002) (upholding authority of Congress to pass the International Parental Kidnapping Crime Act under the Foreign Commerce Power, but analyzing the statute under the three categories of permissible regulation under the *Interstate* Commerce Clause in *Lopez*).

§ 10.03 DORMANT FOREIGN COMMERCE CLAUSE RESTRICTIONS ON STATE ACTIONS

Page 10-7, replace citation to "Denning & McCall" in note 16 with:

Denning & McCall, The Constitutionality of State and Local "Sanctions" Against Foreign Countries: Affairs of State, States' Affairs, or a Sorry State of Affairs?, 26 Hastings Const. L.Q. 307 (1999); Dhooge, The Wrong Way to Mandalay: The Massachusetts Selective Purchasing Act and the Constitution, 37 Am. Bus. L.J. 387 (2000). For recent arguments that they should be upheld, *see* Jenkins, National Foreign Trade Council v. The Commonwealth of Massachusetts: A State Acting As a "Market Participant" Should Trump the Federal Government's Right to Regulate Foreign Affairs Unless Congress Expressly Declares Otherwise, 14 Conn. J. Int'l L. 593 (1999); Porterfield, State and Local Foreign Policy Initiatives and Free Speech: The First Amendment as an Instrument of Federalism, 35 Stan. J. Int'l L. 1 (1999). For post-*Crosby* commentary on state and local sanctions, *see* Symposium, New Voices on the New Federalism, 46 Vill. L. Rev. 907 (2001) (articles by Cleveland, Halberstam, Vazquez and others); Barnico, The Road From Burma: State Boycotts After *Crosby v. National Foreign Trade Council,* 19 B.U. Int'l L.J. 89 (2001); Delahunty, Federalism Beyond the Water's Edge: State Procurement Sanctions and Foreign

Affairs, 37 Stan. J. Int'l L. 1 (2001); Klein & Stern, Back to First Principles: The Constituitonal Rationale for Invalidating Local Sanctions Against Foreign Trade, 33 Law & Pol'y Int'l Bus. 77 (2001); Cao, Comment, Limiting States' Roles in Foreign Commerce: Teaching Old-World Dogs New-World Tricks, 23 Houston J. Int'l L. 349 (2001); Miyaki-Murphy, Comment, In the Wake of *Crosby v. National Foreign Trade Council,* 34 J. Marshall L. Rev. 827 (2001); Moritsugu, Note, The Winding Course of the Massachusetts Burma Law: Subfederal Sanctions in a Historical Context, 34 Geo. Wash. Int'l L. Rev. 435 (2002); Pascoe, Note, Time for a New Approach?: Federalism and Foreign Affairs After *Crosby v. National Foreign Trade Council,* 35 Vand. J. Transnat'l L. 291 (2002); Sendleski, Note, Taking Our Money and Going Home: State Divestment Policy and the Foreign Affairs, Foreign Commerce, and Supremacy Clauses, 24 Suffolk Transnat'l L. Rev. 317 (2001); *see also* Swaine, The Undersea Word of Foreign Relations Federalism, 2 Chi. J. Int'l L. 337 (2001).

Page 10-7, add to the end of note 16:

See also National Foreign Trade Council v. Natsios, 181 F.3d 38 (1st Cir. 1999) (holding unconstitutional Massachusetts law banning firms doing business in Burma from competing for state contracts), *aff'd sub nom.* Crosby v. Nat'l Foreign Trade Council, 530 U.S. 363, 120 S. Ct. 2288 (2000) (striking down state sanctions, but resting decision on preemption; declining to reach dormant Foreign Commerce Clause issue); Antilles Cement Corp. v. Calderon, 288 F. Supp. 2d 187, 199 (D.P.R. 2003) (striking down law prohibiting the use of non-Puerto Rican cement in construction projects funded by Commonwealth or by the United States government); Miami Light Project v. Miami-Dade Co., 97 F. Supp. 2d 1174 (S.D. Fla. 2000) (granting preliminary injunction against local ordinance restricting the transaction of county business with persons or entities that do business with Cuba). For an analysis of the Miami ordinance regarding Cuba, *see* Puentes, Comment, The Politics of Music and Film: The Validity of a Local Government's Cultural Embargo on Cuba, 31 U. Miami Inter-Am. L. Rev. 235 (2000) (concluding that the ordinance violates the Commerce Clause, is preempted by federal law, and offends the First Amendment). *But see* Equal Access Education v. Merten, 305 F. Supp. 2d 585, 608-611 (E.D. Va. 2004) (rejecting argument that state law prohibiting illegal aliens from enrolling in state-sponsored, post-secondary educational institutions violated dormant foreign Commerce Clause doctrine; state admission policies "are by no stretch of the imagination a regulation of foreign commerce").

§ 10.04 STATE TAXATION OF FOREIGN COMMERCE

Page 10-11, add to the end of note 32:

Specifically, the Court held that in addition to the four requirements of *Complete Auto*—that an activity be sufficiently related to the taxing jurisdiction, that the tax be fairly related to the benefits provided the taxpayer, that the tax not discriminate against foreign commerce, and that the tax be fairly apportioned—the tax must neither (i) present an enhanced risk of multiple taxation nor (ii) "impair federal uniformity in an area where federal uniformity is essential." 441 U.S. at 445, 99 S. Ct. at 1820.

§ 10.05 THE INDIAN COMMERCE CLAUSE

Page 10-12, add to the end of note 34:

See generally Laurence, Symmetry and Asymmetry in Federal Indian Law, 42 Ariz. L. Rev. 861 (2000).

[A] The Scope of Congressional Power under the Indian Commerce Clause

Page 10-14, add to the end of note 41:

; *see also* Carpenter, Interpreting Indian Country in *State of Alaska v. Native Village of Venetie,* 35 Tulsa L.J. 73 (1999).

Page 10-14, add to note 42, after "see generally,":

Symposium, Native Americans and the Constitution, 5 U. Pa. J. Const. L. 219 (2003); Symposium, Cultural Sovereignty: Native Rights in the 21st Century, 34 Ariz. St. L.J. 1 (2002);

Page 10-14, add to note 42, after "(1995);" and before "Clinton, supra":

Cleveland, Powers Inherent in Sovereignty: Indians, Aliens, Territories, and the Nineteenth Century Origins of Plenary Power over Foreign Affairs, 81 Tex. L. Rev. 1 (2002);

Page 10-15, add to the end of note 50:

; *see also* King, Note, The Legend of Crow Dog: An Examination of Jurisdiction over Intra-tribal Crimes Not Covered by the Major Crimes Act, 52 Vand. L. Rev. 1479 (1999).

Page 10-16, add to the end of note 53:

But see United States v. Enas, 204 F.3d 915 (9th Cir. 2000) (tribal court jurisdiction over crimes derives from tribe's inherent sovereignty and not from delegation from the federal government; therefore, indictment by both tribal court and federal government not barred by the Fifth Amendment's prohibition on Double Jeopardy under the dual sovereigns doctrine).

Page 10-17, add to the end of note 56:

The power is not, however, unlimited. In 1996, the Court held that the power was not sufficient to abrogate a state's sovereign immunity, which the Court found in the penumbras of the Eleventh Amendment. *See* Seminole Tribe of Florida v. Florida, 517 U.S. 44, 116 S. Ct. 1114 (1996) (divided court). *Seminole Tribe,* which overruled *Pennsylvania v. Union Gas Co.,* 491 U.S. 1, 109 S. Ct. 2273 (1989) (divided court), has been expanded in other cases, and has created a potent barrier against certain exercises of congressional power. *See* Alden v. Maine, 527 U.S. 706, 119 S. Ct. 2240 (1999) (divided court) (extending *Seminole Tribe* to lawsuits against states in state court); College Sav. Bank v. Florida Prepaid Postsecondary Educ. Expense Bd., 527 U.S. 666, 119 S. Ct. 2219 (1999) (divided court) (holding that congressional power under section 5 of the Fourteenth Amendment insufficient to waive state sovereign immunity in patent and trademark actions brought against states in federal court). *Seminole Tribe* and the "*Alden* trilogy," the Fifth Circuit recently held, barred an Indian tribe from seeking ejectment of the State of Texas from land to which the tribe claimed the state obtained title in violation of the Non-Intercourse Act. *See* Ysleta del Sur Pueblo v. Laney, 199 F.3d 281 (5th Cir. 2000). For a sampling of the voluminous commentary on *Seminole Tribe* and its progeny, see generally Symposium, The Eleventh Amendment, 75 Notre Dame L. Rev. 817 (2000) (articles by Pfander, Fletcher, Vazquez, Woolhandler, Jackson, Meltzer, Nowak, Farber, Tidmarsh, Marshall & Cowart); Siegel, Congress's Power to Authorize Suits Against States, 68 Geo. Wash. L. Rev. 44 (1999); Vazquez, The *Alden* Trilogy, 109 Yale L.J. 1927 (2000).

Page 10-17, add to end of Subsection [A]:

For example, Justice Thomas has noted that the Court never has found "any provision of the Constitution that gives Congress the power to alter tribal sovereignty" and concluded that the Indian Commerce Clause could not suffice. He urged the Court to revisit the Court's tribal sovereignty decisions to clear up the doctrinal confusion.[58.1]

[B] The Power of the States over Indians and Indian Tribes

Page 10-17, add to the end of note 60:

But see Seldin, Comment, Interstate Marketing of Indian Water Rights: The Impact of the Dormant Commerce Clause, 87 Calif. L. Rev. 1545 (discussing the ability of states to regulate tribes' sales of indigenous water rights off the reservation).

Page 10-18, add to the end of note 61:

See also Agnew, Note, The Dormant Indian Commerce Clause: Up in Smoke?, 25 Am. Ind. L. Rev. 353 (2000-2001).

[1] The So-Called Dormant Indian Commerce Clause

Page 10-19, add to the end of note 65:

For commentary on using foreign relations law as a prism through which to view federal-state-tribal relations, *see* Fredericks, America's First Nations: The Origins, History and Future of American Indian Sovereignty, 7 J.L. & Pol'y 347 (1999); Borchert, Comment, Tribal Immunity Through the Lens of the Foreign Sovereign Immunities Act: A Warrant for Codification?, 13 Emory Int'l L. Rev. 247 (1999); *see also* O'Melinn, The Imperial Origins of Federal Indian Law: The Ideology of Colonization in Britain, Ireland, and America, 31 Ariz. St. L.J. 1207 (1999).

Page 10-22, add to the end of note 73:

See also Omaha Tribe of Nebraska v. Miller, 311 F. Supp. 2d 816, 822 (S.D. Iowa 2004) (rejecting Indian Commerce Clause-based argument that tribe-owned cigarette manufacturer exempt from statue requiring manufacturers that did not participate in multistate tobacco litigation settlement either to participate or make escrow payments to state based on product sales to state citizens); Ward v. New York, 291 F. Supp. 2d 188, 200 (W.D.N.Y. 2003) (rejecting claim that "dormant" Indian Commerce Clause prohibited state from enforcing direct-shipment ban on cigarettes against tribal-owned mail order cigarette business). For more on the power of states to tax Indians' activities, see generally Carleton, State Income Taxation of Nonmember Indians in Indian Country, 27 Am. Ind. L. Rev. 253 (2002-2003); *see also* Sac and Fox Nation of Missouri v. Pierce, 213 F.3d 566, 583-84 (10th Cir. 2000) (remanding, for further evidence of federal, tribal, and state interests, Kansas tax on motor fuel distributed to tribal retail stations); Ansson, State Taxation of Non-Indians Whom Do Business with Indian Tribes: Why Several Recent Ninth Circuit Holdings Reemphasize the Need for Indian Tribes to Enter into Taxation Compacts with Their Respective State, 78 Or. L. Rev. 501 (1999) (urging tribes to enter into tax compacts with states); Burson, Comment, The Blaze Construction Case: An Analysis of the *Blaze Construction* Tax Cases and the Implications on Avoidance of Taxation in Indian Country, 39 Nat. Resources J. 845 (1999).

[2] Federal Preemption of State Law Affecting Indian Affairs

Page 10-23, add to the end of note 77:

See also Leading Cases—Native American Treaties—State Sovereignty—Compatibility with Indian Treaty Rights, 113 Harv. L. Rev. 389 (1999).

[58.1] United States v. Lara, ___ U.S. ___, ___, 124 S. Ct. 1628, 1647 (2004) (Thomas, J., concurring).

CHAPTER 11

PROHIBITION OF FEDERAL TAXES ON EXPORTS AND PORT PREFERENCES

§11.01 INTRODUCTION: FEDERAL EXPORT TAX CLAUSE

Page 11-4, add to the end of note 6:

See generally Jensen, The Export Clause, 6 Fla. Tax Rev. 1 (2003); Kelly & Amzel, Does the Commerce Clause Eclipse the Export Clause?: Making Sense of *United States v. United States Shoe Corp.*, 84 Minn. L. Rev. 129 (1999).

§11.02 THE MEANING OF "ARTICLES EXPORTED"

Page 11-5, add new footnote 9.1 after **THE MEANING OF "ARTICLES EXPORTED"***:*

One threshold question whose answer has been long assumed, though never squarely stated, is whether the "articles exported" mentioned in the clause refer only to *foreign* exports, or encompasses exports from one state to another. While admitting that no Supreme Court case has addressed the issue squarely, the Court of Appeals for the Federal Circuit recently rejected arguments that the Export Tax Clause should be read to prohibit federal taxes on *interstate* exports. *See* Florida Sugar Marketing and Terminal Association, Inc. v. United States, 220 F.3d 1331, 1338-1339 (Fed. Cir. 2000) ("When viewed in the context of the Convention debates and the entirety of the relevant constitutional text, we see strong indicators that the Constitution's drafters intended only to prohibit taxes on foreign commerce, not interstate shipments."). For the Export Tax Clause's origins, *see supra* § 11.01.

Page 11-10, add to the end of note 30:

For an argument in favor of the Court's approach, but which criticizes the Court for leaving open the possibility for a "user fee" exception to the Export Tax Clause, *see* Kelly & Amzel, supra note 6.

§11.03 "TAX" OR "USER FEE"

Page 11-13, add to the end of note 39:

The HMT was also levied upon imports; the U.S. Court of International Trade recently held that the provisions struck down in *United States Shoe* were severable from other provisions, like the tax on imports. *See* Amoco

Oil Co. v. United States, 63 F. Supp. 2d 1332 (Ct. Int'l Trade 1999). The United States Court of Appeals for the Federal Circuit recently agreed. *See* Thomson Multimedia, Inc. v. United States, 340 F.3d 1355, 1359 (Fed. Cir. 2003) (noting presence of severability clause and legislative history).

Page 11-13, add to the end of note 41:

In a subsequent case, a court held unconstitutional the application of the HMT to the transportation of passengers, a question not addressed by *United States Shoe. See* Carnival Cruise Lines, Inc. v. United States, 8 F. Supp. 2d 877 (Ct. Int'l Trade 1999). Kelly & Amzel, *supra* note 6, argue that "[t]here is nothing in the text, case law or history of the Export [Tax] Clause which suggests that there is a user fee exception to its broad prohibition." *Id.* at 186. They further criticize the Court for suggesting that the "user fee" concept could be imported into the Export Tax Clause. *Id.* at 189.

In contrast to the strict test applied to taxes or fees on exports by *United States Shoe* that invalidated the Harbor Maintenance Tax, the United States Court of Appeals for the Federal Circuit applied the more lenient test of *Massachusetts v. United States,* 435 U.S. 444, 98 S. Ct. 1153 (1978) to evaluate the constitutionality of the Harbor Maintenance Tax as applied to *imports. Massachusetts* requires that charges (i) must not discriminate against constitutionally protected interests; (ii) must be based on fair approximation of the use of some system; and (iii) be fairly apportioned to the total costs to the government of the benefits conferred. As applied to a fee imposed on imports that contained specific exemptions for inland waterways and for the states of Hawaii and Alaska, the Federal Circuit found that there was no evidence of discrimination under the Uniformity or Port Preference Clauses; that the tax was "based upon a fair approximation of the cost of the benefits provided for port users;" and that it was not excessive in relation to the expenditures by the government. Thomson Multimedia, Inc. v. United States, 340 F.3d 1355, 1360-1364 (Fed. Cir. 2003).

Page 11-14, add new paragraph to the end of the first full paragraph on the page:

But in *Consolidated Coal Company v. United States* (2005), a recent case from the Court of Federal Claims, the court refused to adopt the

Moon analysis, holding that a provision of the Surface Mining Control and Reclamation Act of 1977 (SMCRA) requiring producers to pay a "reclamation fee" on coal sold was invalid as applied to coal sold to foreign customers.[47.1] The court acknowledged "the plethora of decisions which have consistently concluded that the reclamation fee, contrary to its title, is actually a tax" and held that, even if SMCRA was passed under Congress's commerce power, that fact did not insulate it from an Export Clause challenge.[47.2] Since it was clearly a tax, imposed on an article for export, it was invalid.

[47.1] Consolidated Coal Co. v. United States, 2005 WL 757176 (Ct. Fed. Cl. 2005), at *16-*17.

[47.2] *Consolidated Coal Co.*, 2005 WL 757176, at *16 ("The Supreme Court has explained that an inquiry under the Export Clause is more strict than an inquiry under other constitutional provisions.").

§11.04 PORT PREFERENCE CLAUSE

[B] Discrimination between States

Page 11-20, add to the end of note 66:

See also Thomson Multimedia, Inc. v. United States, 340 F.3d 1355, 1364 (Fed. Cir. 2003) (holding that "the Clause does not prohibit a facially nondiscriminatory law that has incidental, disparate effects on ports of one or more states"); Amoco Oil Co. v. United States, 63 F. Supp. 2d 1332, 1341 (Ct. Int'l Trade 1999) ("The Port Preference Clause was intended to protect states, as opposed to individual ports or regions, from Congressional regulation that intentionally discriminates against one state's ports to the advantage of another's"; *held,* HMT, as applied to imports, did not violate the Port Preference Clause; no evidence of intent to discriminate against a particular state). *Thomson Multimedia* went on to hold that exemptions from the Harbor Maintenance Tax for domestic unloadings in Alaska and Hawaii and exemptions for unloadings at other ports in the United States when the shipment was from those states did not violate the Port Preference Clause. "The cases do not support the proposition," the court wrote, "that a statute with explicit exemptions of states to *prevent* disparate effects violates the Clause." 340 F.3d at 1364-1365. Congress, it noted, "crafted a narrow exemption to alleviate a disproportionate incidence of the tax on Alaska and Hawaii as a result of their heavy reliance on domestic shipping. . . . To solve this problem, the exemption . . . only applies to domestic unloadings, not to imports or exports. . . . Thus, no advantage arises for international shipping to and from ports of these states, because there is no indication that Alaska and Hawaii are more dependent on international shipping than any other states." *Id.* at 1365. "In short, it is clear that the intent and effect of the exemption was not to provide a preference to the ports of the exempted states at the expense of ports of other states, but rather to provide some relief from the disparate effects the HMT would have had on the shipping-dependent states and possessions." *Id.* at 1366.

[D] "Accidents" of Geography

Page 11-23, first line of note 77, before "For an analogous rationale. . . .":

For a recent application of the "accidents" of geography rationale, *see* Thomson Multimedia, Inc. v. United States, 340 F.3d 1355, 1365 (Fed. Cir. 2003) (concluding that exemptions from the Harbor Maintenance Tax for domestic shipments to and from ports in Alaska and Hawaii did not violate the Port Preference Clause; holding that the Clause "prohibits only intentional, effectual preference of the ports of one state over ports of another state, advantaging certain states' ports by disadvantaging other states' ports");

CHAPTER 12

STATE IMPORT-EXPORT TAXES AND TONNAGE DUTIES

§ 12.05 "IMPOSTS OR DUTIES ON IMPORTS OR EXPORTS"

Page 12-20, add to the end of note 62:

Cf. Florida Sugar Marketing and Terminal Association, Inc. v. United States, 220 F.3d 1331, 1338-1339 (Fed. Cir. 2000) (rejecting Crosskey's evidence that terms "import" and "export" encompassed both interstate and foreign commerce, offered in support of argument that Export Tax Clause prohibiting federal taxes or duties on articles exported from states, applied to interstate exports as well as foreign ones). For the Export Tax Clause, *see supra* §§ 11.01-11.03.

§ 12.06 EXPORTS AFTER THE *MICHELIN TIRE* CASE

Page 12-25, add to the end of note 82:

; see also Ammex, Inc. v. Dept. Treasury, 603 N.W.2d 308, 314 (Ct. App. Mich. 1999) (noting that "an article does not constitute an 'export' if there exists a practical possibility of diversion to domestic markets. . . . Similarly, an article cannot be considered an 'export' within the meaning of the Import-Export Clause if 'it will be used in this country for its designed purpose, before being shipped abroad' "; therefore state tax on gasoline sold at station located close to Canadian border not prohibited by the Import-Export Clause).

Page 12-25, add to the end of note 83:

For a recent example of *Michelin Tire*'s application to a case involving exports, *see* Auto Cargo, Inc. v. Miami Dade Co., 237 F.3d 1289, 1292-1294 (11th Cir. 2001) (upholding imposition of state inspection fee charged for every used, self-propelled vehicle exported through U.S. Customs at county-operated port).

§ 12.07 GOODS IN TRANSIT

Page 12-34, add to the end of note 120:

See Ammex, Inc. v. Dept. Treasury, 603 N.W.2d 308, 314 (Ct. App. Mich. 1999) (state sales taxes on fuel sold at "duty-free" gas station located less than two miles from the Canadian border did not constitute a tax on "exports" prohibited by the Import-Export Clause).

Chapter 13

THE REGULATION OF LIQUOR UNDER THE TWENTY-FIRST AMENDMENT

§ 13.03 THE TWENTY-FIRST AMENDMENT AND THE DORMANT COMMERCE CLAUSE

[A] Transportation and Importation of Liquor into States

Page 13-8, add at end of section [A]:

The *Young's Market* line of cases, however, has been overruled in all but name.[75.1] In *Granholm v. Heald* (2005), a divided Court favored recent cases holding that the dormant Commerce Clause doctrine's nondiscrimination principle applied to state regulation of wine, as it would to the regulation of cheese.[75.2] Striking down laws in Michigan and New York that prohibited the direct shipment of out-of-state wine—but not wine produced locally—to in-state consumers, Justice Kennedy wrote that the Court's more recent decisions "confirm that the Twenty-first Amendment . . . does not displace the rule that States may not give a discriminatory preference to their own producers."[75.3]

75.1 *See infra* § 13.04.
75.2 Granholm v. Heald, __ U.S. __, 125 S. Ct. 1885 (2005) (divided court).
75.3 __ U.S. at __, 125 S. Ct. at 1903

§ 13.04 RESIDUAL COMMERCE CLAUSE RESTRICTIONS ON STATE REGULATION OF LIQUOR

[B] State Economic Protectionism in the Regulation of Liquor

Pages 13-20 and 13-21, omit paragraphs following note 82 and replace with the following:

In recent years, a circuit split had developed on the issue of whether state liquor laws that permitted certain in-state producers, usually local wineries, to ship directly to customers, while prohibiting direct shipment by out-of-state wineries, violated the dormant Commerce Clause doctrine. States argued that section two of the Twenty-first Amendment authorized the differential treatment. Last term, in *Granholm v. Heald* (2005), the Supreme Court held definitively that the Twenty-first Amendment did not trump the dormant Commerce Clause doctrine's nondiscrimination principle.[82]

The laws of New York and Michigan challenged in *Heald* were fairly typical. Both states had a three-tiered system of alcohol sales: producers could sell only to wholesalers, who could sell only to retailers, who could sell to consumers. Out-of-state producers could not obtain licenses to sell directly to consumers, but both states' in-state producers could.[83] The states defended these laws by invoking section two of the Twenty-first Amendment, which, they argued, trumped the dormant Commerce Clause doctrine, including its nondiscrimination principle. The Court, in an opinion written by Justice Kennedy, rejected this view as "inconsistent with our precedents and with the Twenty-first Amendment's history."[84]

After a lengthy review of the history of alcohol regulation, and of Congress's response to the Court's use of the dormant Commerce Clause doctrine to invalidate state liquor regulations through the Wilson and Webb-Kenyon Acts, Justice Kennedy concluded that far from *allowing* any type of discrimination, "[t]he Wilson Act reaffirmed, and the Webb-Kenyon Act did not displace, the Court's line of . . . cases striking down state laws that discriminated against liquor produced out of state" even though they removed dormant Commerce Clause barriers to facially neutral laws that were held to "directly regulate" interstate commerce or otherwise burden it.[85] On the Court's reading, section two of the Twenty-first Amendment was intended "to allow States to maintain an effective and uniform system for controlling liquor by regulating its transportation, importation, and use. The Amendment did not give States the authority to pass nonuniform laws in order to discriminate against out of state goods, a privilege they had not enjoyed at any earlier time."[86]

But what of the *Young's Market* cases? Here the majority was cagey. It said it was "unclear whether the language in *Young's Market* [that the Twenty-first Amendment did not explicitly prohibit discrimination against out-of-state goods by states] was necessary to the result because the Court also stated that 'the case [did] not present a question of discrimination prohibited by the commerce clause.' "[87] That was certainly the *Young's Market*'s holding, but *Heald*'s use of the quotation is extremely misleading because it implies that *Young's Market* involved a facially neutral statute that treated in-state and out-of-state alcohol alike. In fact, the case involved a $500 license fee required of those importing beer from out-of-state; a wholesaler's license, which would permit the sale of domestic or imported beer, could be had for $50.[88] Thus, the entire burden of the license fee fell on wholesalers of out-of-state beer. Even if the *Young's Market* facts were not quite on all fours with the laws challenged in *Heald*, other cases contemporary with *Young's Market* had facts that were.[89] In each case, the Court applied *Young's Market* and permitted state legislation that *Heald* condemned. The *Heald* Court also faulted *Young's Market* for failing "to consider the history underlying the Twenty-first Amendment."[90]

In any event, the Court concluded that the *Young's Market* line of cases were inconsistent with the Court's more recent cases, which "confirm that the Twenty-first Amendment . . . does not displace the rule that States may not give a discriminatory preference to their own producers."[90.1] Here, the Court relied heavily on *Bacchus Imports v. Dias* (1984), and refused invitations to overrule it or limit it to its facts despite that case's own lack of interest in the history of the Twenty-first Amendment.[90.2]

The states argued that their laws served legitimate interests that could not be achieved through nondiscriminatory alternatives. Their main arguments were that the direct shipment ban permitted them (1) to police underage drinking and (2) to ensure accurate and orderly collection of state taxes. The Court rejected both. "The States produce little evidence," the Court wrote, "that the purchase of wine over the Internet by minors is a problem" and cited a Federal Trade Commission report suggesting the opposite.[90.3] "Even were we to credit the States' largely unsupported claim that direct shipping of wine increases the risk of underage drinking, this would not justify" the discrimination since "minors are just as likely to order wine from in-state producers as from out-of-state ones."[90.4]

The states also argued that direct shipment could result in a loss of tax revenue. While the states' tax collection concerns "were not wholly illusory," according to the Court, "their regulatory objectives can be achieved without discriminating against interstate commerce."[90.5]

In a lengthy dissent, Justice Thomas criticized the majority for misapprehending the import of the Wilson and Webb-Kenyon Acts and for disregarding the *Young's Market* cases.[90.6] Thomas pointed out that not only were the states' laws regulating shipment or transportation within the explicit terms of the Webb-Kenyon Act, but that the Act also omitted language present in the Wilson Act requiring in-state and out-of-state alcohol be treated the same.[90.7] Contrary to the majority's conclusion, Thomas argued that "the Webb-Kenyon Act overturned not only [cases barring nondiscriminatory state regulations] but also [cases involving the] 'nondiscrimination' principle."[90.8]

Noting the similarity with the Webb-Kenyon Act itself, Thomas further argued that the plain meaning of section two of the Twenty-first Amendment permitted the laws struck down by the majority, particularly in light of the *Young's Market* cases.[90.9] He also criticized the majority's reliance on *Bacchus Imports* while ignoring the Court's earlier cases. "*Bacchus*' reasoning is unpersuasive," Thomas wrote, "[i]t swept aside the weighty authority of this Court's early Twenty-first Amendment case law" substituting instead a test—a test Thomas accused the majority of abandoning without comment—that only regulations dealing with the Amendment's "core concerns" (mainly, enforcing temperance) fell within the scope of section two.[90.10] "Stripped of *Bacchus*," Thomas concluded, "the Court's holding is bereft of support in our cases. . . . Given the uniformity of our early case law supporting even discriminatory state laws regulating imports into States, then, Michigan's and New York's laws easily pass muster under the Court's cases."[90.11]

[82] Granholm v. Heald, __ U.S. __, 125 S. Ct. 1885 (2005) (divided court).

[83] *Heald*, __ U.S. at __, 125 S. Ct. at 1892. For a detailed description of the Michigan law, *see*__ U.S. at __, 125 S. Ct. at 1893-1894. The New York law was somewhat different than Michigan's. It was theoretically possible for an out-of-state producer to obtain a license that would permit direct shipment, but only if it maintained a physical presence in the state. Despite this possibility, the Court concluded that both states' laws discriminated against interstate commerce. __ U.S. at __, 125 S. Ct. at 1896-1897.

[84] __ U.S. at __, 125 S. Ct. at 1897.

[85] __ U.S. at __, 125 S. Ct. at 1897-1902. For more on the Wilson and the Webb-Kenyon Acts, *see supra* § 9.02.

[86] __ U.S. at __, 125 S. Ct. at 1902

[87] __ U.S. at __, 125 S. Ct. at 1903.

[88] *Young's Market*, 299 U.S. at 60-61, 57 S. Ct. at 78.

[89] *See, e.g.*, Joseph F. Finch & Co. v. McKittrick, 305 U.S. 395, 398, 59 S. Ct. 256, 257 (1939) (upholding Minnesota law prohibiting the importation of certain liquor whose brands had not been registered with the U.S. Patent Office, but exempting locally produced liquor).

[90] *Heald*, __ U.S. at __, 125 S. Ct. at 1903.

[90.1] __ U.S. at __, 125 S. Ct. at 1903.

[90.2] __ U.S. at __, 125 S. Ct. at 1904.

[90.3] __ U.S. at __, 125 S. Ct. at 1905. The report cited three reasons this was so: (1) the preference of minors for types of alcohol other than wine; (2) the availability of more direct means of obtaining alcohol than procuring a credit card and ordering wine over the Internet; and (3) the lack of "instant gratification" inherent in making Internet purchases. *Id.*

[90.4] __ U.S. at __, at 125 S. Ct. 1905-1906

[90.5] __ U.S. at __, 125 S. Ct. at 1906.

[90.6] __ U.S. at __, 125 S. Ct. at 1909 (Thomas, J., dissenting). Justice Stevens also wrote a dissenting opinion faulting the majority for failing to credit the *Young's Market* line of cases, noting that the Justices who applied and interpreted the Twenty-first Amendment then were in a better position than members of the current Court to be aware of the expectations of those proposing and ratifying the amendment. __ U.S. at __, 125 S. Ct. at 1908-1909 (Stevens, J., dissenting).

[90.7] __ U.S. at __, __, 125 S. Ct. at 1910, 1912 (Thomas, J., dissenting).
[90.8] __ U.S. at __, 125 S. Ct. at 1913 (Thomas, J., dissenting).
[90.9] __ U.S. at __, 125 S. Ct. at 1919-1920 (Thomas, J., dissenting).
[90.10] __ U.S. at __, 125 S. Ct. at 1925 (Thomas, J., dissenting).
[90.11] __ U.S. at __, 125 S. Ct. at 1926 (Thomas, J., dissenting).

§13.05 OTHER CONSTITUTIONAL RESTRICTIONS ON STATE REGULATION OF LIQUOR

[F] The Federal Spending Power

Page 13-34, add to the end of note 143:

Some commentators have inferred from *Printz* additional limits on congressional conditional spending power. *See* Hammeke, Note, State Autonomy Implications for Congressional Conditional Spending, 24 Okla. City U. L. Rev. 349 (1999).

TABLE OF CASES

References are to sections.

A

C

D

E

F

G

H

I

J

K

L

M

N

Q

R

S

U

V

W

X

Y

Z

TABLE OF AUTHORITIES

References are to sections.

A

Ann, Comment, A More Convenient Crime: Why States Must Regulate Internet-Related Criminal Activity Under the Dormant Commerce Clause, 20 Pace L. Rev. 189, 3.06[C]

Anson & Schenkken, Federalism, The Dormant Commerce Clause, and State-Owned Resources, 59 Tex. L. Rev. 71, 6.01[A], 7.01

Ansson, State Taxation of Non-Indians Who Do Business with Indian Tribes: Why Several Recent Ninth Circuit Holdings Reemphasize the Need for Indian Tribes to Enter into Taxation Compacts with Their Respective State, 78 Or. L. Rev. 501, 10.05[B][1]

Anstreich, Fisher & Meithke, Jefferson Lines as Ticket to Cyberspace? Taxing Electronic Commerce Services, Tax Notes, July 27, 1998, 3.06[C]

Apple & Burros, Zinfandel by Mail? Well, Yes and No, N.Y. Times, May 19, 1999, 13.03[A]

Areeda, Hovenkamp & Solon, Antitrust Law, 3.04, 7.02[C]

Areeda & Turner, Antitrust Law, 3.05, 5.05[B]

Associated Press, U.S. Seeking Ban on Internet Taxes, N.Y. Times, Oct. 1, 1999, 3.06[C]

Associated Press, Wineries Complain of Federal Threat, N.Y. Times, Oct. 11, 1999, 13.03[A]

Ausness, Preemption of the State Tort Law by Federal Safety Statutes: Supreme Court Preemption Jurisprudence Since *Cipallone*, 92 Ky. L.J. 913 (2003-2004), 5.06[D]

Avery, Comment, State Oil Spill Prevention Laws and Intertanko: When Is State Law Preempted?, 6 Ocean & Coastal L.J. 119, 5.06[E]

B

Badawi, Comment, Unceasing Animosities and the Public Tranquility: Political Market Failure and the Scope of the Commerce Power, 91 Cal. L. Rev. 1331 (2003), 5.04[A]

Baden, Note, When the Open Road is Closed to Juveniles: The Constitutionality of Juvenile Curfew Laws and the Inconsistencies Among the Courts, 37 Val. U. L. Rev. 831 (2003), 3.11[C]

Bair, Note, The Dormant Commerce Clause and State-Mandated Preference Laws in Public Contracting: Developing a More Substantive Application of the Market Participation Exception, 93 Mich. L. Rev. 2408, 6.06[H][2][b], 7.06

Baker, Conditional Federal Spending After *Lopez,* 95 Colum. L. Rev. 1911, 5.04[B]

Baker, A Strict Scrutiny of the Right to Travel, 22 U.C.L.A. L. Rev. 1129, 3.11

Balderson Note, *Birbrower, Montalbano, Condon & Frank, P.C. v. Superior Court*: A Defensible Outcome but a Striking Example of the Need to Reform Unauthorized Practice of Law Provisions, 36 San Diego L. Rev. 871, 6.06[H][1][c]

Barber, Necessary and Proper Clause, *in* 3 Ency. Amer. Const., 5.01[B], 5.04

Barnett, The Delegation of Legislative Power by Congress to the States, 2 Am. Pol. Sci. Rev. 347, 9.02

Barnett, Necessary and Proper, 44 U.C.L.A. L. Rev. 745, 5.01[B]

Barnett, New Evidence of the Original Meaning of the Commerce Clause, 55 Ark. L. Rev. 847, 1.01, 2.01, 2.03, 3.01, 3.04, 5.01

Barnico, The Road From Burma: State Boycotts After *Crosby v. National Foreign Trade Council,* 19 B.U. Int's L.J. 89, 5.06[D], 7.02[D], 10.03

Barrett, State Taxation of Interstate Commerce, Direct Burdens, Multiple Burdens or What Have You, 4 Vand. L. Rev. 496, 8.07

Barton, An Institutional Analysis of Lawyer Regulation: Who Should Control Lawyer Regulation —Courts, Legislatures, or the Market? 37 Ga. L. Rev. 1167 (2003), 6.06[H][1][c]
Bassinger, Note, Dormant Commerce Clause Limits on State Regulation of the Internet: The Transportation Analogy, 32 Ga. L. Rev. 889, 3.06[C], 8.01
Bauerle, Congress' Commerce Clause Authority: Is the Pendulum Finally Swinging Back?, 1997 Det. C.L.-Mich. St. U.L. Rev. 49, 5.04[A]
Bauerly, Balancing the Scales: The 1996 Telecommunications Act and Eleventh Amendment Immunity, 50 Fed. Comm. L.J. 399, 3.06[B]
Baxter, Daniel Webster and the Supreme Court, 1.02[A]
Baxter, One and Inseparable: Daniel Webster and the Union, 1.02[A]
Baxter, The Steamboat Monopoly, 1.02[A], 1.03
Beale, The Unintended Consequences of Enhancing Gun Penalties: Shooting Down the Commerce Clause and Arming Federal Prosecutors, 51 Duke L.J. 1641, 3.13[B]
Beard, An Economic Interpretation of the Constitution, 1.01
Beard, Regulation of Pipe Lines As Common Carriers, 3.02[F]
Beck, The New Jurisprudence of the Necessary and Proper Clause, 2002 U. Ill. L. Rev. 581; cf. Beck, The Heart of Federalism: Pretext Review of Means-Ends Relationships, 36 U.C. Davis L. Rev. 407, 5.01[B]
Bederman, Admiralty Jurisdiction, 31 J. Mar. L. & Com., 189, 3.02[C]
Bederman, Food Libel: Litigating Scientific Uncertainty in a Constitutional Twilight Zone, 10 DePaul Bus. L.J. 191, 12.08
Beerman, Comment, State Involvement in the Promotion of Export Trade: Is It Time to Rethink the Concept of Federalism as it Pertains to Foreign Relations?, 21 N.C. J. Int'l.L. & Comm. Reg. 187, 10.03
Benoit, The Privileges and Immunities Clause of the Fourteenth Amendment: Can There Be Life After Death?, 11 Suffolk U. L. Rev. 61, 6.06[H][3]
Benson, The Supreme Court and the Commerce Clause, 1937-1970, 5.02, 5.03
Berger, Comment, Phoenix Grounded: The Impact of the Supreme Court's Changing Preemption Doctrine on State and Local Impediments to Airport Expansion, 97 Nw. U. L. Rev. 941, 5.06[E]
Berger, Federalism: The Founders' Design, 2.02
Berger, Interstate Commerce: A Response to Sanford Levinson, 74 Tex. L. Rev. 785, 5.04[A]
Berger, Judicial Manipulation of the Commerce Clause, 74 Tex. L. Rev. 695, 5.04[A]
Berman, *Guillen* and Gullability: Piercing the Surface of Commerce Clause Doctrine, 89 Iowa L. Rev. 1487 (2004), 5.01[A], 5.04[G]
Beth, The Slaughter-House Cases — Revisited, 23 La. L. Rev. 487, 6.06[I][6]
Beveridge, The Life of John Marshall, 1.02[A]
Bickel, The Least Dangerous Branch, 5.06[F], 6.02[C]
Bickel & Schmidt, IX History of the Supreme Court of the United States: The Judiciary and Responsible Government, 1910-21, 2.03, 2.04, 3.02[E], 5.01[A]
Biden, The Civil Rights Remedy of the Violence Against Women Act: A Defense, 37 Harv. J. on Legis. 1, 5.04[E]
Bikel, The Silence of Congress, 41 Harv. L. Rev. 200, 6.01[A]
Bilder, The Role of States and Cities in Foreign Relations, 83 Am. J. Int'l. L. 821, 10.03

Bradley, Federalism and Federal Criminal Law, 55 Hastings L.J. 573 (2004), 3.13[B], 5.04[G], 5.04[H][9]

Braun, Drobny & Gessner, www.commercial_terrorism.com: A Proposed Federal Criminal Statute Addressing the Solicitation of Commercial Terrorism Through the Internet, 37 Harv. J. on Legis. 159, 3.06[C]

Breen, The Travel Act: Prosecution of Interstate Acts in Aid of Racketeering, 24 Am. Crim. L. Rev. 125, 3.13[B]

Brennan, The Constitution of the United States: Contemporary Ratification, 27 Tex. L.J. 433, 12.04

Brickey, Crime Control and the Commerce Clause After *Lopez,* 46 Case W. Res. L.J. 801, 5.04[A]

Brignac, Recent Development, The Commerce Clause Justification of Endangered Species Protection: *Gibbs v. Babbitt,* 79 N.C. L. Rev. 873, 5.04[H][7]

Brody, Hocking the Halo: Implications of the Charities' Winning Brief in *Camps Newfound/Owatonna, Inc.,* 27 Stetson L. Rev. 433, 3.14

Broll, Comment, The Economic Liberty Rationale of the Dormant Commerce Clause, 49 S.D. L. Rev., 824 (2003-2004), 6.01[A]

Brown, The Commercial Power of Congress Considered in the Light of Its Origin, 1.01, 5.01

Brown, Constitutionalizing the Federal Criminal Law Debate: *Morrison, Jones* and the ABA, 2001 U. Ill. L. J. 983, 5.04[H][5]

Brown, The Open Economy: Justice Frankfurter and the Position of the Judiciary, 67 Yale L.J. 219, 6.02[C], 9.01

Brown, Ratification of the Twenty-first Amendment to the Constitution of the United States: State Convention Records and Laws, 13.02

Brown, State Court Attempts to Limit the Applicability of the Federal Arbitration Act in a Post-*Lopez* World, 56 U. Miami L. Rev. 1051, 5.04[C], 5.04[G], 5.05[C]

Buck, Note, *General Motors Corp. v. Tracy,* 20 Energy L.J. 345, 8.05

Bunch, The Original Understanding of the Privileges and Immunities Clause: Michael Perry's Justification for Judicial Activism or Robert Bork's Constitutional Inkblot?, 10 Seton Hall Const. L.J. 321, 6.06[H][3]

Burdick, Law of the American Constitution, 2.02

Burk, Federalism in Cyberspace, 28 Conn. L. Rev. 1095, 3.06[C]

Burk, How State Regulation of the Internet Violates the Commerce Clause, 17 Cato J. 147, 3.06[C]

Burson, Comment, The *Blaze Construction* Case: An Analysis of the *Blaze Construction* Tax Cases and the Implications on Avoidance of Taxation in Indian Country, 39 Nat. Resources J. 845, 10.05[B][1]

Buzbee & Shapiro, Legislative Record Review, 54 Stan. L. Rev. 87, 5.01[C], 5.04[B]

C

Caballero, Foreign Multinationals and the Commerce Clause: Should the States Mind Their Own Business?, 41 Tax Law. 785, 10.03

Cain, Comment, The Civil Rights Provisions of the Violence Against Women Act: Its Legacy and Its Future, 34 Tulsa L.J. 367, 5.04[E]

Chiang, Comment, State Income Taxation of Out-of-State Trademark Holding Companies, 70 U. Chi. L. Rev. 1533 (2003), 8.06
Choper, The Scope of National Power Vis-a-Vis the States: The Dispensability of Judicial Review, 86 Yale L.J. 1552, 5.04[A], 5.05
Choper, Taming Congress's Power Under the Commerce Clause: What Does the Near Future Portend?, 55 Ark. L. Rev. 731, 5.04[G]
Choper & Yin, State Taxation and the Dormant Commerce Clause: The Object-Measure Approach, 1998 Sup. Ct. Rev. 193, 8.01
Choper & Yoo, The Scope of the Commerce Power After *Morrison,* 25 Okla. City Univ. L. Rev. 843, 5.04[B], 5.04[G]
Chuang, Note, Who Should Win the Garbage Wars? Lessons from the Low-Level Radioactive Waste Act, 72 Fordham L. Rev. 2403 (2004), 6.06[B]
Clark, Comment, Give 'Em Enough Rope: States, Subdivisions and the Market Participant Exception to the Dormant Commerce Clause, 60 U. Chi. L. Rev. 615, 7.06
Clausing, Debate on Internet Taxes Takes Political Turn, N.Y. Times, Sept. 13, 1999, 3.06[C]
Clausing, House Passes Bill to Restrict Online Liquor Sales, N.Y. Times, Aug. 3, 1999, 13.03[A]
Cleveland, Powers Inherent in Sovereignty: Indians, Aliens, Territories, and the Nineteenth Century Origins of Plenary Power over Foreign Affairs, 81 Tex. L. Rev. 1, 10.05[A]
Clevenger, Internet Pharmacies: Cyberspace Versus the Regulatory State, 15 J.L. & Health 165, 3.06[C]
Clinton, The Dormant Indian Commerce Clause, 27 Conn. L. Rev. 1055, 10.05, 10.05[A], 10.05[B][1]
Cockfield, Transforming the Internet into a Taxable Forum: A Case Study in E-Commerce Taxation, 85 Minn. L. Rev. 1171, 3.06[C]
Coenen, Business Subsidies and the Dormant Commerce Clause, 107 Yale L.J. 965, 6.04[1], 6.06[G][1]
Coenen, The Impact of the *Garcia* Decision on the Market-Participation Exception to the Dormant Commerce Clause, 1995 U. Ill. L. Rev. 727, 7.01
Coenen, State User Fees and the Dormant Commerce Clause, 50 Vand. L. Rev. 795, 3.03, 6.01[A], 7.01, 8.06, 12.02[D], 12.10, 12.10[C]
Coenen, Untangling the Market-Participant Exception to the Dormant Commerce Clause, 88 Mich. L. Rev. 395, 7.01, 7.07
Coenen & Hellerstein, Suspect Linkage: The Interplay of State Taxing and Spending Measures in the Application of Constitutional Antidiscrimination Rules, 95 Mich. L. Rev. 2167, 6.06[G][2]
Cohen, Congressional Power to Validate Unconstitutional State Laws: A Forgotten Solution to an Old Dilemma, 35 Stan. L. Rev. 387, 9.02, 9.03
Cohen, Handbook of Federal Indian Law, 10.05[A], 10.05[B][1]
Coleman, A Step Backwards: Carjacking and the Commerce Clause, 16 J. Law & Comm. 113, 5.04[A]
Collins, Economic Union as a Constitutional Value, 63 N.Y.U. L. Rev. 43, 6.01[A]
Comment, 8 J. Air. L. 498, 3.03
Comment, 21 Ill. L. Rev. 166, 3.02[C]
Comment, Constitutional Limitations on State Long Arm Jurisdiction, 49 U. Chi. L. Rev. 156, 3.02[C]

D

Dennis, Federalism, Electric Industry Restructuring, and the Dormant Commerce Clause: *Tampa Electric co. v. Garcia* and State Restrictions on the Development of Merchant Power Plants, 43 Nat. Res. J. 615 (2003), 3.07

Devins, Congress as Culprit: How Lawmakers Spurred on the Court's Anti-Congress Crusade, 51 Duke L.J. 435, 5.04[B]

Devins, Congressional Factfinding and the Scope of Judicial Review: A Preliminary Analysis, 50 Duke L.J. 1169, 5.01[C]

Dhooge, The Wrong Way to Mandalay: The Massachusetts Selective Purchasing Act and the Constitution, 37 Am. Bus. L.J. 387, 10.03

Dickerson, The Navigation Acts and the American Revolution, 11.04

Diederich, Municipalities Regain Control Over Trash — "Flow Control" Revisited, 35 Urb. Law. 687 (2003), 6.06[B]

Diehl, Is the IP Holding Company Dead?, 37 Md. Bar 43 (Jan./Feb. 2004), 8.06

Douglas, Note, The Violence Against Women Act and Contemporary Commerce Power: Principled Regulation and the Concerns of Federalism, 1999 Utah L. Rev. 703, 5.04[E]

Dowling, Interstate Commerce and State Power, 27 Va. L. Rev. 1, 6.01[A], 6.04

Dowling, Interstate Commerce and State Power — Revised Version, 47 Colum. L. Rev. 547, 6.01[A], 9.01[4]

Dowling, The Methods of Mr. Justice Stone in Constitutional Cases, 41 Colum. L. Rev. 1160, 6.04

Dowling & Hubbard, Divesting an Article of Its Interstate Character: An Examination of the Doctrine Underlying the Webb-Kenyon Act, 5 Minn. L. Rev. 100, 9.04

Drahozal, On Tariffs v. Subsidies in Interstate Trade: A Legal and Accounting Analysis, 74 Wash. U.L.Q. 1127, 6.06[G][1], 6.06[G][2]

Drahozal, Preserving the American Common Market: State and Local Governments in the United States Supreme Court, 7 Sup. Ct. Econ. Rev. 233, 6.02[C]

Dral & Phillips, Commerce by Another Name: The Impact of *United States v. Lopez* and *United States v. Morrison,* 68 Tenn. L. Rev. 605, 5.04[A], 5.04[G]

Dreifke, Note, The Foreign Commerce Clause and the Market Participation Exception, 25 Vand. J. Transnat'l L. 257, 7.02[D]

Dunham, Gross Receipts Taxes on Interstate Transactions, 47 Colum. L. Rev. 211, 8.02, 8.07

E

Early & Weitzman, A Century of Dissent: The Immunity of Goods Imported for Resale From Nondiscriminatory State Personal Property Taxes, 7 Sw. U. L. Rev. 247, 12.04

Eastman, A Fistful of Denials: The Supreme Court Takes a Pass on Commerce Clause Challenges to Environmental Laws, 2004 Cato Sup. Ct. Rev. 469, 5.04[G]

Eban, Diplomacy for the Next Century, 5.06[B]

Edson, *Quill's* Constitutional Jurisprudence and Tax Nexus Standards in an Age of Electronic Commerce, 49 Tax Law. 893, 8.06

Eisgruber & Sager, Congressional Powers and Religious Liberty After *City of Boerne v. Flores,* 1997 Sup. Ct. Rev. 79, 6.06[I]

Elliot, Debates on the Adoption of the Federal Constitution, 1.01

F

Freund, Foreword to Powell, Vagaries and Varieties in Constitutional Interpretation, 4.03, 6.01[A]
Freund, Memorandum on Civil Rights Act of 1964, 2.04
Freund, The Police Power: Public Policy and Constitutional Rights, 2.04, 4.02
Freund, Umpiring the Federal System, 54 Colum. L. Rev. 561, 6.02[C], 9.04
Freyer, Harmony and Dissonance: The *Swift* and *Erie* Cases in American Federalism, 2.05[A]
Frickey, Congressional Intent, Practical Reasoning, and the Dynamic Nature of Federal Indian Law, 78 Cal. L. Rev. 1137, 10.02[B][1], 10.05[A]
Frickey, The Fool on the Hill: Congressional Findings, Constitutional Adjudication, and *United States v. Lopez,* 46 Case Western Res. L. Rev. 695, 5.01[C], 5.04[B]
Frickey, Marshalling Past and Present: Colonialism, Constitutionalism, and Interpretation in Federal Indian Law, 107 Harv. L. Rev. 381, 10.05[B][1]
Frickey & Smith, Judicial Review, the Congressional Process, and the Federalism Cases: An Interdisciplinary Critique, 111 Yale L.J. 1707, 5.01[C]
Fried, Order and Law: Arguing the Reagan Revolution, 5.06[G]
Friedman, Charting the Course of Commerce Clause Challenge, 55 Ark. L. Rev. 1055, 5.01[C]
Friedman, The Sometimes-Bumpy Stream of Commerce Clause Doctrine, 55 Ark. L. Rev. 981, 5.01[C]
Friendly, Federal Jurisdiction: A General View, 3.13[A]
Friendly, The Gap in Lawmaking—Judges Who Can't and Legislators Who Won't, 63 Colum. L. Rev. 787, 2.05[B]
Friendly, In Praise of Erie—and of the New Federal Common Law, 39 N.Y.U. L. Rev. 383, 2.05[A]

G

Gannet, The New Federalism, the Spending Power, and Federal Criminal Law, 89 Cornell L. Rev. 1 (2003), 5.04[B]
Gardbaum, The Nature of Preemption, 79 Cornell L. Rev. 767, 5.06, 5.06[B]
Gardbaum, Rethinking Constitutional Federalism, 74 Tex. L. Rev. 795, 5.06[B]
Gasaway, The Problem of Tort Reform: Federalism and the Regulation of Lawyers, 25 Harv. J.L. & Pub. Pol'y 953, 5.04[A]
Gavit, The Commerce Clause, 6.01[A], 6.02[B]
Gavit, State Highways and Interstate Motor Transportation, 21 Ill. L. Rev. 559, 3.02[E]
Gaylord, Note, State Regulatory Jurisdiction and the Internet: Letting the Dormant Commerce Clause Lie, 52 Vand. L. Rev. 1095, 3.06[C]
Gerhardt, On Revolution and Wetland Regulations, 90 Geo. L.J. 2143, 5.04[G]
Gergen, The Selfish State and the Market, 66 Tex. L. Rev. 1097, 6.06[G][1], 6.06[H][1], 7.01
Gerhardt, The Curious Flight of the Migratory Bird Rule, 31 Envt'l L. Rep, 5.04[G]
Gillette, Business Incentives, Interstate Competition, and the Commerce Clause, 82 Minn. L. Rev. 447, 6.06[G][1]
Gillette, Lawyers, Guns and Commerce: *United States v. Lopez* and the New Commerce Clause Doctrine, 46 DePaul L. Rev. 823, 5.04[A]

H

Hellerstein, State's Power to Tax Foreign Commerce Dominates Supreme Court's 1978 Agenda, 51 J. Tax. 106, 8.14[A]

Hellerstein, State Taxation of Electronic Commerce, 52 Tax L. Rev. 425, 8.01

Hellerstein, State Taxation of Interstate Business: Perspective on Two Centuries of Constitutional Adjudication, 41 Tax Law. 37, 8.08

Hellerstein, State Taxation and the Supreme Court: Toward a More Unified Approach to Constitutional Adjudication, 75 Mich. L. Rev. 1426, 8.08, 12.01

Hellerstein, Taxing Electronic Commerce: Preliminary Thoughts on Model Uniform Legislation, Tax Notes, May 12, 1997, 3.06[C]

Hellerstein & Coenen, Commerce Clause Restraints on State Business Incentives, 81 Cornell L. Rev. 789, 6.06[G][1]

Hellerstein & Hellerstein, State Taxation (2nd ed.), 3.06[B], 4.05[A], 8.01, 8.06, 8.07, 8.08, 8.11, 8.13[B]

Hellerstein, McIntyre & Pomp, Commerce Clause Restraints on State Taxation After *Jefferson Lines,* 51 Tax L. Rev. 47, 6.07[C], 8.01, 8.01[K]

Hellwege, Law Enforcement, Legislators Grapple with Child Sexual Exploitation on the Net, Trial, March 2000, 3.06[C]

Henderson, Congress, Courts and Criminals: The Development of Federal Criminal Law, 1801-1829, 3.13[A]

Henderson, The Position of Foreign Corporations in American Constitutional Law, 6.06[D]

Henkin, Foreign Affairs and the United States Constitution, 10.02, 10.03, 11.01, 11.02, 12.04

Henkin, Infallibility Under Law: Constitutional Balancing, 78 Colum. L. Rev. 1022, 6.05

Henning, Foreward: Statutory Interpretation and the Federalization of Criminal Law, 86 J. Crim. L. & Criminology 1167, 3.13[A]

Hinds, State Taxes and the Import-Export Clause, 14 Am. J. Tax Policy 73, 12.01

Hirsch, An Economic Analysis of the Constitutionality of State Preference Laws, 14 Int'l Rev. L. & Econ. 299, 6.06[H][1][a]

Hodas, State Responses to Global Warming: Is It Constitutional to Think Globally and Act Locally? 21 Pace Envt'l L. Rev. 53 (2003), 6.06[B]

Hodson, The Dormant Commerce Clause and the Constitutionalizing of Intrastate Groundwater Management Programs, 62 Tex. L. Rev. 537, 6.06[C][2]

Hoke, Preemption Pathologies and Civic Republican Values, 71 B.U.L. Rev. 685, 5.06[B]

Hoke, Transcending Conventional Supremacy: A Reconstruction of the Supremacy Clause, 24 Conn. L. Rev. 829, 5.06[B]

Holdsworth, The First Bank of the United States, 3.09

Holdsworth & Dewey, First and Second Banks of the United States, 3.09

Holman, After *United States v. Lopez,* Can the Clean Water Act and the Endangered Species Act Survive Commerce Law Attack?, 15 Va. Env. L.J. 139, 5.04[A]

Holmes, Collected Legal Papers, 6.02[C]

Holmes, The Common Law, 1.03

Hong, Note, And ''Cloning'' Makes Three: A Constitutional Comparison Between Cloning and Other Assisted Reproductive Technologies, 26 Hastings Const. L. Q. 741, 5.04[A]

Houck, Environmental Law and the General Welfare, 16 Pace Envt'l L. Rev. 1, 6.06[B]

Houghton & Friedman, Lost in [Cyber]Space?, Tax Notes, Sept. 15, 1997, 3.06[C]

K

Kohnke, Comment, Can Congress Do That?: An Analysis of the Federal Prohibition on Marijuana Possession, 19 Miss C. L. Rev. 381, 5.04[H][2]

Kopel & Reynolds, Taking Federalism Seriously: *Lopez* and the Partial Birth Abortion Ban Act, 30 Conn. L. Rev. 59, 5.04[A], 5.04[E], 5.04[F][1]

Korot, Note, *Waste Management Holdings v. Gilmore*: The Anything but Dormant Problem of Interstate Waste, 13 Vill. Envt'l L.J. 315, 6.06[B]

Kraakman, Taking Discounts Seriously: The Implication of "Discounted" Share Prices as an Acquisition Motive, 88 Colum. L. Rev. 891, 6.06[E][3]

Kramer, The Arrogance of the Court, Wash. Post, May 23, 2000, 5.04[G]

Kramer, Putting the Politics Back into the Political Safeguards of Federalism, 100 Colum. L. Rev. 215, 5.04[A]

Kronman, Alexander Bickel's Philosophy of Prudence, 94 Yale L.J. 1567, 6.02[C]

Kropf, The Failure of *United States v. Lopez*: Analyzing the Violence Against Women Act, 8 S. Cal. Rev. L. & Women's Studies 373, 5.04[E]

Kurland, The Privileges and Immunities Clause: "Its Hour Come Round at Last"?, 1972 Wash. U. L.Q. 405, 6.06[H][3]

Kurland & Lerner, The Founders' Constitution, 2.03

Kurtz, Comment, Does the Violence Against Women Act Do Violence to the Limits of Congressional Power?, 34 San Diego L. Rev. 1047, 5.04[E]

Kyvig, Repealing National Prohibition, 13.01

Kyvig, Sober Thoughts: Myths and Realities of National Prohibition After Fifty Years, *in* Alcohol and Order: Perspectives on National Prohibition, 13.01, 13.02

L

Landman, Creation of a Less Perfect Union: The Implications of *General Motors v. Tracy* for Commerce Clause Analysis of State Taxation, 30 Conn. L. Rev. 1121, 8.05

Landmark Briefs and Arguments of the Supreme Court of the United States (vol. 60), 2.04

Langevoort, The Supreme Court and the Politics of Corporate Takeovers: A Comment on *CTS Corp. v. Dynamics Corp. of America,* 101 Harv. L. Rev. 96, 6.06[E][2]

Larsen, Discrimination in the Dormant Commerce Clause, 49 S.D. L. Rev. 844 (2003-2004), 6.01[A]

Lasser, "Lit Theory" Put to the Test: A Comparative Literary Analysis of American Judicial Tests and French Judicial Discourse, 111 Harv. L. Rev. 689, 8.10

Laughlin, The Law of United States Territories and Affiliated Jurisdiction 3, 12.04

Lawrence, Toward a More Coherent Commerce Clause: A Proposed Unitary Framework, 21 Harv. J.L. & Pub. Pol'y 395, 6.01[A]

Lazarus, Note, The Commerce Clause Limitation on the Power to Condemn a Relocating Business, 96 Yale L.J. 1348, 6.06[G][1]

Lazarus, Restoring What's Environmental About Environmental Law in the Supreme Court, 47 U.C.L.A. L. Rev. 703, 6.06[B]

Leading Cases — Native American Treaties — State Sovereignty — Compatibility with Indian Treaty Rights, 113 Harv. L. Rev. 389, 10.05[B][2]

Lee, The Federal Air Commerce Act, 12 A.B.A.J. 371, 3.03

Leman, The Birds: Regulation of Wetlands and the Limits of the Commerce Clause, 28 U.C. San Diego L. Rev. 1237, 5.04[A]

M

McLaughlin, FCC Jurisdiction Over Local Telephone Under the 1996 Act: Fenced Off?, 97 Colum. L. Rev. 2210, 3.06[B]

Merritt, Commerce!, 94 Mich. L. Rev. 674, 7.01

Mesnikoff, Disposing of the Dormant Commerce Clause Barrier: Keeping Waste at Home, 76 Minn. L. Rev. 1219, 6.06[B]

Michel, Comment, *Hood v. Du Mond:* A Study of the Supreme Court and the Ideology of Capitalism, 134 U. Pa. L. Rev. 657, 8.02

Mikhail, Reversing the Tide Under the Commerce Clause, 86 J. Crim. L. & Criminology 1493, 5.04[A]

Miller, Interstate Branching and the Constitution, 41 Bus. Law. 337, 6.06[E]

Miller, Note, The First Amendment and Legislative Bans of Liquor and Cigarette Advertisements, 85 Colum. L. Rev. 632, 13.05[A]

Miller, Note, The Wine is in the Mail: The Twenty-first Amendment and State Laws Against the Direct Shipment of Alcoholic Beverages, 54 Vand. L. Rev. 2495, 6.06[F], 13.03[A], 13.04[B]

Miller, The Latest Phase of the Original Package Doctrine, 35 Am. L. Rev. 364, 4.05[C]

Mincavage, Comment, Title III of the Violence Against Women Act: Can It Survive a Commerce Clause Challenge in the Wake of *United States v. Lopez*?, 102 Dickinson L. Rev. 441, 5.04[E]

Mitchell, Comment, Conditional Federal Funding to the States: The New Federalism Demands a Close Examination for Unconstitutional Conditions, 48 U. Kan. L. Rev. 161, 5.04[B], 5.04[G]

Miyaki-Murphy, Comment, In the Wake of *Crosby v. National Foreign Trade Council,* 34 J. Marshall L. Rev. 827, 5.06[D], 7.02[D], 10.03

Monaghan, Constitutional Fact Review, 85 Colum. L. Rev. 229, 5.01[C]

Monaghan, The Supreme Court, 1995 Term—Comment: The Sovereign Immunity Exception, 110 Harv. L. Rev. 102, 10.05[A]

Moritsugu, Note, The Winding Course of the Massachusetts Burma Law: Subfederal Sanctions in a Historical Context, 34 Geo. Wash. Int'l L. Rev. 435, 5.06[D], 7.02[D], 10.03

Montejano, Note, When Welfare Reform Crosses the Line: A Look Behind the Scenes of *Saenz v. Roe* and California's Battle over Durational Residency Requirements, 4 Tex. F. on C.L. & C.R. 275, 3.11

Moore, State and Local Taxation: When Will Congress Intervene?, 23 J. Legis. 171, 8.08

Moore, State and Local Taxation of Interstate and Foreign Commerce: The Second Best Solution, 42 Wayne L. Rev. 1425, 8.08

Moriarty, Comment, Parental Wiretapping: Should Federal Courts Provide a Civil Remedy in a Family Law Matter, 48 U. Kan. L. Rev. 397, 5.04[A]

Morris & Booher, A Case for National E-Mail Regulations: State UCE Statutes Have Infirmities, 70 Def. Counsel J. 1 (2003), 3.06[C]

Morris, Commentary, Interstate Commerce and the Future of State Sales and Use Taxes, 54 Ala. L. Rev. 1393 (2003), 3.06[C], 8.05, 8.06

Morrison, Workman's Compensation and the Maritime Law, 38 Yale L.J. 472, 9.04

Moulton, The American Transportation Problem, 3.03

Multistate Tax Commission, Model Regulations, Statutes and Guidelines, 8.11

Murphy, Personal Jurisdiction and the Stream of Commerce Theory: A Reappraisal and a Revised Approach, 77 Ky. L.J. 243, 6.06[D]

O

P

Pann, The Dormant Commerce Clause and State Regulation of the Internet: Are Laws Protecting Minors from Sexually Explicit Predators Constitutionally Different than Those Protecting Minors from Sexually Explicit Materials?, 2005 Duke L. & Tech. Rev. 8 (2005), 3.06[C]

Parkinson, Congressional Prohibitions of Interstate Commerce, 16 Colum. L. Rev. 367, 2.03

Pascoe, Note, Time for a New Approach?: Federalism and Foreign Affairs After *Crosby v. National Foreign Trade Council,* 35 Vand. J. Transnat'l L. 291, 5.06[D], 7.02[D], 10.03

Patterson, Does the Commerce Clause Value Public Goods?: *West Lynn Creamery v. Healy,* 44 Cath. U. L. Rev. 977, 6.06[E][1]

Patterson, Note, A Brewing Debate: Alcohol Direct Shipment Laws and the Twenty-first Amendment, 2002 U. Ill. L. Rev. 761, 6.06[F], 13.03[A], 13.04[B]

Peake, Note, South Carolina Loses a Battle in the Hazardous Waste Wars: Using the Dormant Commerce Clause to Invalidate South Carolina's Hazardous Waste Laws in *Environmental Technology Council v. Sierra Club,* 76 N.C. L. Rev. 650, 6.06[B]

Percival, ''Greening'' the Constitution — Harmonizing Environmental and Constitutional Values, 32 Envtl. L. 809, 6.06[B]

Perino, Fraud and Federalism: Preempting Private Securities Fraud Causes of Action, 50 Stan. L. Rev. 273, 5.06[C]

Perlman, A Bar Against Competition: The Unconstitutionality of Admission Rules for Out-of-State Attorneys, 18 Geo. J. Legal Ethics __ (forthcoming 2004), 6.06[H][1][c]

Phillips, Hoist by Own Petard: When a Conservative Commerce Clause Interpretation Meets Conservative Tort Reform, 64 Tenn. L. Rev. 647, 5.04[A]

Pietila, Note, ''[W]e're Doing This to Ourselves'': South Dakota's Anticorporate Farming Amendment, J. Corp. L. 149, 6.05

Pinoto, Takeover Statutes: The Dormant Commerce Clause and the State Corporate Law, 41 U. Miami L. Rev. 473, 6.06[G]

Piraino, A Proposal for the Antitrust Regulation of Professional Sports, 79 B.U. L. Rev. 889, 3.10

Pirnot, Note, *United States v. Wilson*: Did Interstate General Substantially Affect Interstate Commerce?, 77 N.C. L. Rev. 361, 5.04[A]

Polelle, A Critique of the Market Participation Exception, 15 Whitt. L. Rev. 647, 7.01

Pollak, Foreword, 5.04[A]

Pomper, Recycling *Philadelphia v. New Jersey:* The Dormant Commerce Clause, Post-Industrial Natural Resources and the Solid Waste Crisis, 137 U. Pa. L. Rev. 1309, 6.06[B]

Porterfield, State and Local Foreign Policy Initiatives and Free Speech: The First Amendment as an Instrument of Federalism, 35 Stan. J. Int'l L. 1, 10.03

Post, Gambling on Internet Law, American Lawyer, Sept. 1998, 3.06[C]

Potts, State Taxing Schemes Discriminating in Violation of the Foreign Commerce Clause, 46 Tax Law. 555, 8.14[D]

Powell, Child Labor, Congress and the Constitution, 1 N.C. L. Rev. 61, 2.04

Powell, Contemporary Commerce Clause Controversies Over State Taxation, 76 U. Pa. L. Rev. 773, 8.02

Powell, Insurance as Commerce in Constitution and Statute, 57 Harv. L. Rev. 937, 3.08[B]

Powell, The Original Understanding of Original Intent, 98 Harv. L. Rev. 907, 5.04

Powell, Physics and Law, 58 Harv. L. Rev. 1072, 3.05, 3.06[A]

R

S

T

U

V

W

Y

Z

INDEX

References are to sections.

G

H

I

O

P

U